Philosophy and Film

Philosophy and Film

edited and with an Introduction by
Cynthia A. Freeland
and
Thomas E. Wartenberg

Routledge   New York & London

Published in 1995 by
Routledge
29 West 35th Street
New York, NY 10001

Published in Great Britain in 1995 by
Routledge
11 New Fetter Lane
London EC4P 4EE

Library of Congress Cataloging-in-Publication Data

Philosophy and film / edited by Cynthia A. Freeland and Thomas
E. Wartenberg
     p.   cm.
     Includes bibliographical references and index.
     ISBN 0-415-90920-1 (cloth) — ISBN 0-415-90921-X (pbk.)
     1. Motion pictures — Philosophy.   I. Freeland, Cynthia A.
     II. Wartenberg, Thomas E.

PN 1995.P499   1994   94-37854
791.43—dc20   CIP

To my grandmothers,
Dorothy Kent Freeland Parker (1905–1986)
and Dorothy Alice Evans Wright
—CF

To my son, Jacob Benjamin Wartenberg
—TW

Contents

Acknowledgments

We would like to thank the following authors and publishers for their permission to reprint previously published material:

Stanley Cavell's essay "The Thought of Movies" originally appeared in the *Yale Review* (Winter, 1983). Used by permission of the author and publisher.

Nickolas Pappas' essay "Failures of Marriage in *Sea of Love* (The Love of Men, the Respect of Women)" contains material previously published in "A Sea of Love Among Men," *Film Criticism* 14 (1990): 14–26. Used by permission of the editor, Lloyd Michaels.

Naomi Scheman's essay "Missing Mothers/Desiring Daughters: Framing the Sight of Women," is a shortened version of an essay by the same title published in *Critical Inquiry* 15 (Autumn 1988): 62–89. Used by permission of the University of Chicago Press.

George Wilson's essay "Morals for Method" contains material previously published in *Narration in Light: Studies in Cinematic Point of View* (Baltimore and London: The Johns Hopkins University Press, 1986). Used by permission of the author and publisher.

Preface

This anthology had its origin in a discussion in the fall of 1991 that took place at the Au Bon Pain Cafe in Cambridge, Massachusetts. The two editors are old friends, having both attended graduate school at the University of Pittsburgh. We were in Cambridge at the same time, so we decided to have coffee and catch up with each others' lives. When the talk turned to our work, we were surprised to find that we were both working on the papers about film that are contained in this volume. The reason for our mutual surprise was that we each thought of the other as still working in the field that we had left graduate school trained in: ancient philosophy, in the case of Cynthia; Kant and nineteenth-century German philosophy, in the case of Tom. Although we knew that we shared an interest in aesthetics, we were genuinely startled to find that our intellectual careers—which we each thought of as taking a circuitous path of its own—had led us to the same place: the philosophic study of film.

The surprising coincidence of our interest in the serious study of film led us to the idea of editing an anthology together. Among the various reasons for it was our sense that there were many more philosophers working on film than we knew about or than were willing to admit it. Our hope in publishing this volume is that it will play a role in legitimating film as a philosophic interest.

In shaping this volume, we asked a wide range of philosophers to contribute. The contributors to this volume are separated not only by their philosophic commitments and their method of approaching film, but also by the stage of their careers. We have included writing by both well-established philosophers of film and relative newcomers to the field. We think that this variety indicates the character of film study by philosophers.

Philosophy has changed a great deal as an intellectual discipline in American colleges and universities since the two of us were graduate students some twenty years ago. We think that this volume marks some of the changes in that discipline and in our own pursuit of it. We hope that it will encourage others in their desire to continue to change the face of American philosophy.

We want to thank Anna May Dion and Laurie Dion for their help in preparing this manuscript. Without their assistance, we would have been unable to complete this project.

TEW—NORTHAMPTON, MA
CF—HOUSTON, TX

Introduction

Philosophy and Film

The scholarly study of films is one of the fastest growing areas of research in academia. Different disciplines have appropriated film to their own distinctive questions and methods of study. Literary scholars construct readings of film "texts," while historians use films in courses on the history of wars, protest movements, or pioneer voyages. Sociologists and anthropologists view films as fruitful fields for the exploration of social and cultural issues concerning family structures, urban violence, teenage rebellion, sexual initiation rites, or religious taboos. Feminist scholars from many different disciplines study films to highlight their concerns with the representation of gender, sexuality, patriarchic power relations, and canon formation.

The premise of this volume is that philosophy has its own unique perspective to bring to the exploration of film. We have deliberately invited contributions from only professionally designated "philosophers," with the aim of demonstrating that philosophy has the potential to make distinctive and valuable contributions to the study of film. There are two groups of readers who may be surprised by this claim.

First, many students of American philosophy will not likely see film as a central topic for philosophic discussion. We hope that they will be surprised to find how many significant philosophic issues surface in the analyses of films in this volume. These range from broad questions about the relations between science and value theory to specific questions about knowledge and perspectivism, authenticity and social relations, and modern vs. post-modern views on the nature of representation. For the most part, the authors in this volume share the view that the relationship between philosophy and film is not one-way: While philosophy can bring out important aspects of films, film also can challenge philosophy to think of itself and its questions in new ways. We hope that as a result, this volume will stimulate philosophers to see that thinking about films is an interesting avenue for philosophic investigation.

Second, students of film may also wonder about what in particular philosophers have to offer to their field. Our hope is that they will come to appreciate the clarity, rigor, and significantly new critical voices and traditions that philosophers bring to the study of film. We believe that the contributions of philosophers will encourage consideration of broader alternatives to those currently dominant in cinema studies. Philosophers are generally wary of adopting any specific theoretical vocabulary and simply applying it to the study of any area. As a result, authors in this volume tend to eschew the highly theorized vocabulary of film studies and employ a more ordinary vocabulary for addressing films. The virtues of this approach can be seen in many of the essays included here.

The philosophic study of film applies its particular disciplinary perspective and methods to produce critical analyses of some of the most basic assumptions now dominant in film studies. Much of the early and influential work in film studies has addressed themes that could well be described as philosophical: Is film a language, and if so, how is it constructed, and how does it communicate? If film is an art form, what constitutes its uniqueness, and what makes works in this medium excellent? How do people construct, study, interpret, and criticize works of art generally, and films in particular? What is the nature of filmic representation? Though film studies is a recent, still emerging field, certain points of view on these issues have acquired prominence. In much of current film studies, these positions have become standard without a critical examination of serious alternatives using the methods and standards common to philosophy. While our understanding of film has been significantly advanced by film studies' discussion of the questions these positions raise, issues relevant to film yet unapproached by film studies have been addressed by philosophers from Plato onwards. Similarly, there is a lengthy philosophical tradition discussing some of the central concepts employed in film studies about knowledge, evidence, point of view, perspectivism, and objectivity. Philosophers studying film are aware of the need to subject the basic assumptions of a discipline to critical study. They approach the study of film cognizant of these theoretical issues and enrich their interpretations by addressing them.

Our own view of the philosophical enterprise of studying film draws upon the work of what might seem to be the very disparate twentieth-century philosophers, Michel Foucault and Nelson Goodman. While Goodman's analytic American pragmatism and Foucault's French post-structuralism are not often mentioned in the same breath, we think that they share an important approach that is useful in thinking about film. Both thinkers regard artworks of all kinds as symbolic systems with complex internal structures that enable them to play significant cognitive functions within certain contexts. To play these cognitive roles, the artworks' symbol systems must be interpreted—a project that may often seem simple and uncomplicated, because of our familiarity with their codes or representational devices. In other words, these complex symbolic structures always function within a pragmatic epistemic context where users, or viewers, "read" them as presenting a world. When we engage in such reading, both Foucault and Goodman emphasize, we are doing a kind of thinking and learning.

Foucault analyzes works of art such as Velazquez's *Las Meninas* and Magritte's *This is Not a Pipe*, showing that they contain an entire system of representational thought, what he calls an *episteme*, that is both characteristic and revelatory of the age in which they were produced. As he shows for *Las Meninas*, an artwork may even self-consciously encapsulate the contradictions of an era by its own creative reflections upon the systems of representation it employs. Applying Foucault's point to film, we can ask both how individual films embody conventions of representation that make them characteristic for their time, and how they themselves think about—indeed, philosophize upon—these conventions.

Goodman similarly allows artworks a significant role in demonstrating and shaping our visions of our world. He argues that the major aim of art is to contribute to and enlarge upon our understanding of a world. This means it is a mistake to draw naive contrasts between art, which is somehow "subjective," and science, which "objectively" aims at truth. Goodman articulates criteria that make either scientific hypotheses or artworks successful: he cites such features as clarity, elegance, and above all something he describes as "rightness of rendering." Rightness of rendering should not be taken in a realist sense to involve getting at the way the world "really" is. Both science and artworks create worlds that seem right in relation to our needs and habits (or what can become our habits).

On either of these approaches to films as artworks, we may respect films as themselves reflective, world-creating, philosophical achievements. After all, in watching films, we are drawn into the worlds that they seem to reveal. By using photography, sound, editing, special effects, and vivid characterization, films can persuade their audiences to believe in the worlds that they present. What makes films suitable objects for critical reflection is precisely their ability to create such worlds, for we can attend to various features of the worlds created by films. Film worlds can construe human relations, give us a picture of everything as rational and run by God, or of our lives as free or fated, or of whether we should be pessimistic or blithe. A film can represent ourselves to ourselves, depicting a world in which people are beautiful or ugly, romantic or bland, evil or amusing.

It is precisely our effort to become aware of the features of such film-worlds that gives rise to philosophic criticism of film. There are various different aspects of the process and result of world creation that can be attended to critically. The project of reflecting on a film becomes much like the project of assessing a philosophical system. There are many questions that can be asked about a film and its world, depending upon our interests and goals. While we may begin by asking very general questions about the ways in which films create their worlds, we may end up asking such specific questions as: Is the world of this film coherent? Is it a world in which we would like to live? What aspects of human relationships does it highlight? How does it represent them? Does it help illuminate "our" world?

We recognize that the philosophers writing in this volume may not share the particular conception of the study of film that we have briefly articulated here. Philosophers as a group are no more united than, say, literary scholars or sociologists. The variety of different methodologies and approaches that characterize contemporary philosophy might make it seem doubtful that there is enough unity to philosophy itself for a volume of contributions by philosophers to make a coherent statement. At least one prominent contemporary philosopher, Richard Rorty, has argued that philosophers should give up their claims to having any particular field of expertise, regarding themselves instead as members of a continuing cultural conversation, commonly linked by their shared forbears, questions, and approaches.

There are sure to be those included in this volume who would disagree with Rorty. While we might all see ourselves as the inheritors of a conversation that includes the names Plato, Aristotle, Descartes, and Kant, it is unlikely that everyone in this volume could agree to counting as shared forbears certain other names that appear here as part of the ongoing conversation of philosophy: Marx, Emerson, Hegel, Foucault, James, Peirce, Baudrillard, Goodman, Kristeva, and Irigaray. We have deliberately invited contributions to this volume by philosophers from widely divergent schools of thought: analytical, "Continental," Marxist, feminist, pragmatist, post-modern, anti-post-modern, classical. Our aim has been to highlight the creative diversity of approaches and perspectives that do in fact get counted as philosophical by participants in the discipline.

The essays in this volume approach film in many different ways and with a wide range of philosophic commitments. These differences manifest themselves in different stances that are taken in regard to the nature of film as an object of study. The theoretical perspective that a particular philosopher accepts determines the type of object that he or she takes film to be and, along with that, the sort of approach that is required to understand its nature. Different ontological understandings of film produce different types of philosophic criticism of film.

For many philosophers, the least controversial approach to film is one that assimilates films to other aesthetic objects. Philosophy of art has always looked at specific kinds of art: Plato and Aristotle examined tragedy, Kant looked at landscape gardens, Hegel at all the art forms of his time. More recently, philosophers have continued in this tradition as we find Danto examining abstract painting, Kivy, opera, and Baudrillard, Disneyland and the Pompidou Centre. The questions philosophers pursue in considering aesthetic objects may vary according to these objects themselves. Films may be examined by looking at traditional sorts of questions that have been raised about other sorts of aesthetic objects, e.g., in virtue of what are they excellent? What are the standard parts of a film, how do these parts work, what function do they play or effect do they aim at? etc. One may also conceptualize the examination of film on the model of how we look at artworks in other mediums.

The present volume contains a number of essays that approach films as aesthetic objects. George Wilson focuses on films as complex representations that may be better understood by categorizing and studying their narrative patterns and structures. He borrows from literary theory here, making appropriate adaptations in considering how films use point of view to create their stories. Harvey Cormier discusses modernism in film, more specifically in *2001*, in relation to Greenberg's well-known views on modernism in painting. Cynthia Freeland relates her consideration of spectacle in horror films to Plato's critical attack on ancient tragedy in his *Republic*, and Aristotle's defense in the *Poetics*.

But there are also significantly new and different aesthetic questions about films, including questions that are medium-specific. For example, Douglas Kellner, Stanley Cavell, and Thomas Wartenberg discuss how the popular, non-elitist status of film art affects the way we conceptualize our inquiries. Kellner considers Spike Lee's aesthetic choices by comparison to those of Brecht, focusing on the particular roles played in both artists' work by their diverse political inspirations in either Marx or Malcolm X. Cavell defends his conviction that it is legitimate to draw aesthetic comparisons between such popular film comedies as *The Philadelphia Story* and *Pennies from Heaven* and the plays of Shakespeare. Like Cavell, Wartenberg is interested in ways in which films reflect upon the history of their own medium. He shows that *Some Like It Hot* is not only alluded to in *White Palace*, but is a key subtext that not only determines meaning but that allows the film to reflect upon the nature of film as a medium. A different sort of approach is taken by Noël Carroll, who asks what makes film the specific type of art object it is. Carroll's concern is to distinguish film from other types of aesthetic objects, to specify the nature of film as an aesthetic medium.

But films can also be philosophized about on the assumption that they are everyday objects, things we encounter in our everyday experience that begin somehow to confound us when we reflect on them. We can puzzle over them in the way that philosophers have so often done about other ordinary things—a practice that notoriously leads some people to regard philosophers as rather strange. As St. Augustine observed, when he thought about the nature of time, he stopped being able to understand what he could ordinarily comprehend perfectly well. Again, philosophers always have sought to ask and answer deep questions by creating wonder and puzzlement over what may appear in our everyday experiences to be simple: Thales' water that showed the essence of the universe, Descartes' wax that failed to reveal any essence except that of extended matter, Hume's billiard balls that created fundamental doubts about causation, Marx's table that encapsulated commodity fetishism, etc.

Much of what makes films puzzling is that, despite their role in our everyday lives, they pose a variety of epistemological problems. They are like other so-called ordinary objects that function somehow to enhance our representations of the world—like mirrors, windows, paintings, photographs, television screens, binoculars, telescopes. All these are familiar devices that enhance our vision, and that we know how to "use," but may not understand. How do they work? How is it we can read them? To what extent can we "trust" them to give us the "truth"?

Stanley Cavell meditates on such issues in his essay in this volume, admitting that he sometimes adopts a defensive attitude in explaining his philosophical interests in film. He resists the interpretation of movies "as specialized commodities manufactured by an industry designed to satisfy the tastes of a mass audience." What then are films, "these mysterious objects called movies, ...unlike anything else on earth"? Cavell notes films' paradoxical qualities of being evanescent and yet recorded; he further speculates concretely about many Hollywood movies' quintessential "Americanness." Naomi Scheman's essay subjects Cavell's understanding of film to critical inspection. Scheman asks whether Cavell's celebration of Hollywood film can be maintained in the face of the feminist film theorists' analyses of such film as objectifying women. By reading the "women's genre" of melodrama for its restrictions and gaps in depicting the maternal gaze, Scheman begins theorizing a feminist account of both knowledge and vision.

In her contribution to this volume, Karen Hanson speculates about the prominence of another view of films as objects that is prevalent in the field of film studies. This approach may reflect less a conception of the specific nature of film objects than one of what it is to construct a theoretical analysis of any kind of object. On this approach, films are regarded as worthy matters for investigation in much the way that scientists might take up anything as the objects of their study—from quasars to sharks, or schizophrenia to flu viruses. In a nutshell, films are treated as "data" that require both classification and explanation. Hanson argues that this paradigm relies upon often naive and unexamined assumptions about the nature of scientific "explanation" and theory-building. She challenges the belief that an informative "scientific" or classificatory theory of film objects would be either essential or useful for producing evaluational schemes. She puzzles over why this paradigm seems to have become so dominant in film studies, and suggests instead that we might profitably borrow from intriguing recent developments in value theory (ethics and aesthetics) which resist the attractions of generalized systematization.

Instead of raising questions about the nature of the "objects" that films are, philosophers may view them "transparently" in the sense that they treat the film as an illustration or test of a philosophical theory. Here the focus is not so much on films as representational systems but on films as stories about characters and actions. Using this approach philosophers analyze films as providing examples of the viability of a specific claim or theory that they wish to defend. In this approach to film, the film becomes a stage in a philosophic argument.

Films then function like the concrete examples philosophers have always used to illustrate their conceptions of virtue, vice, or political and social interaction. Taking this approach, philosophers follow much the same course that has been adopted by philosophers of literature: films are like novels, plays, or stories. They may be treated as offering particularly acute, detailed, and concrete illustrations of certain kinds of moral problems and of attempted resolutions of these problems. This is the strategy that Julie Inness takes in her essay on the concept of passing in *Europa, Europa*. She uses the narrative of the film to resolve a puzzle that she sees in our usual understanding of passing and why people find it difficult when it seems to provide benefits that they desire.

An alternative use of film as an example in a philosophic argument involves the use of a philosophic theory as a means of interpreting films. Both Nickolas Pappas and Kelly Oliver approach film in this way. Pappas uses Irigaray's analysis of gender relations as a means of understanding The *Sea of Love* and other films in the genre he calls "the Case of the Unmarried Woman." He argues that the ways in which these films present both women and men and the relationships between them can be understood by reference to Irigaray's theory and, in particular, her understanding of how men use women as means of homoerotic contact. Oliver uses Ingmar Bergman's classic film *Persona* in order to undermine the Hegelian-Lacanian understanding of self-other relationships. She shows that the narrative of *Persona* illustrates the validity of Julia Kristeva's theory of the origin of self-consciousness as opposed to that of Hegel-Lacan. Here, the film functions as a means of adjudicating between two rival theories, playing the role of an experiment in scientific theory by allowing us to have a field in which to judge which of two theories is more successful in helping us understand the film.

But treating a film as an example of a moral vision does not mean one is limited to viewing the film story in itself as just an illustration or test of a theory. Philosophers can also view the film story as a whole—character, author, director, and all—as itself thematizing and reflecting upon the moral or social concerns the film raises. In doing so, philosophers may also develop critical questions about a film's moral vision, for example, about its use of stereotypical modes of representation in presenting issues of race, class, and gender. Such interpretations depart from the film's own perspective and show how the film unwittingly mobilizes attitudes that are morally or socially suspect. In these examinations philosophers dig deeply into key issues of race, class, and gender so as to locate the positions described by films in the context of ethical or social theories, broadly considered. This concern is exemplified by Douglas Kellner's discussion of the representations of race and gender in Spike Lee's *oeuvre*. Robert Gooding-Williams focuses on the question of racism in the representation of African Americans in Hollywood cinema. Using the idea of the "black cupid," he argues that black characters that seem to eschew the racism of early Hollywood portrayals really reinscribe that racism in a more sophisticated manner.

Thomas Wartenberg's analysis of *White Palace* combines both of these approaches. On the one hand, he shows how the film uses an "unlikely couple" to make a philosophic statement about authenticity, how human beings can achieve a more adequate life in a relationship with another human being from a different group. On the other hand, he argues that the film's ending employs a simplistic understanding of social difference that undercuts the film's own message.

The essays in this book, then, demonstrate the wide variety of concerns that philosophers have in approaching film, and the different methods that they use to analyze them. Whether regarding films as primarily objects of aesthetic appraisal, epistemological puzzles, or especially vivid and complex illustrations of social and political viewpoints, the authors of these essays bring to bear a rich and diverse tradition of philosophic reflection as a means of enriching their interpretations of these films.

Toward the conclusion of her article, Karen Hanson quotes from William James's essay "The Sentiment of Rationality." James there describes two directions that our philosophical efforts to understand may take. First, philosophy is most typically known for what he labels its "theoretic" passion, the systematizing passion that aims to produce order out of chaos or to simplify a diverse manifold by profound, general, reflective observations about truths. By contrast to this better known enterprise James lists an equally important "sister passion" that aims at insight through a deeply particular and thorough acquaintance with individual objects. Here the drive is toward particularity, clarity, and integrity of perception. Hanson asks here, "Can we, out of our ordinary and individual experience, make exemplary claims about film?" We believe that both these passions may produce illuminating and rich philosophical film studies, and so we have tried to gather together examples illustrating both.

In fact, we have placed the essays in this volume along a continuum of philosophic reflection between the two poles envisioned by James. At the start are essays by Cavell, Hanson, Wilson, and Carroll that address the "manifold" of theorizing about film by asking large questions about how and why we may want to philosophize about films. Of course, despite their wide scope, these essayists may also cite and consider specific examples, including *The Philadelphia Story*, *Lady from Shanghai*, and *Pennies from Heaven*.

Part Two includes essays by Scheman, Pappas, Freeland, Gooding-Williams, and Wartenberg that focus primarily on categories of films—unlikely couple, realist horror, melodrama, etc.—with the aim of describing and asking questions about the significance of a film genre. Here again the essays may reflect at length upon individual films, such as *White Palace*, *Bill of Divorcement*, or *Henry: Portrait of a Serial Killer*, but with the primary goal of exploring how they fit into a larger pattern of films, in terms of their ideological messages or representational practices.

Finally, Part Three contains essays by Cormier, Kellner, Inness, and

Oliver that aim at a significant level of engagement with the details of individual films, highlighting a variety of concerns about these films, ranging from their aesthetic strategies to their moral visions. The films discussed here include *2001*, *Do the Right Thing*, *Malcolm X*, *Europa, Europa*, and *Persona*.

Moving from the general to the specific, the essays in this volume illustrate the range of concerns and approaches that philosophers exhibit when writing about film. Despite their diversity, these essays are united in their belief that philosophers have interesting things to say about films, and that films can be used as a means of addressing issues within philosophy. Although the field of philosophy of film is a young one, our hope is that this volume can mark an important step in its maturation into an important sub-discipline, of interest to both serious students of film and of philosophy.

part one ▌**General Perspectives**

1 The Thought of Movies

Stanley Cavell

It must be the nature of American academic philosophy (or of its reputation), together with the nature of American movies (or of their notoriety), that makes someone who writes about both, in the same breath, subject to questions, not to say suspicions. The invitation to deliver this year's Patricia Wise Lecture is the first time I have been questioned about this combination of concerns, or obsessions, by a group of people committed to sitting quietly for the better part of an hour while I search for an answer.

The question has, I think without fail, come my way with philosophy put first: How is it that a professor of philosophy gets to thinking about Hollywood films?—as though becoming a professor of philosophy were easier to accept than thinking and writing about movies. So defensive have I grown that it took me a while to recognize that for most of my life the opposite direction of the question would have been more natural: How is it that someone whose education was as formed by going to the movies as by reading books, gets to thinking about philosophy professionally?

For a long time I believed the connection to be a private crossroads of my own. It became explicit for me during that period in my life, I learned later, in a calmer time, to call my identity crisis. After college, in the late 1940s, I was accepted by the extension program of the Julliard Conservatory as a composition major, following some two years of increasing doubts that music was my life. Almost as soon as I arrived in New York and established myself in school, I began avoiding my composition lessons. I spent my days reading and my nights in a theater, typically standing for the opera or a play, and then afterwards going to a film revival on 42nd Street, which in the late forties was a rich arena within which to learn the range and randomness of the American talkie. What I was reading all day I privately called philosophy, though I knew no more about what other people meant by the word than I knew why it was in philosophy that I was looking for the answer to the question my life had become.

Since I had spent my undergraduate years torn between the wish to be a writer and the fact of composing music for the student theater—for anything ranging from numbers for our annual musical revues to incidental music for nothing less than *King Lear*—what I learned in college would scarcely, I mean by European standards, have added up to an education at all. But I was encouraged to go on learning from the odd places, and the odd people, that it pleased my immigrant, unlettered father and my accomplished mother to take me to—he who was in love with the learning he never would have, and she who while I was growing up made a living playing the piano for silent movies and for vaudeville. The commonest place we went together was to movies. So while before I entered college I would not have heard a performance of, say, the Beethoven Ninth, and lacked any obvious preparation for it in the history of music and of German culture, I had known enough to attend carefully, for example, to the moves of Fred Astaire and Ginger Rogers and Jerome Kern, so that when the chorus in the last movement of the Ninth sings the two principal themes in counterpoint, the ecstasy this caused me had been prepared by my response to the closing of *Swingtime,* in which one of the pair is singing again "A Fine Romance" while the other is singing again "The Way You Look Tonight." This would not have constituted the preparation I claim for high art unless it had gone beyond cleverness. It is essential that each of the Kern songs is as good individually as it is, so that when the pair modify and cast them together in the reprise, each can be seen capable, so to speak, of meaning the separate song he and she have on their minds.

In the same way the lyrics of such songs were preparation for the high poetry I had yet to discover. In my early adolescence lines such as

> Heaven, I'm in heaven
> And the cares that hung around me through the week
> Seem to vanish like a gambler's lucky streak
> When we're out together dancing cheek to cheek

was what I thought of as poetry—nothing else will be poetry for me that cannot compete with the experience of concentration and lift in such words. It seems to me that I knew this then to be an experience not isolated from the behavior and the intelligence of the words with one another, nor only, in addition, of the wit and beauty of invoking the gambler's run of luck, but that it was an experience of these (though I would have lacked as yet words of my own in which to say so) together with the drama of using the vanishing of the streak, which is a bad thing, as a simile for the vanishing of cares and the access to heaven, which is a good thing— as if beyond bad and good there were a region of chance and risk within which alone the intimacy emblematized or mythologized in the dancing of Astaire and Rogers is realizable. Eventually I would be able to note that happiness and happenstance spring from the same root, that the pursuit of happiness—whether this is an occasion for a step into selfhood or into nationhood—requires the bravery to recognize and seize the occasion, or as Emerson had put it, "the courage to be what you are." I am not claiming that I, then, on 42nd Street, had already planned my book on the Hollywood comedy of remarriage; but rather that that book is in part written in loyalty to younger versions of myself, some of whom were, or are, there. Certainly I can sympathize with Steve Martin's half-crazed hero in the recent *Pennies from Heaven* when he says, crying from the heart about the songs he peddles and believes, "Listen to the words!" And I am, I guess, claiming that that younger version of myself, playing hooky from Julliard and in the poverty of his formal education reading all day and spending half the night in theaters, was already taking to heart Henry James's most memorable advice to aspiring writers. In "The Art of Fiction" James says:

> The power to guess the unseen from the seen, to trace the implications of things, to judge the whole piece by the pattern, the condition of feeling life in general so completely that you are well on your way to knowing any particular corner of it—this cluster of gifts may almost be said to constitute experience.... Therefore, if I should certainly say to a novice, "Write from experience and experience only," I should feel that this was rather a tantalizing monition if I were not careful immediately to add, "Try to be one of the people on whom nothing is lost."

By the time the time came for me to write my book about a set of Hollywood romances (*Pursuits of Happiness*), I had come to count on myself as one of the people willing not to be lost to his or to her experience, hence to count on being able to survive the indignities of sometimes guessing unconvincingly and of sometimes tracing things in thin air. So, for instance, in my book I build a sense of the shared structure of the comedies of remarriage out of an understanding of Shakespearean romance; and I discuss the blanket in *It Happened One Night* in terms of the censoring of human knowledge and aspiration in the philosophy of Kant; and I see the speculation of Heidegger exemplified in the countenance of Buster Keaton; and I find in *The Awful Truth* that when the camera moves away from an imminent embrace between Cary Grant and Irene Dunne to discover a pair of human figurines marking the passage of time by skipping together into a clock that has the form of a house, that in that image something metaphysical is being said about what marriage is, that it is a new way of inhabiting time, and moreover that that is a way of summarizing the philosophy, among others, of Thoreau and of Nietzsche.

So I suppose I should not be surprised that this book of mine has met with some resistance from its reviewers. More than once it has been called pretentious. Put aside for the present the possibility that its ideas are poorly executed or voiced in the writing—there is nothing I can do about that now. If that is not the whole story, then the charge of pretension must have to do with the connections I make between film and philosophy; at any rate, the charge levelled against either separately would hardly be worth responding to. But what in the connections may strike one as pretentious? It is important to me to bring out what I find to be a harmless way of issuing the charge, and a harmful way.

The harmless way takes the connections as a matter of preference, and on this basis I can see that one who is not familiar with the texts I mention may prefer that I not drop their names. I have two excuses for doing so. First, since I find in movies food for thought, I go for help thinking about what I understand them to be thinking about where I go for help in thinking about anything, to the thinkers I know best and trust most. Second, as is typical of a certain kind of American, I find what I do to be pertinent to any and all of my fellow citizens, and I secretly believe that if they saw it as I do, they would all immediately devote themselves to doing it too. This accounts in part for an American's readiness to lecture his fellows, a practice that made an impression on de Tocqueville during his visit to us in the 1830s, the decade before Thoreau moved out to Walden to prepare his kind of lecturing, or dressing down. It is a practice some will find insufferable and others generous. The practice raises for me the issue whether Americans have anything to their name to call a common cultural inheritance, whether you can name three works of high culture that you can be sure all the people you care about have read or seen or heard. This lack of assured commonality would be another part of the cause for our tendency to lecture rather than to converse with one another.

The harmful way of charging my book with pretension takes it for granted that philosophy and Hollywood movies occupy separate cultural intentions, with nothing to say across their border, indeed with not so much as a border between them. The immediate harm in this view lies in its closing off an exploration of what those Americans to whom it matters may be said to have instead of a common inheritance of high culture, namely an ability to move between high and low, caring about each also from the vantage of the other. This has its liabilities, naturally; for example, of indiscriminateness and of moments of incomprehensibility to the outside learned world. But it also, to my mind, accounts for what is best, or special, in our work; for example, for the reach in Thoreau's prose from the highest sublimity to the lowest pun. I am reminded that de Tocqueville also remarked a liveliness among the populace of our democracy that he missed in his populace at home and which he attributed to the fact that in America there is genuinely public business which requires learning and intelligence to take part in. This seems to me the condition for the kind of mutual respect called upon in putting together the high and the low.

For someone, or most people, to take for granted that there is no border between philosophy and movies, for this to carry its apparent conviction, there must be available fairly definite, if unconscious, interpretations both of what philosophy is and of what the Hollywood movie is. Philosophy would have to be thought of as a more or less technical discipline reserved for specialists. But this would just interpret what it is that makes philosophy professional; and however internal that state is to philosophy and indeed to the growing professionalization of the world, it does not say what makes philosophy philosophy.

I understand it as a willingness to think not about something other than what ordinary human beings think about, but rather to learn to think undistractedly about things that ordinary human beings cannot help thinking about, or anyway cannot help having occur to them, sometimes in fantasy, sometimes as a flash across a landscape; such things, for example, as whether we can know the world as it is in itself, or whether others really know the nature of one's own experiences, or whether good and bad are relative, or whether we might not now be dreaming that we are awake, or whether modern tyrannies and weapons and spaces and speeds and art are continuous with the past of the human race or discontinuous, and hence whether the learning of the human race is not irrelevant to the problems it has brought before itself. Such thoughts are instances of that characteristic human willingness to allow questions for itself which it cannot answer with satisfaction. Cynics about philosophy, and perhaps about humanity, will find that questions without answers are empty; dogmatists will claim to have arrived at answers; philosophers after my heart will rather wish to convey the thought that while there may be no satisfying answers to such questions *in certain forms*, there are, so to speak, directions to answers, *ways to think*, that are worth the time of your life to discover. (It is a further question for me whether directions of this kind are teachable, in ways suited to what we think of as schools.)

It would not become me to proceed, in speaking on this occasion of my interest in movies, other than by way of faithfulness to the impulse to philosophy as I conceive it. Apart from the best I can do in this attempt, I would not have approached the question whether the same sensibility that is drawn to and perplexed about philosophy is drawn to and perplexed about movies.

There is, I suggested, an interpretation of Hollywood movies that is the companion of the interpretation of philosophy as a specialized profession. This interpretation takes movies as specialized commodities manufactured by an industry designed to satisfy the tastes of a mass audience. Conventional capitalists as well as conventional Marxists can equally take such a view. It is no more false than is the interpretation of philosophy as a profession, but is no less partial, or prejudicial. Just as it would be possible to select films carefully with an idea of proving that the film can attain to art (people interested in such selections will on the whole not include Hollywood talkies in this selection), so one could heap together abysses of bad and meretricious movies with an idea of proving one's bleakest view of Hollywood. These are not my interests, and have nothing special to do with assessing the life of movies.

What interests me much more in these terms about Hollywood is that for around fifteen years, say from the middle thirties to the early fifties, it provided an environment in which a group of people, as a matter of its routine practice, turned out work as good, say, as that represented by the seven movies forming the basis of my book on remarriage comedies— work, that is to say, as good, or something like as good, as *It Happened One Night* (1934), *The Awful Truth* (1937), *Bringing Up Baby* (1938), *His Girl Friday* (1940), *The Philadelphia Story* (1940), *The Lady Eve* (1941), and *Adam's Rib* (1949)—work that must participate in any history of film as an art that I would find credible. I am not, perhaps I should say, claiming that this work is the best work in the history of world cinema, nor that these films are better than the experimental or nonfiction films contemporary with them. I am, I guess, claiming that they are good, worthy companions of the best; and also that we have as yet no way of knowing, no sufficient terms in which to say, how good they are. So it is no part of my argument to insist that major work can only come from such an environment or to deny that significant movies continue to be made in Hollywood. But I expect that no one still finds that they come almost exclusively from there, and routinely, say every other week, something like twenty or twenty-five times a year. Over a period of fifteen golden years, that comes to between three hundred and four hundred works, which is a larger body of first-rate or nearly first-rate work than the entire corpus of Elizabethan and Jacobean drama can show.

How could we show that it is equally, or anyway, sufficiently, *worth* studying? Now we are at the heart of the aesthetic matter. Nothing can show this value to you unless it is discovered in your own experience, in the persistent exercise of your own taste and hence the willingness to challenge your taste as it stands, to form your own artistic conscience, hence nowhere but in the details of your encounter with specific works.

It is time for some more extended examples. I choose two principally, one beginning from a question I have about a moment in *The Philadelphia Story*, the second from a question I have about the mood of *Pennies from Heaven*.

The Philadelphia Story is in some ways the central member of the remarriage comedies brought together in *Pursuits of Happiness*, but beyond allowing me the pleasure of saying something consecutive about my commitment to these comedies, the example here is meant to isolate for attention one of those apparently insignificant moments in whose power a part of the power of film rests. If it is part of the grain of film to magnify the feeling and meaning of a moment, it is equally part of it to counter this tendency, and instead to acknowledge the fateful fact of a human life that the significance of its moments is ordinarily not given with the moments as they are lived, so that to determine the significant crossroads of a life may be the work of a lifetime. It is as if an inherent *concealment* of significance, as much as its revelation, were part of the governing force of what we mean by film acting and film directing and film viewing.

We need always to be returning to the fact of how mysterious these objects called movies are, unlike anything else on earth. They have the evanescence of performances and the permanence of recordings, but they are not recordings (because there is nothing independent of them to which they owe fidelity); and they are not performances (because they are perfectly repeatable).

If what I might call the *historical* evanescence of film will be overcome when the new technologies of video cassettes and discs complete the work of late-night-television and revival theaters, and the history of movies becomes part of the experience of viewing new movies—a relation to history that we take for granted in the rest of the arts—this should serve to steady our awareness of the *natural* evanescence of film, the fact that its events exist only in motion, in passing.[1] This natural fact makes all the more extraordinary the historical fact that films are still on the whole viewed just once and reviewed on the basis of just one viewing, hence that the bulk of the prose even dedicated movie-goers read about movies is the prose of reviewing, not the demanding criticism and the readings and appreciations one takes for granted as being devoted to other arts. It will compensate my having to choose examples that I cannot be assured we have in common if doing so serves to bring this contingency of film viewing and reading into question.

The moment in *The Philadelphia Story* occurs late, when Katharine Hepburn, hearing from Jimmy Stewart that he did not take advantage of her drunken state the previous night, turns from the assembled audience and says, in a sudden, quiet access of admiration, "I think men are wonderful." Nothing further comes of the line; its moment passes with its saying, like a shadow passing. Struck with the strangeness of this moment, I found in composing *Pursuits of Happiness*—and it is something that one of my reviewers, and on the whole a sympathetic and learned one, found more hysterically inappropriate than any other of my perceptions—that to my ear this line alludes to the moment in *The Tempest* at which Miranda exclaims, "How beauteous mankind is!" Evidently I had not, for that reader, made sufficiently clear my general need for the Shakespearean connection in relation to remarriage comedy; nor had I gained sufficient credit with him to get him to put his sense of appropriateness in abeyance for the moment and specifically to try out what I called an allusion amounting almost to an echo. This is something I am going to ask you to consider doing. Let me go over what I am basing myself on in such cases.

The point of the title "remarriage" is to register the grouping of a set of comedies which differ from classical comedy in various respects, but most notably in this, that in classical comedy the narrative shows a young pair overcoming obstacles to their love and at the end achieving marriage, whereas comedies of remarriage begin or climax with a pair less young, getting or threatening their divorce, so that the drive of the narrative is to get them *back* together, together *again*. The central idea I follow out along various paths, but *roughly* the idea is that the validity or bond of marriage is assured, even legitimized, not by church or state or sexual compatibility (these bonds, it is implied, are no deeper than those of marriage), but, by something I call the willingness for remarriage, a way of continuing to affirm the happiness of one's initial leap; As if the chance of happiness exists only when it seconds itself. In classical comedy people made for one another find one another; in remarriage comedy people who *have* found one another find that they are made for each other. The greatest of the structures of remarriage is *The Winter's Tale*, which is together with *The Tempest*, the greatest of the Shakespearean romances.

But I want the Shakespearean connection with remarriage comedy also for less stupendous structural reasons. Shakespearean romantic comedy lost out, so a way of telling the history goes, to the newer Jonsonian comedy of manners as setting the standard for the future of the English stage. Now I claim that the emergence of film, especially of the talkie, discovered another theater, several centuries later, for that older, Shakespearean structure. Some features of the older comedy that found new life on film are, for example, that it is the woman rather than the man who holds the key to the plot and who undergoes something like death and transformation; that there is some special understanding she has with her father, who does not oppose (as in conventional comedy) but endorses the object of her desire; that the central pair are not young, so that the issue of chastity or innocence, while present, cannot be settled by determinations of literal virginity; that the plot begins and complicates itself in a city but gets resolved in a move to a world of nature—in Shakespeare this is called the green world or the golden world; in four of the seven major Hollywood comedies of remarriage this world is called Connecticut.

But such structural connections are in service of a further reason for the Shakespearean connection, namely to locate the mode of perception called upon in movies, at least in movies of this kind. The connection in effect implies that what allows film to rediscover, for its own purposes, Shakespearean romance, is that unlike the prose of comic theatrical dialogue after Shakespeare, film has a natural equivalent for the medium of Shakespeare's dramatic poetry. I think of it as the poetry of film itself, what it is that happens to figures and objects and places as they are variously molded and displaced by a motion-picture camera and then projected and screened. Every art, every worthwhile human enterprise, has its poetry, ways of doing things that perfect the possibilities of the enterprise itself, make it the one it is; each of the arts has its own poetry, of course, so has each sport, and so, I am sure, have banking and baking and surgery and government. You may think of it as the unteachable point in any worthwhile enterprise.

I understand it to be, let me say, a natural vision of film that every motion and station, in particular every human posture and gesture, however glancing, has its poetry, or you may say its lucidity. Charlie Chaplin and Buster Keaton live on this knowledge, and perhaps bring it to its purest expression; it is my claim in *Pursuits of Happiness* that the Hollywood talkie finds an equivalent for this expressiveness, this expression of lucidity, in the way certain pairs of human beings are in conversation. (An implied threat to their happiness is that they are, somehow because of this fortune, incomprehensible to everyone else in the world they inhabit.) Any of the arts will be drawn to this knowledge, this perception of the poetry of the ordinary, but film, I would like to say, democratizes the knowledge, hence at once blesses and curses us with it. It says that the perception of poetry is as open to all, regardless of birth or talent, as is the ability to hold a camera on a subject, so that a failure to perceive, to persist in missing the subject, which may amount to missing the evanescence of the subject, is ascribable only to ourselves, to failures of our character; as if to fail to guess the unseen from the seen, to fail to trace the implications of things—that is, to fail the perception that there is something to be guessed and traced, right or wrong—requires that we persistently coarsen and stupefy ourselves.

Business people would not run a business this way; this was something Emerson admired about American business; it is why Thoreau asks for what he calls "a little more Yankee shrewdness" in our lives. And Emerson and Thoreau are the writers I know best who most incessantly express this sense of life as missed possibility, of its passing as in a dream, hence the sense of our leading lives of what they call quiet desperation. The movies I name comedies of remarriage find happiness in proposing that there is relief from just that Emersonian loss, that there are conditions under which opportunities may be discovered again and retaken, that somewhere there is a locale in which a second chance is something one may give oneself. (It is my argument about *The Philadelphia Story* in *Pursuits of Happiness*—which I won't try to go into here—that the Philadelphia in its title is the site of the signing of the Declaration of Independence and the Constitution of the United States, so that America is the name of the locale of the second chance, or it was meant to be. Remarriage is the central of the second chances.)

Now I'm taking that apparently insignificant moment of *The Philadelphia Story*, the evanescence of the seven syllables, "I think men are wonderful," as one in which a character is taking such an opportunity, and the movie proposing one to us. It may help to note that the companion line from *The Tempest*—"How beauteous mankind is!"—is also seven syllables long and that both lines occur at the late moment in their dramas at which the principal female is about to undergo a metaphysical transformation. The Hepburn character is to move from the state of chaste goddess (a state each of the four men in her life either accuses her of or praises her for) into what she calls feeling like a human being; and in *The Tempest*, in response to Miranda's exclamation, Ferdinand's father asks whether she is a goddess, to which Ferdinand replies:

> Sir she is mortal,
> But by immortal providence she's mine.

By the way, while the line of Miranda's I am measuring Hepburn's with does not contain the word "wonderful," its more familiar, wider context runs this way:

O wonder!
How many goodly creatures are there here!
How beauteous mankind is! O brave new world
That has such people in it!

Remember that *we* are what has become of the new world, the idea and the fact of which so fascinated Shakespeare and his age.

If one is interested enough to go this far with the conjunction of Hollywood comedy and Shakespearean romance, one will be bound to ask what the point of such a moment is, I mean why this crossroads of wonder is marked so carefully in these dramatic structures. My answer for the comedies of remarriage would run in something like the following way. I think of them, as a group, to be dedicated to the pursuit of what you might call equality between men and women (and of this as emblematic of the search for human community as such—but I am letting this pass for the present), the pursuit of their correct independence of, and dependence upon, one another. What the comedies of remarriage show is that, as the world goes, there is an unfairness or asymmetry in this pursuit, because women require an education for their assumption of equality, and this must be managed with the help of men. The first task for her, accordingly, is to choose the best man for this work. Because of the history between them—both their private history and the history of their culture—they are struggling with one another, they have justified grievances against one another; hence I sometimes characterize these movies as revenge comedies. If their relationship is to go forward the pair must get around to forgiving one another, and, continuing the asymmetry, it must primarily be the woman who forgives the man, not just because she has more to forgive but because she has more power to forgive. And yet in these movies it may be hard to see what the particular man in question needs such radical forgiveness for. He has done nothing obvious to harm the woman, and the specific charges the women bring against the men—Clark Gable's disdainfulness in *It Happened One Night*, Cary Grant's craziness in *The Awful Truth*, and his deviousness in *His Girl Friday*, and his gorgeous thirst in *The Philadelphia Story*; Henry Fonda's sappiness in *The Lady Eve*; Spencer Tracy's forcefulness, even brutishness, in *Adam's Rib*—these are features the woman honors as well as hates the man for, which is doubtless why she can forgive him. It is not fully explicit until the last of the definitive remarriage comedies, *Adam's Rib* in 1949, that what the woman has against the man is fundamentally the simple villainy of his *being* a man; hence that is what her happiness with him depends on her getting around to forgiving him for. The form this takes in the line from *The Philadelphia Story* about men being wonderful, I take, accordingly, as an expression of admiration at the sheer fact of their separateness, wonder as it were that there should be two sexes, and that the opposite one is *as such* admirable. This is hardly the end of anger between them; there are always their differences. But it is a kind of promise to spend as long as it takes—say till death do them part—to work out what those differences are, what they come to.

At some point—always supposing that one can believe that a conjunction of Shakespeare and Hollywood comedies is not hysterically inappropriate—a more sympathetic doubt about the conjunction may seem called for, prompting one to want to know how *serious* I am about it, whether when I say, for example, that film has a natural power of poetry equivalent to the power of Shakespeare's dramatic poetry, I really mean poetry in the same sense. Here I might just respond by saying that that is not a question to which I have an answer apart from the thinking and the writing I do and have done, about movies among other matters. But I want to pause, before turning to my concluding example, to sketch an answer more openly philosophical, in particular one that accounts more openly for the periodic appearance of Emerson and Thoreau in my thoughts, those here tonight and those in *Pursuits of Happiness.* Because while my insistence on writing about philosophy and movies in the same breath, insisting on both of them, but especially on their conjunction, as part of my American intellectual and cultural inheritance—while this has caused me a certain amount of professional tension, it has caused no more than my insistence on inheriting Emerson and Thoreau as philosophers.

Do I really mean philosophers? In the same sense that Plato and Descartes and Kant are philosophers? While this is not a moment to argue the point, I take the moment to ask you to conceive the following possibility: that Emerson and Thoreau are the central founding thinkers of American culture but that this knowledge, though possessed by shifting bands of individuals, is not culturally possessed. It would be an expression of this possibility that no profession is responsible for them as thinkers. Mostly they do not exist for the American profession of philosophy; and the literary professions are mostly not in a position to preserve them in these terms. They are unknown to the culture they express in a way it would not be thinkable for Kant and Schiller and Goethe to be unknown to the culture of Germany, or Descartes and Rousseau to France, or Locke and Hume and John Stuart Mill to England. I do not think it is clear how we are to understand and assess this fact about our cultural lives, but you can see that someone with my interests might wish not to miss the occasion for noting the fact out loud in the nation's capital.

(Here I am seeing our reception of our best writers, like our reception of the best Hollywood movies, as part of America's tendency to over-

praise and undervalue its best work, as though the circus ballyhoo advertising of Hollywood movies were covering doubts we have that they are
really any good at all. I guess this is a preachy thing to say; and maybe
that is what's meant sometimes when I'm called pretentious. But preach-
iness is equally part of the American grain in me, a risk you can run hanging around Emerson and Thoreau as much as I have lately. It is a tone
associated in remarriage comedies especially with Katharine Hepburn's
high-mindedness. She gets lectured about it by the men in her life,
repeatedly dressed down. And once, in *Adam's Rib*, Spencer Tracy allows
himself to say to her, "You get cute when you get causey." Of course this
makes her sore. And I think I know just how she feels.)

But now if our central thinkers are unpossessed, unshared by us, it will
not be expected that we can readily come to intellectual terms on the issues
that matter most to us, as say the fundamental issues of art and of philosophy can matter to us. Emerson and Thoreau fully knew this difficulty in
getting themselves understood. I have taken as a parable of Emerson's ded-
ication of himself as a writer the following sentences from one of his early,
most famous essays, "Self-Reliance":

> I shun father and mother and wife and brother when my genius calls
> me. I would write on the lintels of the door-post, *Whim*. I hope it is
> somewhat better than whim at last, but we cannot spend the day in
> explanation.

Two remarks about this. First, shunning father and mother and wife
and brother is, according to the New Testament, required of you when
the Lord calls you and you seek the kingdom of heaven. And according
to the Old Testament, writing on the lintels of the door is something you
do on Passover, to avoid the angel of death, and it is also where writings
from Deuteronomy are placed, in mezuzahs, to signify that Jews live within and that they are obedient to the injunction of the Lord to bear his
words and at all times to acknowledge them. So Emerson is putting the
calling and the *act* of his writing in the public place reserved in both of
the founding testaments of our culture for the word of God. Is he being
serious?

My second remark about Emerson's passage is that it acknowledges his
writing to be posing exactly the question of its own seriousness. In the
parable I just cited, he both declares his writing to be a matter of life and
death, the path of his faith and redemption, and also declares that *everything* he writes is Whim. I understand this to mean that it is his mission
to create the language in which to explain himself, and accordingly to
imply both that there is no such standing discourse between him and his
culture, and that he is to that extent without justification before himself.

The course open to him is to stake the seriousness of his life, his conviction, on what, before his life's work, we will have no words for: call it whim. So if I answer that my insistence on, for example, aligning movies and Shakespeare and philosophy is based on whim, you will know how to take me.

Now I'm ready to offer as my concluding example, to challenge our convictions in the worth of movies as subjects of thought, *Pennies from Heaven,* a much less lucky movie than, say, the seven thirties comedies I listed in the original genre of remarriage. Those movies are likeable and comprehensible enough to be worth taking and treasuring as light comedies, without working to consciousness any more of the material in *Pursuits of Happiness* than occurs to you casually. Whereas if the brilliance of *Pennies from Heaven* doesn't strike you right off, if you don't become convinced at any rate fairly swiftly that the shocking juxtaposition of attitudes it presents is part of a study, among other things, of the unsettling power of movies, it is likely to seem too unpleasant and confused to think about at all. It is bound to be somewhat hard to think about since it is a Hollywood musical that apparently seeks to undermine the conventions that made possible the Hollywood musical. The subsequent paradox is that its success depends on its undermining itself. If it absorbs the power of conviction of the Hollywood musical then it has not undermined that power. If on the other hand it does not absorb the power of the Hollywood musical then it lacks the power of conviction altogether. It would answer this paradox to say: This movie has the conviction of a work that undermines the conventional sources of conviction in its medium, precisely by reconceiving the sources of that conviction. This sounds like something that might be said of the course of modernism in the other major arts; it is a reason I have sometimes said that art now exists in the condition of philosophy, since it has always been the condition of philosophy to attempt to escape itself, which for several centuries has taken the form of each new major philosopher wishing to repudiate the past of the subject—I mean repudiate it philosophically. As famous, and successful, as any such effort in the arts is Bertolt Brecht's repudiation of theatricality by means of theater itself; theater, hence, reconceived. But in thinking about movies this is so far merely words; it is an idea that has no commonly appreciated and acknowledged realization in film itself. It tells us nothing about whether, for example, *Pennies from Heaven* succeeds or fails in the new terms we allow for it. The moral remains that nothing but the details of the individual work can tell.

Take the two most obvious details in which this film calls into question the conventions of classical Hollywood musicals, the fact that they employ the dubbing of voices, and the fact that they go to any fictional lengths in order to motivate realistically their fantastic songs and dances. When the small time hero, refused financing by the banker, breaks into a happy duet with him, his voice dubbed by a woman's; or, when the crippled mumbling beggar takes on an athletic, dazzlingly mounted performance of the title song; the violence of emotion I felt as I stared at the conventions of the Hollywood musical brought to trial was only increased by the fact that I found the numbers expert and gripping. So if *Pennies from Heaven* is parody, it is at the same time tribute, homage: it acknowledges that the reputedly naive musicals on which it lives were as artful and as mysterious as anything it can claim for itself. It shows that conventions of the Hollywood musical are deeper than we may have thought, that their discovery of human desires and satisfactions cannot be undone or outpaced merely by exaggerating them, and indeed in no obvious way at all. And if this is true of the Hollywood musical, where in successful film, or in art generally, is it not true?

Yet this film fails its own knowledge at the end and strikes, to my ear, so false a note as to help ensure its lack of consideration. What happens is this. The hero is arrested for a terrible crime we know has been committed by the crippled beggar, and the film's examination of the human voice and the sentiments of popular song climaxes with the hero's finding his own voice not in song but in plain speech as, on the gallows, he speaks the words of what may be recognized as the verse to the song "Pennies from Heaven." To ask a writer's words to be so sound that they can be said on the gallows is an ambitious test of writing; I find that these words, said by Steve Martin, passed well enough. If so, then nothing should stand in the way of the fiction's happy ending. The Governor might have driven up in a limousine, his way cleared by screaming motorcycles, and sung a song of pardon to our hero. Instead the movie slinks to a conclusion by having the hero reappear to his sweetheart for no reason within the fiction, mouthing something like, "We've worked too hard not to get a happy ending." This is roughly to suppose that the conventions that lend the movie its power are disposable at will.

How wrong this is is reinforced if we notice that the climax of the movie alludes to a more famous dramatic work with pennies in its title, the Brecht-Weill *Threepenny Opera*, which concludes with its bourgeois criminal hero singing on the gallows and being brought a reprieve by a messenger on horseback. So in failing to find out how to say that its hero deserves a pardon, perhaps in the form of an ironic consolation, *Pennies from Heaven* is faithless at once to its Hollywood medium and to its source in the Brechtian theater of estrangement.[2]

Let us end on this movie's other and most dangerous moment of imitation and homage, the reenactment by Steve Martin and Bernadette Peters of the Astaire-Rogers routine on Irving Berlin's "Let's Face the Music and Dance." What the movie is studying here most extravagantly is the nature of what is called our identification with the figures of drama. This reenactment, along with the voices that take over the characters as they go into song, reveals the identification with figures on film not as a process of imitating them but as a product of being possessed by them. Now of all the impersonations one might have tried of the distinctive stars in the history of Hollywood, from Chaplin to Gable and Hepburn, the one no normal person in his right mind would have tried to translate from the realm of fantasy into the public realm is the sense of himself in an Astaire routine: no one else could perfectly enough lend his body to the demands of that spirit. So one must ask how good the Martin-Peters enactment is of this impossible possession. And I find the answer to be that it is convincing enough to make me ask how convincing the original is, whether *it* fulfills its own dramatic invitation to face the music and dance.

I note that it is perhaps the most weirdly motivated of all the memorable Astaire productions. He prefaces the dance with a little drama in which he loses his money at a casino and then, wandering outside with a pistol to use on himself, sees a woman in an evening gown mount a parapet; he grabs her before she can leap, throws away the pistol, and begins the song and dance. Described in this way, apart from its experience, it may be wondered how they get through all this without laughing.[3] But within the experience, or in remembering such experiences, we know that Astaire has thought about what motivates dancing, about what provides its occasions, as well as anyone who ever lived; so we had perhaps better think further about it in the present case.

The little opening drama, in which the actions set in music are neither spoken, nor sung, nor danced, invokes the condition of mime, of what the Elizabethans called a dumb show, of the sort used in *Hamlet* by the players of the play-within-the-play who act out their drama silently before they speak their parts. If you take this undanced prelude or invitation to dance in this way, as a kind of prophecy or parable of Astaire's understanding of his dancing, then he can be taken to be declaring that it is meant as a removal not from life but from death. Though the idea of escaping life is a more common view of dance and of comedy, and I guess of art in general, than Astaire's idea of redeeming death, it is no less metaphysical. Astaire's view of dancing as facing the music, as a *response* to the life of inexorable consequences, which turn out to be the consequences of desperate pleasures, would then be a concrete translation of what such a thinker as Nietzsche meant by dancing (as when Zarathustra speaks urging: "Raise up your hearts, my brothers, high, higher! And don't forget your legs! Raise up your legs, too, good dancers...!)—something I guess he would have learned, among other things, from Emerson, from such a passage in another of Emerson's early essays as this: "All that we reckoned settled shakes and rattles; and literatures, cities, climates, religions, leave their foundations and dance before our eyes." Can an Astaire-Rogers dance, projected on a screen, be this good? How good would this good have to be?—This is serious business.

Postscript

It was pointed out to me by a student at Yale, on my return for other matters some months after I had given a version of this lecture there, that the ending of *Pennies from Heaven,* which I criticize as faithless to its sources in the Hollywood musical and in Brechtian theater in its avoidance of a stance toward the hero's threatened execution, is readable as a further reflection of the hero's fantasy life, hence as his last moments on the gallows. We hadn't more than a few minutes in which to pursue the idea, so I may have misunderstood what he said. My response is this.

Dennis Potter's novelized version of the material for *Pennies from Heaven* fairly obviously does not know what its own end should be, whether part of the hero's fantasy life, or a further appeal on its behalf, or some final regret that there is no use in such appeal, or a complaint against society for not listening more carefully, or a complaint against the songs for being dismissable. Regarded as the prospectus for a movie, these alternatives may well have seemed undecidable, for the movie must work its own way into such matters. The possibility that the movie takes the option of adopting the hero's fantasy is one that crossed my mind, but it makes matters worse, I think, than I said, worse than making some cheap fun of itself.

The hero's prior bursts into song and dance have the effect of authenticating his inner life, convincing us not only of its existence but of the justice, however mad in imagery (in, some might say, the Utopianism), of its demands. An accomplishment worthy of any art. After these outbursts, it followed (as a kind of price of their elations) that the film's return to grim reality was a return to something no less indebted to the Hollywood past than its treatment of the musical is. A way to tell the structure of *Pennies from Heaven* is as one that alternates musical absorptions of Hollywood (of the thirties and early forties) with counter-absorptions of that same Hollywood; the counter-absorptions work as a kind of negative Utopianism to match the mad positive Utopianism of its music and its music's words. An obvious source for the returns, the counter-absorptions, is such a "woman's film" or "tearjerker" (as if we knew what these are) as George Stevens's *Penny Serenade* of 1941, with Irene Dunne and Cary Grant. I suppose this is deliberate, not only because of the connection in name, but because one of the married pair in the earlier film (in this case the woman) is a hawker of popular music (of records, not sheet music), and a spinning record recurrently punctuates the narration as the film works its way through the death of an innocent and the death of innocence. A less specific source of the counter attitude to reality, to reality as consisting of a planet without music, seems to me something like a Fritz Lang *film noir* early in his American career, for example, *You Only Live Once* of 1937, also about a loser condemned to die for a crime of which he is innocent, which also ends (almost) in a prison yard, with a succeeding ironic fantasy of freedom.

The sources of negative or dashed Utopianism will be harder to recognize than those of the musical numbers, but the alternation of genres provides at once an interpretation of the hero's sensibility, of the commonness of his craziness, and an insight of significance into the Hollywood of its golden age, namely that it depicted a unified world, a universe. The "fugitive couple" of certain of its melodramas are negations of just those pairs in certain Hollywood comedies who are hardly less isolated from society, hardly less incomprehensible to it, but whose isolation and incomprehensibility work themselves out with fortune more willing to smile. (The happier pairs have easier access to money. It remains to be determined how far this is the difference that matters, and how far it is the symbol of the difference.)

It is up to each of us to find our participation in these high-hat highs and low-down lows. Now if the conclusion of *Pennies from Heaven* is to be identified as the hero's fantasy, and it is to be taken on the model of his earlier bursts into song, then, since it has no follow-up, it forces us to read his fantasy as merely some apparently well-understood, ironic escape from some well-understood reality.

And this seems to me faithless at once to the hero's inner life, refusing the just appeal in its tawdriness; and to the freedom it seemed to assign us in determining our relation to these events; and to the power of film itself, whose dangers and values of seduction it had honored, if feared, in its own production, but now seems, in an act of self-disrespect, to claim to transcend—to claim some privileged position from which to assess the value of movies, of fantasy, of art, of such freedom as we can find the means to express and hence to claim. Far be it from me to deny the connection between high and low tawdriness, or escape; but to discount them is not something we need art for, high or low.

I take this moment to avert a related ambiguity in what I was saying in my lecture. When I note the extraordinary persistence of the conventions in viewing movies just once (interspersed with the odd cult-object viewed countless times), and reviewing them on the basis of one viewing, I am objecting not to the practices in themselves but to their dominance, and lack of assessment, in general movie culture. Certainly I am not recommending repetitive viewing to no particular point, as the better alternative. On the contrary, the casual, or surprised, appeal to memorable passages has a value that studiedness may sacrifice, a value not merely of spontaneity (whatever that is), but of a depth that only a certain immediacy will capture, as by surprise. The sacrifice of literary immediacy to studiedness is more familiar ground, and I can imagine that the practical difficulties in the way of checking one's reactions to the events of film (for all the technology of casettes etc.), or one's recall of them, may at some time have a leavening effect on our literary culture, remembering the value there was (however practically necessitated by its own economy) in citing common literary works from memory, a time when a smaller literary world had works in common, a time (except for such things) not to be envied. It resulted in some misquotation (of a particular kind), but its outcome was of contexts in which one recognized the point of having a memory, a public memory. This is something I want from an eventual film culture as much as I want film's rigorous, orderly study. Such is my justification for continuing to explore *Pennies from Heaven* on the basis of one viewing. My excuse is not having had it available since needing to see it again. (*How hard did I look for it? A new question for one's intellectual conscience.)

Notes

This essay appeared in the Winter 1983 issue of the *Yale Review*. It was delivered on May 20, 1982, at the Kennedy Center in Washington D.C., under the sponsorship of the American Film Institute as the Second Annual Patricia Wise Lecture. I was told, in my invitation to prepare the lecture, that the idea of the series was to provide an occasion for writers and scholars not centered within the film community to describe the importance to their work, or to contemporary culture, of the existence of movies. I found I wanted to use the occasion to respond with fair consecutiveness to the repeated quizzing I have been subjected to over the years about my interest in film, especially on the publications of my books about film, *The World Viewed* (1971), and *Pursuits of Happiness: The Hollywood Comedy of Remarriage* (1981), the publications which, I assumed, had produced the invitation to me to give the Wise Lecture. So I am glad for the opportunity to have the lecture printed essentially as it was delivered, with no effort to remove what I had been careful to include within it—my sense of its occasion.

1 Norton Batkin took me back to this idea. His work represented by *Photography and Philosophy*, the doctoral dissertation he submitted to the Department of Philosophy at Harvard in May 1981, goes far with it, into the nature of photography's stillness.
2 I have added a postscript that amplifies this claim.
3 Arlene Croce testifies to such a feeling in her elegant and useful *The Fred Astaire and Ginger Rogers Book* (New York: Vintage Books, 1972), 88.

2 ▮ Provocations and Justifications of Film

Karen Hanson

Serious film study often takes the form of *theory*. Is there any reason why this should be so? I want to approach this question by examining some of the contingencies of film theory, especially its attempted alignment with science. Science seems to have grown out of the refinement of common sense and from a desire to understand and control the forces of nature. How do we understand the growth of film theory? What motivates it?

Despite the fact that film has provoked an enormous amount of need for explanation, the puzzle of the impetus to theory construction may yet be overlooked. Consider a commonly accepted account of the generation of film theory, here articulated by Noël Carroll:

> One reason for [the large body of theoretical writing] is that film is an art form that was invented not only in living memory but self-consciously. It is a medium that had to prove that it was an art form.... [F]ilm had to legitimize its place in our culture. And the way that it initially set about getting itself taken seriously was to prove that it was an art.... This was the first task of film theory.[1]

One might think that the only—and a sufficient—way for a medium to prove it is an art form is for it to be the medium of what evidently are works of art. The task of getting taken seriously would then fall to film-makers, not film theorists. If film theorists are thought crucial, is it because those who find this account tenable take it as obvious that all art requires the support of theory, that, in the absence of theory, nothing can be, or be recognized as, art? Or is it that all art *now* requires theory, that we, in the modern or postmodern age, demand it? Or is it that a *young* art cannot stand without the help of theory?

The idea remains undeveloped that theory's testimony is required to achieve or bestow standing or recognition, but the idea is given urgency by the antecedent assertion of the requirement of legitimacy. If we pause at this earlier point, too, however, we might well wonder: Why did anything—let alone the claim to be art—need to be proved, and to whom? The usual assumption is that film is from the start popular; it *has* a place in our culture. If that place were analyzed solely in, say, commercial or economic terms; or if film were understood simply as diversion, as a medium of amusement and relaxation, is it clear that a question of "legitimacy" would press itself upon us? When a new technology—from the telephone to the computer—becomes popular, there does not seem to be an inevitable second step, "getting itself taken seriously." And we are not so dour as to insist that every popular new mode of diversion—consider, for example, football or basketball—must "legitimize its place in our culture." When pressed, the adversion to the necessity of legitimacy seems less a satisfying explanation for the appearance of theory than the disclosure of a puzzling attitude itself in need of explanation.

What here motivates the issue of legitimacy? The common account suggests that it is film's claim to the title "art" that is under theoretical scrutiny. But the account also suggests that that claim is entered for film precisely *by* theory. The very question of legitimacy thus seems an artifact of theory. The idea that *film* needs to legitimize itself then looks like a *displacement* of whatever fear, anxiety and embarrassment may typically underlie the issue of legitimacy. It is not, then, the invention and immediate popularity of film, but the intervention of and attraction to theory that raises the question, perhaps itself needs, legitimacy.

The subtext of the commonly accepted explanation for the enterprise of film theory is the revelation of a discomfiture of, in, thought. For reasons unknown, film is supposed to have had to prove itself an art and to meet some question about its legitimacy; film theory is then supposed to appear, called into being to examine film's case and serve as an advocate. The ready acceptance of this transparently inadequate explanation suggests an eagerness to avoid some deeper issues: what is it about film that provokes sustained thought, and what are the directions such thought might take? Examination of the received account, with its displaced problem of legitimacy, should make us wonder: Do we feel the need for an excuse for thinking hard about film? And do we assume that certain objects of thought—e.g., art—insure thought's legitimacy? What are the difficulties in supposing that thought might have to proceed with no fixed guarantors of legitimacy?

One might forestall these questions by advancing a general cultural piety about the inherent value of virtually any intellectual activity. Indeed, those who reflect on reflections about film sometimes assume that not just the legitimacy but also the aim of theorizing is adequately conveyed by the claim that we are seeking knowledge or understanding. A distinction is then quickly drawn between practical knowledge—concerning such matters as camera angles, focus, lighting, camera and projection speeds, and so on—that might be useful to filmmakers, and another, more general product of a more general inquiry, something that springs not from professional needs but from our most general, our human, interest in understanding our world and everything in it. Inquiry of the second sort is often compared, indeed sometimes said to be one, with science. So, for example, Dudley Andrew, in introducing his account of the major theories of film, says:

> Film theory is another avenue of science, and as such is concerned with
> the general rather than the particular. It is not concerned primarily with
> individual films or techniques, but with what might be called the cine-
> matic capability itself.[2]

The comparison or identification with science is grounded on a number of more or less clear assumptions. One is explicitly stated: science is understood to concern itself with the general rather than the particular, or with the particular only insofar as it can be understood as an instance of the more general. Thus a distinction is drawn between film criticism, which makes claims about particular films, and film theory, which makes claims about the medium. Implicit in the attachment to the idea of science are, *inter alia*, some commitment to systemization and to objectivity and a supposition that among the desiderata that control the enterprise are the ideals of truth and explanatory power.

All of these features that are taken to be characteristic of science are, of course, philosophically contested. Their functions, their very meanings in the activities acknowledged as science are matters in continuous dispute. That film theorists exhibit little awareness of the history and the present state of these disputes is perhaps unsurprising and, at first glance, no cause for disparagement. We do not, after all, expect, say, a chemist to attend to all the conceptual debates about the nature of objectivity or the character of confirmation, causation, or explanation. Behind our self-assurance about a justifiable division of efforts, however, there may be a vague confidence that the practices of particular sciences have working standards to which all their practitioners are answerable. Indeed, much philosophy of science, especially in recent decades, has proceeded on the self-conscious assumption that one of the routes to clarifying the signal concepts of science is to study the operation of those concepts in the everyday practice of scientists. So, for example, if we want to understand the notion of confirmation, part of what we shall need to do is become familiar with the actual use of this concept in ongoing science—what does and does not count as confirmation, the relations between confirmation and corroboration, prediction, observation, experimental results, and so on, in the communities and institutions of science.

Philosophers may then continue to analyze, explicate, and argue about the proper understanding of these key concepts; and, during periods of methodological controversy or theoretical crisis, scientists themselves may find the philosophic discussion unavoidable. The fact remains, however, that at least during periods of what is called "normal science," there is operational agreement among the members of the scientific community concerning the notions that structure the presentation and evaluation of scientific claims.[3] There are publicly shared standards of acceptable methodology, shared judgments of the pertinence of specific results or observations, shared convictions about what count as problems, shared hypotheses about what might be relevant to the resolution of controversial cases or to progress on outstanding issues.

Is there this sort of operational agreement in film theory? Among the questions film theorists may need to ask themselves—or rather, among the questions that must be asked of those who understand film theory as a science—are those that probe the evaluative criteria for theoretical claims. Is there a working framework, generally acknowledged, for *testing* hypotheses? Do all parties to the enterprise share a sense of what counts as *evidence*, what *confirms*, or *disconfirms*, a theory? Dudley Andrew says that "[f]ilm theorists make and verify propositions about film."[4] Though the idea of verification is notoriously vexed, philosophically, the history and character of that vexation need not necessarily concern someone such as Andrew, someone who wants to claim film theory is a science, so long as it is reasonably clear how verification—or falsification, or confirmation or corroboration, or disconfirmation—is operationalized in the discipline. But, again, is this clear?

A philosophically-minded defender of the idea that film theory is science might try to dismiss all worries about exactly how observations are supposed to warrant general theoretical claims by reminding us, first, that no particular observation, no finite number of observations, can *ever* fully confirm a general statement, unless we know we have observed all cases covered by the general statement.[5] Furthermore, no particular observation ever compels the revision or abandonment of a theory. Even if, for example, we could understand film theory's being "concerned with the general" to be cashed out as its offering subsumptive patterns of explanation, and explanations of the most rigorous deductive sort—the theory's general laws serving as major premises in valid deductive arguments having true observations and even accurate predictions as their conclusions—logic would not require theory change in the event of a failed prediction or a recalcitrant observation. We may just as easily, and sometimes more responsibly, dismiss the observation as erroneous or attribute the failed prediction to an inaccurate or inadequate specification of the factual circumstances in which the theory's laws were applied. The fact is that, even in the best of circumstances, even in the paradigm examples of science, scientific methods are themselves theory-dependent: theoretical claims are not uniquely related to observational predictions in the sense that each theoretical statement will imply a particular, or a set of particular, observations; the observational consequences of a theory are always derived not just from the theory in question but, holistically, from that theory *and* a set of auxiliary hypotheses, assumed conditions, or background theories.

These philosophical points about the relations between theory and observation are, however, utterly misconceived as a defense of the construal of film theory as science; for the salient fact about science is precisely that these philosophical concerns about theory and observation do not cloud its normal practice. Within each discipline or domain of science, there is a fairly clear working sense of the confirmatory value of particular types of observation, of the number of tests or observations reasonably required for the abandonment or the provisional acceptance of a theory, of the relative need to suspect an observation of being faulty, of the extent to which a given theory or portion of theory should be considered relatively immune or relatively susceptible to revision, of the background theories that are appropriately employed, and so on. Do we see this sort of pragmatic consensus in the field of film theory?

It might of course be suggested that, if we do not, it is perhaps because film theory, though a science, is not, or not yet, in a period of "normal" science. Doubts about the aptness of the scientific model, however, might only be heightened by this analysis. Even if the histories of the sciences, even the *exemplary* sciences, the natural sciences, are punctuated by periods of theoretical crisis, times when questions of the relation between theory and evidence are alive and unsettled within practice itself; and even if theories in the exemplary sciences are sometimes abandoned not because of experimental results or observations but because of the attractiveness of alternative theories; still, insisting on the identification of film theory with science by embracing the idea that film theory exists in a state of extended theoretical crisis would seem a self-defeating stance. For the very idea of extended, perpetual, theoretical crisis should itself prompt some puzzlement about the *character* of film theory's claims. Is there something about them that invites not testing but contesting, something that is not just the dispositional fallibility of science but an active resistance to resolution? In any case, we should now wonder, what would *support* the assumption that film theory is science, that this is the best way to understand the nature of its claims?

Crucial to the self-conception of science, after all, is some idea that its accounts are descriptive, not evaluative. Science must be said to value truth, and the norms that are supposed to govern its search for truth—standards of coherence and consistency, allegiance to impartial testing, etc.—may be ones we find admirable. Nonetheless, the results of adherence to the norms of science are, given the context of a distinction between fact and value, supposed to be value-free. This does not, of course, mean they are devoid *of* value. Scientific truths may be sought for their instrumental value, and thus it is that the mention of the scientific aim of accurate prediction is often immediately followed by discussion of the possibility of control. Moreover, human interests, preferences, values, may set research agendas; indeed *particular* political values, the interests and preferences of *particular* people or groups may not only set the agendas but in fact influence the interpretation of results.[6] But scientific results—observational laws and theories—are supposed to have objectivity, to stand beyond or despite anyone's wishes or desires. Scientific findings may be used to advance human weal or woe, but their welcome or unwelcome import for human affairs is supposed to be no part of their content.

While there is controversy about the extent to which the institutions of science have maintained value neutrality, debate even about whether the aspiration makes sense, whether there *is* a realm or level of *facts* unmixed with values, the self-conception of science still stands in sharp contrast to the open commitment to evaluation often evidenced by film theory. Sciences, particularly social sciences such as economics and sociology, may certainly take an interest in value judgments, but these sciences understand themselves to be aiming for objective accounts, neutral descriptions, of the facts of subjective preferences. Film theory often understands itself to be *advancing* particular preferences, or grounding or justifying one or a set of evaluative claims. It is worth noting that Dudley Andrew, after asserting that film theory is a science and affirming that *auteur* theory—because it is a "way of ranking directors in a hierarchy of worth," because all it does is "[organize] our film history…and [make] us sensitive to certain aspects of it, showing us what movies we have valued or ought to begin valuing"—is "properly speaking, …not a theory at all but a critical method," then finds it possible and appropriate to organize his treatment of proper film theories by canvassing, among other fixed features, what he takes to be their inevitable pronouncements on or implicit answers to the question of the value of film.[7] Some account of film's ultimate human purpose is a categorical feature of all film theory, according to Andrew, and this feature is disclosed, he says, as we note each theory's responses to "questions which seek the goal of cinema in man's universe. Once raw material has been shaped by a process into a given significant form, what does this mean for mankind?"[8]

Andrew's version of an Aristotelian analysis—he takes himself to be employing an adaptation of the *Physics'* account of four "causes"—material, efficient, formal, and final—will not strike a responsive chord among practicing scientists. Modern science does not seek ultimate purposes behind or within the phenomena it studies, and it is not part of the business of science to offer accounts of "the meaning for mankind" of the objects of its research.

Nonetheless, some metatheoretical attention to the important role of valuation in film theory may yet seem to allow for a closer fit with the practices of the sciences. For example, Noël Carroll also affirms that the major film theories all offer an answer to the question, "What is the value or role of cinema?", and he says that film theories differ from filmmaking guides and manuals in that film theories "attempt to elucidate each process...of articulation [composition, editing, sound, etc.] in terms of its commitment to a particular determinant feature and to the value of film."[9] Now if the notion of "value" is taken to be essentially equivalent to the idea of "role," then film theory might perhaps after all be trying to position itself as a branch or subdivision of one of the social sciences. Film theorists would then not themselves be *making* evaluative judgments about cinema; they would merely be describing the *function* of cinema in the dynamics of some other social events or processes. Functional analyses and teleological explanations are common not only in the social sciences but also in biology, where the Aristotelian idea of final ends may have been abandoned, but purposive or teleological locutions are, at the least, important heuristics. Biologists investigating some detail of the structure of an organism or a particular natural process often ask, "What is the purpose of this structure?", "What is this process *for?*"; and they are helped to an understanding of a phenomenon by a consideration of the way in which it functions to preserve or continue life. Is this the model of thought we discern when film theory tries "to elucidate each process...of articulation in terms of its commitment to the value of film"?

The nature and status, in science, of teleological explanations is itself a complicated matter, but some simple points may here need attention. It must first be remembered that modern biology's teleological claims can generally be recast to eliminate teleological language. Consider, for example: "Insulin is released into the bloodstream in order to metabolize glucose"; "This butterfly's pattern of coloration is designed to disguise it from predators." The vital process of glucose metabolism can also be described biochemically, in terms of non-purposive chemical reactions; and the facts concerning glucose metabolism's *being* a vital process can be stated apart from any supposition that, from the point of view of dispassionate science, life *has* a value—compared to, say, death or nonexistence. The claim about the butterfly may be regarded as a sort of shorthand version of an evolutionary explanation of the coloration, an explanation in terms of variation and natural selection, an account that involves no notion of design or of goals and that rests on no ideas of the ultimate "meaning for mankind," of the fact of survival.

Now there certainly can be teleological claims about film that can be recast into nonteleological terms. "The camera exposes film in order to capture images" may be a way of putting a fact about how the camera works that can also be conveyed by a description of the mechanical features of the camera, identification of the relevant laws of optics, and a specification of some photochemical reactions. And there certainly can be, indeed there are, modes of studying film that fit the paradigms of the social sciences. Consider, for example, historical examination of the value of certain sorts of films in building or maintaining patriotic sentiment; or psychological studies of the role that violent and pornographic movies might play in shaping viewers' attitudes toward women. But if, for example, Siegfried Kracauer claims that the value of film is grounded on its capacity to record and reveal reality, and he questions the cinematic validity of German expressionist film, is it plausible to take his remarks as attempts at social science, descriptive accounts of the social role of film?[10] If Rudolph Arnheim claims that what we see when we look at a film is importantly different from what we see when we look at the physical world, and that it is just these differences that film must exploit in order to secure the values inherent in art, should we understand him to be offering a functional analysis?[11] Could we reasonably consider Arnheim's apparent assumption that art is a goal *worth* aiming for "just a heuristic," a device of thought adopted only to uncover the value-neutral facts?

When film theorists make recommendations about the proper, the best, the "valid" uses of film, it is not at all obvious that those recommendations can be reduced to the technical claims and the elliptical hypotheticals characteristic of applications of the exemplary social sciences. (Compare, for example, "The best public opinion polls have properties p,q,r,s...", which has the force of something like "To obtain [or, '*If* you want to obtain...'] the most accurate data about public opinion, a poll must have [or, 'then you must employ a poll with] properties p,q,r,s....') Insofar as film theory is unabashedly pervaded by the film theorist's critical evaluative judgments—about *film*, not just about observations supporting *claims* about film—the self-conception of the enterprise appears quite different from the self-conception of the exemplary sciences.[12] Insofar as film theory is concerned with establishing the categorical worth of film or some film phenomenon, it goes beyond the value-neutrality that is supposed to be a formal feature of the functional analyses of biology and the social sciences.

Given the recurrent difficulties in fitting much of the practice of film theory into the mold of the sciences, we might wonder anew whether there really are any good grounds for the identification or assimilation. How important, how telling, is film theory's interest in systemization? Sciences certainly are concerned with systemization, but to say this is not yet to distinguish science from a range of other endeavors, including, in particular, some kinds of philosophy. It is worth noting that the scientific pursuit of systemization is usually allied with its quest for explanations. The character of this linkage is a complicated and important matter, to which we shall return; but, for now, the fact of this connection should remind us that the ideal of systemization can take a variety of forms. The catalog of the Library of Congress, for example, is a triumph of systemization, but this triumph cannot be seen as fueled by or propelling explanatory power; for systemization and explanation are not here on the same track. How is systemization understood in film theory?

Andrew Tudor says this:

> ...[T]he expression 'theory of film' has been applied to any attempt to make general assertions about the meaning of the medium. While generalization is undoubtedly a necessary component of 'theory', all generalizations do not constitute theories.... There is also an issue of method involving the *systemization* of our thought. The film theorist is distinguished from the film essayist (who might also make general statements) by his stress on the systematic. To theorize is, of necessity to invoke the criterion of logical consistency, and so logically to interrelate various diverse elements into theories.[13]

If we leave aside Tudor's apparent confusion about the notion of logical consistency—logical consistency in no way implies logical interrelations of "various diverse elements"; a standard of logical consistency can be met by a set of utterly unrelated propositions, for logical consistency requires merely the avoidance of contradiction—we may pull two rather

different threads out of this knot of ideas about systemization. One reading, the one probably most faithful to Tudor's intent, takes us in the direction of substantive organization, the building of a structure *of* thought.
Systemization accordingly involves finding or making a pattern in, of, our
ideas, observations, or theoretical laws. Systemization as system-building
might thus be a matter of generalizing about our observations, then bringing a number of generalizations under a yet more general "covering law"
from which they can be deduced, and then in turn subsuming that law
and others under a still more general cover, and so on; or it might be a
matter of resting chains of inferences on a foundational claim accepted as
true *a priori*.[14] Or it might take—it *has* taken, in both science and philosophy—yet other forms.

But stressing *systematic* thought, the other gloss on the necessity of systemization, need not entail system-building. We can be systematic *in* our
thinking—orderly, methodical—even when we have no interest in producing a theory. Systematic thought is often a feature of good problem-
solving in a variety of contexts—from the humblest practical affairs
("Don't cry; I have a *plan* to *find* your lost mitten! We'll retrace our steps,
looking as we go, until we see where you dropped it"), to matters of life
and death ("Your symptoms are compatible with a number of diagnoses;
let's run some tests to see if we can eliminate some possibilities and get a
clearer handle on what's really wrong"), to the most recondite of abstrac-
tions ("If we can just prove this lemma, we can produce a proof of the
whole theorem"). Now systematic thought, as well as system-building, is
surely also a part of good science. And a refusal to brook logical inconsis-
tencies—though it will not positively *construct* substantive ties among one's
thoughts—is an important characteristic of the properly methodical
thinker, and a cast of mind crucial to the operation of some other features
of what is sometimes called "scientific thinking."

A willingness to revise inconsistent beliefs and to withdraw claims in
the face of good evidence or good arguments against them, together with
a willingness to subject claims to critical scrutiny and careful tests, is surely part of the ideal scientific temperament; but that temperament may be
just as desirable in other domains of thought, and in activities within those
domains unconnected with the building of systems. If these attitudes are
taken to further, even to define, *rational* inquiry in every domain—from
philosophy to the affairs of practical life—and yet they are understood to
be most fully, most systematically, realized in the institutions and methods of science, we can see yet another, and a different kind of, attraction
to the idea that film theory is, or should be, a form of science.

A version of this idea seems to animate Noël Carroll's attack on contemporary film theory and his vision for improvement. He complains that "the confusion of belles lettres, on the one hand, with scientific and philosophical reasoning, on the other, is one of the most egregious problems in contemporary film theory," and he asserts that the way to demonstrate and correct this confusion is to assess all theoretical claims "with the rigor one would apply to any scientific hypothesis."[15] We may initially accept the implicit identification of scientific and philosophical *reasoning* , taking it for granted that *anything* that pretends to be reasoning must be constrained by appropriate logic, must show the relevance, adequacy, and plausibility of the premises used to derive conclusions, and so on. The idea of *assessing* all theoretical claims may also be appropriately associated with the spirit of rationality of both philosophy and science. But what, specifically, *is* the "rigor" applied to scientific hypotheses? Carroll describes his own stategy of assessment as a combination of "noting [the] logical and empirical failings" of contemporary film theory and presenting alternative accounts. The construction of rival accounts is crucial, according to Carroll, for thus he is "following the traditional method of scientific debate, …attempting to show the shortcomings of contemporary film theory by demonstrating that there are more attractive, competing theories that offer better explanations of the data at hand."[16]

The details of this alignment of science, film theory, and philosophy are themselves in need of assessment. What makes a theory "more attractive"? Are there clear criteria for "better explanations"? Philosophers of science, from Aristotle to the present, have remarked on the existence of a variety of patterns of explanation. In the course of our present discussion we have had occasion to note both the deductive or covering law model and functional or teleological explanations, and to this list of common patterns we should add probabilistic or statistical explanations and genetic or developmental explanations. Arguments have been and continue to be made about the relations between these patterns and about the extent to which scientific explanations, or explanations in anything that should be counted as science, can be reduced to the covering law pattern, with the probabilistic form understood as a variant of the deductive model. Whether or not a unitary conception of explanation can be found that is regarded as adequate for science, however, it is clear that many of our everyday requests for explantions are *not* requests for covering laws. Suppose a filmviewer asks, "Why was the same actor cast as both the Beast and as Beauty's brother's friend?" An appropriate answer here will cite *reasons* and *purposes*. A causal explanation would not be to the point, even if it were available, even, that is to say, if psychological science had reached a stage where it could cite the general laws of behavior from which this par-

ticular action could be deduced. (Or physics the laws predicting this disposition of matter, etc.)

What counts as a good, what counts as a better, explanation is highly
context-dependent, and context-dependent in a *variety* of specific ways.
If we merely note that explanations are always addressed, explicitly or
implicitly, *to* someone or some cognitive community, we can begin to spell
out some dimensions of context. An account of human sexuality that
would be a good explanation to a three-year old will not be adequate to
the interests of a community of biologists. The reverse holds, too, however, and it would be a mistake to suppose that the explanation we give
to the child is just a crude, scaled-down version of the ones sought by the
biologists. The child's *interests*, and thus what best satisfies them, may be
genuinely *different* from, and not just primitive prototypes of, the biologists'. Furthermore, if we confine our attention just to a community of
scientists, and take their interests to be defined by their discipline, we shall
still find that what gets counted as a good or a better explanation cannot
be sorted out if all we have at our disposal are formulaic notions of "fitting
the facts" or neat assumptions about the undesirability of postulating theoretical entities. Unobservable entities may be cheerfully postulated, if
doing so seems to bring a range of heretofore unrelated phenomena under
a common cover. Descriptive accounts may be idealized, so that, it is
understood, they do not quite fit the facts as we encounter them, do not
quite capture our experience. And the working notion of a better explanation is itself theory-dependent: the way in which a proposed explanation fits or fails to fit a science's present theoretical framework; the extent
to which, the points at which, acceptance of the explanation would require
revision of prevailing theory—these factors play definite roles in the scientific community's assessment of an explanation's merits.

Similarly, there is no fixed or domain-independent metric with which to
measure the attractiveness of a theory. Certainly a number of characteristics are usually cited as theoretical virtues—testability, empirical adequacy, simplicity, parsimony, explanatory power—but there is lively debate
about the appropriate conception of many of these; and, on any plausible
view of these notions, it is not at all clear that the virtues are inevitably
positively linked or mutually reinforcing.[17]

All these considerations should make us considerably less sanguine about
the prospects of film theory's borrowing from science a clear, context- and
content-neutral method of ranking explanations and appraising theories.[18]
Science does not have such a method to loan; and, even if it did, it is not
obvious that the questions film raises for us are always of a sort that a scientific *kind* of explanation will satisfy, or that productive reflection on film,

even when it aims to be systematic, is always seeking *explanations*.

In "The Sentiment of Rationality," William James suggests that a drive to understand things can move us in two radically different directions—orderly thought can step back from confusing phenomena, to see patterns in the chaos; or it can plunge forward, to focus more closely on one element at a time. The first route he calls "theoretic"—"the facts of the world in their sensible diversity are always before us, but our theoretic need is that they should be conceived in a way that reduces their manifoldness to simplicity"—and he calls this need "the philosophic passion *par excellence*."[19] (Think of the division of the world into mind and matter, the reduction of mind to matter, or matter to mind.) But, of course, this passion is expressed in science as well, and, in fact, all the examples James gives ("Who does not feel the charm of thinking that the moon and the apple are, as far as their relation to the earth goes, identical; of knowing respiration and combustion to be one...?") are drawn from the achievements of science. The *other* route to the rational understanding sought by philosophy is motivated by what James describes as "a sister passion," "a rival" to the passion for simplification:

> This is the passion for distinguishing; it is the impulse to be *acquainted* with the parts rather than to comprehend the whole. Loyalty to clearness and integrity of perception, dislike of blurred outlines, of vague identifications, are its characteristics.[20]

The stirrings of the "sister passion"—for specificity, detail, distinctions, a clarity of cognition unrelated to theory-construction—have lately been strongly felt in philosophical ethics, where the cultural role and the intellectual and practical value of moral theory are under serious examination. There is a revival of interest in the prospects for casuistry, and there are efforts both to borrow from old and to describe new ways of being reflective and critical about moral matters, without presuming the necessity of any covering theory of right and wrong, obligation, or the good for humankind. Philosophical aesthetics, too, has lately shown comparatively little interest in grand theories of art and beauty.

For a variety of reasons, these trends in ethics and aesthetics are worth pondering. It is not just that we can suddenly find alternative models for critical and metacritical reflection, models that might better fit many of our interests in film. After all, these traditional, established areas of philosophy, with their fields sometimes grouped together, tendentiously, as "value theory," might, naturally, rather than science, have been the first, the orienting, point of comparison for the relatively young practice of film theory; and in fact film theory is, and has been, often understood as a practice of aesthetics. It is crucial to remember, however, that moral philosophy and aesthetics have themselves often sought self-understanding by positioning their practices in relation to the natural sciences, occasionally claiming structural alignment.

The recurrent attraction of this alignment should not be blithely dismissed as indicative of a yearning for the cultural prestige of modern science. It may be, rather, that scientific theory seems to provide, or suggest that there can be, a compass point in otherwise uncharted territory.[21] The very idea of critical judgments and evaluative claims ungrounded by a fixed framework of standards, something akin to science's "prevailing theory," can be disconcerting. It may seem to leave the status of such judgments unclear, the force of such claims inherently suspect. But perhaps these prospects need to be faced, explored.

Perhaps there are some questions about film, the philosophic questions, that require, or seek, self-legitimating answers, not solutions based on well-corroborated theories or objective causal accounts. Even among philosophers such as James and the other pragmatists, who stress the continuity of science and philosophy, the practice of philosophy is understood to involve no special knowledge and to offer no disciplinary guidance to observation, no fixed procedures for accumulating the evidential support of data. Peirce notes that

> [i]n the special sciences facts are set over against theories, because it is the business of those sciences to connect the special phenomena which they discover with the general experience they derive from other sources. But philosophy embraces all experience. Its direct data are the familiar phenomena found everywhere....[22]
>
> [Philosophy] is an experiential...science, but [it] rests...on phenomena which lie open to the observation of [everyone], every day and hour.[23]

Still, even if film study were to be practiced not as science, or a special science, but as a philosophy of common experience, deeply indulging James's "sister passion" for clarity and detailed acquaintance, it might yet achieve something akin to the generality so frequently cited as a mark of genuine theory. Consider the Kantian picture of aesthetic judgment, as sketched by Stanley Cavell, where the task of the critic is not to discount or overcome subjectivity, "but to master it in exemplary ways"; or consider Cavell's own view of the way in which our knowledge of the conditions of our lives is marshalled in philosophical activity—with the conviction "that if we could articulate it fully we would have spoken for all..., found the necessities common to us all."[24] The assertion of one's own experience as exemplary, as representative, any claim to speak for all, of course raises in a different form the issue of legitimacy. Can we, out of our ordinary and individual experience, make exemplary claims about film?

If that question is left for another occasion, it must still be remarked that it is a philosophic question—and it is raised by film. There may be no confirmed theory of film in terms of which we can seek a satisfying answer, but pressing the question will, in the end, reveal as much about our conception of philosophy as about our understanding of film. Would what we find then settle, or would it raise in a new form, the question of thought's legitimacy?

Notes

1 Noël Carroll, *Philosophical Problems of Classical Film Theory* (Princeton: Princeton University Press, 1988), 4.

2 Dudley Andrew, *The Major Film Theories* (Oxford: Oxford University Press, 1976), 4.

3 The phrase is Thomas Kuhn's, and his account of this sort of historical interval, and of the contrasting periods of crisis and what he calls "paradigm shifts," occurs in his *The Structure of Scientific Revolutions* (Chicago: University of Chicago Press, 1962). The phrase "normal science" has currency even among those who disagree with Kuhn's account.

4 Andrew, *Major Film Theories*, 3.

5 The problem is, of course, the universal *form* of the purported general laws, and this is no more and no less a problem for statements about film than it is for statements about anything else. Consider a version of the standard illustration: For fifty years our community of researchers has engaged in intense birdwatching, and we have seen nothing but white swans. Nonetheless, all it takes is one black swan, somewhere in the world, to falsify the claim that all swans are white. The illustration reminds us how tenuous our inductive grip may be, even when we have made lots of observations, even if our methods are resolutely empirical. Still, it might in fact provoke special anxieties about the evidence for universal generalizations about *film*, an invented and evolving medium.

6 Feminist discussion of the specific possibility of androcentric bias is well summarized in Evelyn Fox Keller's "Feminism and Science," in *Sex and Scientific Inquiry*, eds. S. Harding and J. O'Barr (Chicago: University of Chicago Press, 1987), 233–46.

7 Andrew, *Major Film Theories*, 5, 4.

8 Andrew, *Major Film Theories*, 7.

9 Carroll, *Classical Film Theory*, 14.

10 See Siegfried Kracauer, *Theory of Film* (Oxford: Oxford University Press, 1960).

11 See Rudolph Arnheim, *Film As Art* (Berkeley: University of California Press, 1957).

12 The self-identification, even the academic categorization, of the *theorist* does not, by itself, offer a substantial challenge to this claim. So, for example, the fact that Arnheim is a professional psychologist cannot be taken as proof—or even strong evidence—that *Film As Art* is simply the normal practice of psychological science. (Einstein was a physicist, but sometimes he engaged in the philosophy of science. Noam Chomsky is in linguistics, but some of his writing is philosophical, some is political, etc.)

13 Andrew Tudor, *Theories of Film* (New York: Viking Press, 1974), 9–10.

14 The phrase is usually credited to William Dray. See his *Laws and Explanations in History* (Oxford: Oxford University Press, 1957).

15 Noël Carroll, *Mystifying Movies—Fads and Fallacies in Contemporary Film Theory* (New York: Columbia University Press, 1988), 32.

16 Carroll, *Mystifying Movies*, 7.

17 For a good overview of the nature and problems of scientific explanation and theory choice, a classic text is Ernst Nagel's *The Structure of Science* (New York: Harcourt, Brace, and World, 1961). An anthology that provides a good update, with a helpful sampling of current, "post-positivist" philosophy of science, is *The Philosophy of Science*, eds., R. Boyd, P. Gasper and J.D. Trout (Cambridge, Massachusetts: MIT Press, 1991).

18 Indeed, Carroll's own central metatheoretical assumptions—his preference for "piecemeal" theorizing and his suspicion of any approach that "attempts to answer all our questions about filmic phenomena in terms of a unified theoretical vocabulary with a set of limited laws" (*Mystifying Movies*, 8)—assumptions he evidently takes to exemplify a scientific approach, could be seen as strikingly at odds with some signal features of modern natural science, where there is a continual push for greater generality of theory, where constraints on and clarification of vocabulary license departures from ordinary language, and where unified patterns of explanation are highly prized.

19 William James, *The Will to Believe and Other Essays in Popular Philosophy* (New York: Dover Publications, 1956), 65.

20 James, *The Will to Believe*, 66.

21 It is a fact, perhaps an ironic one, that the nature of *theorizing* in the *humanities* generally, and not just in connnection with film, is relatively unexamined. The aims and standards of this set of practices remain underconceptualized and pragmatically unclear.

22 Arthur Burks, ed., *Collected Papers of Charles Sanders Peirce, vol. 8* (Cambridge, Massachusetts: Harvard University Press, 1958), 85.

23 Burks, *Papers of Peirce, vol. 7*, 314.

24 Stanley Cavell, *Must We Mean What We Say* (New York: Charles Scribner's Sons, 1969), 94, 96.

3   Morals for Method

George M. Wilson

In a wide variety of classical narrative films, there are central characters whose perception and comprehension of their personal circumstances are shown to be dim, distorted, and severely restricted in relation to their need to see and understand the situations in which they act. The film viewer, from a position outside the relevant fictional world, sees how these characters' ways of apprehending the depicted action collide with the facts that their outlooks have failed to encompass. Thus, the audience is given object lessons in the faltering dynamics of perception over a period of time. However, it is equally the case, and equally important, that many films raise questions about the actual and potential illusions of spectatorship at the cinema. The morals that can be found about perceptual malfunction and misalignment *within* the boundaries of the film also effectively double back upon the viewers themselves. Naturally, the illusions of the film spectator tend to differ from those to which the various film characters succumb, but the revelations about viewer vulnerability are enough to undermine the apparent security of what has probably seemed to be a superior style of judiciously distanced observation. Object lessons about the "privileged" and "innocent" activity of film-mediated perception are therefore offered up as well.

I open with this observation in part because it contradicts a major motif in much structuralist and poststructuralist writing on film. It is often maintained, roughly, that the strategies, forms, and techniques of classical cinematic narrative lock members of an audience into an epistemic position that makes it impossible for them to criticize either their own habits of perception in film viewing or the modes of perceptual intelligence that the films themselves display. (We shall look more carefully at a version of this "prison house of movies" thesis in a moment.) Now, here is one site at which the more limited enterprise of understanding point of view in film can impinge forcefully upon what purports to be a much larger and more basic claim of a general theory of film. For it seems that the plausibility that has been attributed to the claim I have mentioned is almost wholly a function of the grand obscurity with which it is normally formulated combined with a wholesale failure to think through even the limited implications of a minimally adequate account of cinematic point of view. In any case, this is a thesis I wish to develop.[1]

Perhaps it will be helpful here to sketch out some components of narrational perspective which are of central importance to the present discussion. Certainly, it should be obvious from even the following brief outline how a sizeable variety of strategies of film narrative can arise under each of the headings that I will offer.

The proper viewing of a given film may require that members of its audience be situated at a certain *epistemic distance* from their usual habits of perception and common-sense beliefs. As noted, a spectator who is to achieve even a rudimentary understanding of a segment of film narrative must draw nonstop upon the incredible diversity of perceptual knowledge that we ordinarily and untendentiously assume we have about actual things and processes. This knowledge includes, of course, our more trustworthy beliefs about the nature and operation of the extra-cinematic world and about the ways they manifest themselves to us. It also includes, as a smaller but still important part, our prior knowledge of the techniques and conventions of film narrative and narration. In some films only part of this knowledge is meant to have application to the fictional world portrayed, while other strands of this knowledge are meant to be set in abeyance. It may be crucial to a correct viewing of such a film that our normal belief that things work in such-and-such a way is not fulfilled by *these things* appearing in *this* narrative. The result, when the strategy is successful, may be a view of our world as observed from a distanced metaphysical perspective. Therefore, assumptions about what features of our shared common-sense picture of the world are and are not projectable upon the world as pictured in a given film will help to constitute the viewer's epistemic base.

It is a different matter to inquire after the *epistemic reliability* of a film's narration. As a film proceeds, an audience's understanding of narrative developments depends not only upon its assimilation of the information with which it is directly presented but also upon its grasp of an imposing complex of inferences that it must make, consciously or unconsciously, from the visual manifolds that it is shown. It actually underscores the present point that it is probably impossible to lay down a definite boundary between what is strictly seen and what is merely inferred. A large and complicated part of the function of any film narration is to present immediately just enough material so that the desired inferences will reliably be drawn. But there is always an actual or potential gap between the inferences that will be made and the inferences that would, by some reasonable standard, be justified. Where a substantial disparity exists between the two classes, questions are implied either about the narration's power to construct a satisfactory fictional narrative or about the audience's acceptance of that power. Any film narration, whether trivial or intricately problematic, is marked by implicit assumptions about the relations between actual and justifiable inferences made on its basis.

Finally, questions can also always be raised about the relations between the information that the audience progressively acquires concerning dramatic issues in the film and the information that one or several characters is shown to possess about the same topic. In other words, our *epistemic alignment* with the characters may vary from case to case. A number of different kinds of relation are possible here, and there are a number of different ways in which the narrative can set them up. As a rule, the audience enjoys an epistemic position superior to that of the fictional agents. The perception of these agents, after all, is confined within a line of narrative action which they cannot survey. However, this advantage may exist in limited respects only, and, in more extreme cases, no significant audience privilege may exist. Once again, the assumptions that underlie these relations of proximity to and distance from the characters help to shape the total way in which they enter the appraising spectator's consciousness. These are examples of questions about the epistemic authority of the film narration. We often can give a general characterization of the kinds of facts about the narrative which the narration is authorized to show, or we can specify certain signifcant overall constraints that exist upon the way in which that range of facts is shown. The remarks above concern themselves with the authority of the narration defined in relation to the situation of the characters, but, as we shall see, other poles of definition may be used as well.

The types of narrational assumption which are picked out within these three categories are not intended to exhaust the factors that pertain to cinematic point of view. Even allowing for a vagueness in that concept which leaves plenty of room for stipulation about what it is to include, this first, short taxonomy can and should be enlarged.

Let us return now to the view that classical film essentially restricts the epistemic situation of its viewer in a radical and deplorable fashion. Because it is impossible to examine all of the formulations of the view in question, I shall concentrate upon the version that figures centrally in a well-known and influential essay by Colin MacCabe.[2] MacCabe's argument turns upon his explication of a concept of a "classic realist text," a concept that he takes to be exemplified both in the standard nineteenth-century novel and in classical narrative films. The basic conventions of the latter are, according to MacCabe, the descendants of conventions of the former. He states that "a classic realist text may be defined as one in which there is a hierarchy among the discourses which compose the text, and this hierarchy is defined in terms of an empirical notion of truth." (153) Fortunately, this "definition" is partially amplified in connection with literary fiction as follows: "In the classical realist novel the narrative prose functions as a metalanguage that can state all of the truths in the object language—those words held in inverted commas [quotations of the characters' speech]—and can also explain the relation of this object language to the real. The metalanguage can thereby explain the relation of the object language to the world and the strange methods by which the object languages attempt to express truths which are straightforwardly conveyed in the metalanguage." (153)

The misuse of the "metalanguage/object language" distinction in this passage leaves the purported amplification murky, but MacCabe pretty clearly has in mind as "the metalanguage" the sentences of a novel which represent the speech acts of the narrator. (It will include everything except the quoted inner and outer speech of the characters.) Furthermore, what makes a literary text one that is "classic realist" is that its narrator has certain general characteristics. First, it seems that the narrator must be relatively omniscient, having the authority to bring together, reliably and without identification of a source of knowledge, the diverse kinds of material needed to explain the behavior, thoughts, and speech acts (the "discourses") of the characters. Second, because we are told that "the narrative discourse simply allows reality to appear and denies its own status as articulation," the classic realist narrator must be substantially undramatized and unselfconscious about the activity of narration. (154) In other words, when the pseudo-logical and pseudo-metaphysical jargon is cleared away, it turns out that MacCabe is traveling on the more familiar terrain of literary point of view.

Leaving aside all questions about the adequacy of MacCabe's conception of the traditions of the nineteenth-century novel, his presentation of this conception is used to set the conditions that a classic realist text in film must meet. He asks, "does this definition carry over into films where it is certainly less evident where to locate the dominant discourse?" Unsurprisingly, his answer is affirmative.

It seems to me that it does.... The narrative prose achieves its position of dominance because it is in the position of knowledge and this function of knowledge is taken up in the cinema by the *narration* [italics mine] of events. Through the knowledge we gain from the narrative we can split the discourses of the various characters from their situations and compare what is said in these discourses with what has been revealed to us through narration. The camera shows us what happens—it tells the truth against which we can measure discourses. (155)

Consolidating his view, MacCabe adds that "the narrative of events—the knowledge which film provides of how things are—is the metalanguage in which we talk of the various characters in film." (156)

Therefore, the "dominant discourse" of classical film is supposed to be a form of visual narration such that:

1. it yields a form of epistemic access that is superior to the vantage points of the characters,

and

2. it fulfills expected standards of explanatory coherence (explains "how things are" in relation to the characters).

Further, the original stipulation that the dominant narration is defined by "an empirical notion of truth" hints at the idea that

3. it is meant to establish a level of objective truth about the characters and their situations which the viewer is able to discern through ordinary perception and commonsense forms of inference.

That MacCabe envisages something such as condition 3 is supported by the last part of the following remark: "The narrative discourse cannot be mistaken in its identifications because the narrative discourse is not present as discourse—as articulation. The unquestioned nature of the narrative discourse entails that the only problem that reality poses is to go and look and see what *Things* there *are*." (157) Moreover, the earlier part of this quotation (and similar claims in MacCabe's essay) suggest that film narration is classic realist only if:

4. the film does not acknowledge its status as an intentional construction whose function is to depict a world of fiction,

and, related to this,

5. its image track is presented as overall transparent.

Finally, given the necessary existence of the properties described in 1. through 5. in the classic realist text, it follows for MacCabe that films with these properties "cannot deal with the real as contradictory"; and, in addition, they "ensure the position of the subject in a relation of dominant specularity." (157) What these charges amount to is not easy to make out, but the imputed consequences unquestionably sound pernicious.

Throughout his discussion, MacCabe presupposes that all classical narrative films are classic realist texts in the usage he wishes to establish. Indeed, the technical concept is introduced as a means of capturing the essential form and nature of traditional films. This presupposition, combined with his dark allegations about their putative limitations, is the basis of his demand for radically alternative, nonnarrative forms. Nevertheless, none of the five conditions listed above—with one possible exception—is uniformly exemplified even in Hollywood genre films. Let us briefly take up each of these conditions in the stated order.

About condition 1. It is true that most classical films adopt an essentially unrestricted narrational authority and do so in the service of an ideally objective overview of the narratives they portray. However, the predominance of this mode coexists with the option of film narration which operates, in a systematic and principled manner, under one or another global restriction upon what it is authorized to show and, through the editing, to juxtapose. I argue for the need for a theory of a point of view capable of accommodating everything from an extended, directly subjective rendering of a character's field of vision to a wholly unpsychologized schema of selection which mirrors some of the limitations governing human observation universally. Between these two extremes is a range of intermediate "nonomniscient" possibilities, each of which is notably distinct in its effects and implications from the others. Any framework of restricted narrational authority which has been consciously worked out determines the angle at which the viewer's experience of the film intersects the experience of the film's characters. It therefore helps to define the degree to which the viewer is entitled to assume that the film-mediated information is or is not mediated in turn by a reflected subjectivity or is otherwise conditioned by constraints on access which the other characters may or may not share. Whenever such issues of mediation or contraint occur, the epistemic superiority of the viewer's position is not assured. These issues can be subtle and complex, but MacCabe writes as if this kind of consideration can never seriously arise.

Most classical films satisfy the second condition of explanatory coherence. They have been designed to provide answers to the chief dramatic questions raised by the assorted dilemmas faced by the characters and to accomplish this in a manner that makes the resolutions of these questions definitive and clearly marked as such. And yet, a classically styled movie (such as *You Only Live Once*[3]) may appear on the surface to answer its highlighted questions fully and adequately while, at the same time, revealing in more muted ways that these surface answers ought to be suspect and that a more stable closure is difficult, if not impossible, to supply.

When this acknowledgment of explanatory incompleteness is a key factor organizing the film's narration, I call that narration "rhetorically unreliable." The existence of this possibility already violates condition 2. But, alternatively, even when a film does contain the basis of a coherent resolution, it may be that the material that constitutes that basis has not been marked so as to signal overtly the explanatory force it bears. Usually, such a film will offer at least the outlines of a superficial closure, which the implicit explanatory counterstructure is intended to outweigh. In one good sense, this sort of narration is also unreliable, because its more overt gestures of resolution are likely to mislead; its true explanatory coherence will be opaque. It does not matter whether we count this explanatory opacity as violating condition 2 or not. It patently represents a sophisticated epistemic possibility that MacCabe's analysis certainly does not envisage.

The precise import of condition 3 is hard to pin down. MacCabe actually says that the classic realist text "fixes the subject in a point of view from which everything becomes obvious," but, taken literally, this is absurdly too strong. (161) I have supposed, in stating 3, that he means to maintain that whatever significance a classical film presents or expresses is knowable by "obvious" methods of observation and inference. This at least allows that the actual deployment of those methods may be indefinitely complicated. All that is required is that any such method is to be more or less familiar from commonsense practices of belief formation. It does not matter that this condition continues to be extremely vague, because any further specification will still be contravened by films that are epistemically distanced from any commonsense picture of the world that we hold. A film may force us to discover new patterns of perceptual intelligibility in the narrative action it depicts if we are to locate a unifying order and meaning in that action as it nonstandardly unfolds. When we have been distanced from our habitual styles of visual comprehension, it may take a deviant metaphysics or epistemology to yield a satisfactory configuration of sense within the film. Von Sternberg's *The Scarlet Empress* and *The Devil Is a Woman* are striking examples of this strategy.

We really do not need new grounds for rejecting the universal applicability of condition 4. It has already been noted that a film may tacitly acknowledge the inadequacy of some of its surface forms and structures. However, there are films that have characters who stand in some privileged relation to the film narration. Several possibilities of this kind may occur, but one among them is especially important for the topic of cinematic self-reference and self-acknowledgement. That is, a film may contain a character who embodies certain of the leading epistemic qualities of the narration and, thereby, of the implied film maker as well (for example,

Letter from an Unknown Woman). Or, beyond this, such a character may assume a metacinematic power to which the narrative events appear to respond (*The Devil Is a Woman*). No doubt there are other, similar relationships of characters to film narration to be exploited, but it is difficult to survey the range in a perspicuous way. In any case, it is plain that the presence of a character who is seen as standing in for an implied film maker not only acknowledges the cinematic artifact but permits an elaborate articulation of the nature of that acknowledgment. Condition 4 can seem an invariant of classical narrative film because the relatively effaced narrational styles of these films and the limitations upon theme and subject matter which they typically observe tend to force the self-consciousness of the narration to appear recessively behind the foregrounded mechanisms of plot. This concession, however, makes it no less a mistake to ignore the striking ways in which self-consciousness can and does occur.

A film whose narration is directly subjective throughout (such as *The Lady in the Lake*) is a counterexample to the last condition of overall transparency of the image track. Still, this sort of counterexample is of marginal interest; the transparency of the image comes closest of the five conditions to being a genuine norm of the traditional cinema. I understand "transparency" to mean that the individual shots of a film are designed to license viewers to take up the impression of having direct perceptual access to the visual appearance of items and events in the fictional world. Naturally, most films that exemplify overall transparency contain shots that do not meet this description, but then these departures from the norm will be suitably flagged and rationalized for what they are. For example, point of view shots from a character's perspective are fairly common, but, within a context of overall transparency, they are presented as direct *quotations*, provided by the narration, of a slice of a character's visual experience. Transparency assures the audience of an extensive base of information, guaranteed to be reliable, about the ways in which the fictional world and its constituents look and sound. Nevertheless, as extensive and important as this reliable foundation generally is, it is, in another way, a quite minimal base of information. Transparency, by itself, does not guarantee that the ambiguities, uncertainties, and outright contradictions that a manifold of appearances may generate over time will be resolved or otherwise explained away. For this reason, transparency potentially leaves open almost all of the issues about what kinds of consistency and intelligibility the appearances given in a film may have. Thus, if transparency is nearly an exceptionless condition of classical narrative film, it is largely because the condition is, in effect, so weak. It is, of course, a feature of many nonclassical, nonnarrative films as well. This relative weakness is often unintentionally obscured in film theory because "transparency" is also used to cover many or all of the first four conditions, but then its proper application is sizably reduced. For instance, transparency seems thus inflated in MacCabe's essay where phrases such as "the empirical notion of truth" merely blot out the relevant distinctions.

I have tried to show, by this brief overview, how badly MacCabe's idea of a classic realist text distorts and impoverishes the possibilities available in traditional films. Like many other authors, he systematically supposes that the customary surface forms and strategies of these films define the limits of their possible concerns and accomplishments. Indeed, because of the variety of degrees of freedom which surface constraints permit, it is easy to deal rather briefly with the fundamental and supposedly congenital limitations that MacCabe imputes to the normal narrative structures. First, he asserts, as I mentioned in passing, that classical film "cannot deal with the real as contradictory." Once again, one is left to guess at the content of this complaint, but it seems to mean that, because he believes that a classical film always purports to establish an objective and intersubjectively available truth about its fictional history, this aim, he infers, precludes the possibility of exhibiting ways in which that very same history might be perceived from different, deeply conflicting perspectives—perspectives whose differences may be ultimately unresolvable. To this objection, my response is fairly simple: its falsity is demonstrated by a significant range of important films. In certain ways, *You Only Live Once* can be cited as an especially pure counterexample, but, in other instances as well there exists a standard, plot-oriented viewing that contradicts at many crucial points the richer and more challenging viewing that can be set forth.

At bottom, MacCabe and others of a similar persuasion are just confused about the nature and extent of the "objectivity" to which the classical forms are typically committed. Transparency, narrowly understood, is a weak commitment, and the superficial requirements of closure and effacement can be satisfied *only* superficially. Actually, I am tempted to assert the contrary of MacCabe's objection. It is in classical narrative film alone that a more or less determinate fictional history is portrayed by visual narration, which can simultaneously sustain both a salient, standard perspective and a distinct, oblique perspective, both of which may be equally and continuously coherent. Be this as it may, the range of possibilities which MacCabe mistakenly denies is central to what the narrative cinema can mean to us. Presumably, the lessons of alternative perspectives in these films are not unrelated to the ways in which we see and comprehend ourselves when we attempt to make a connected narrative out of segments of our own lives and the lives of others.

MacCabe's associated indictment of traditional films is that they "ensure the position of the subject [that is, the viewer] in a relation of dominant specularity." When one first comes across this charge, one feels immediately that dominant specularity is not a position that one, as a sensitive filmgoer, would want to be in. The phrase evokes the picture of a brutish viewer who aggressively glares his films into submission. However, MacCabe's conception is rather the opposite. It is the conception of passive film spectators who, immersed in transparency, allow their perception and understanding of the screen events to be wholly the products of the narrative apparatus. It denotes the relation to film of viewers seduced from the critical use of their perception and understanding by the regimenting dictates of classical narrative and narration. This is the chief target of MacCabe's attack on the classic realist film text, and this passiveness is a phenomenon that merits his rightful, if somewhat overstated, concern. It is not to be denied that normal film viewing is too often intellectually passive and only superficially critical of its object. Far too often conventional films strongly encourage this stolidity and offer few rewards to alertness and analytical reflection. These complaints have over many years acquired the status of truisms, but they are, nonetheless, still true. What is distinctive about the position that MacCabe and other recent theorists occupy is the contention that the forms and strategies of classical film render this situation inevitable—render the practice of the cinema a prison house for the perceptually inert. It is supposed to be in the nature of the forms in question that they forego the possibility of eliciting a radical transformation of vision and a recognition of the vast contingency of the manner in which we ordinarily function as observers of the world. Once again, I can merely repeat that a detailed and rich reading of sample films testifies that these "essentialist" theses are false.

Much poststructuralist writing on film speculates on how it is that subjects are fixed in the position of dominant specularity and on the historical development and ideological consequences of this positioning. Setting aside reservations about how this speculation is usually conducted, I do not question that the specific seductions of the familiar dramatic cinema provide issues to be studied. What I do reject is any theory that makes these seductions a necessary consequence of the forms of classical film and ignores the scattered but triumphant instances that show that this is not the case. If we need a better account of the ideological suasion built into so much commercial film-making, we need just as badly a better account of the flexibility of those forms that make the classical triumphs into concrete, realized possibilities.

Late in his article, MacCabe proposes that "the method of representation (the language, verbal and cinematic) determines in its structural activity…both the places where the object 'appears' and the point from which the object is seen. It is this point which is exactly the place allotted to the reading subject." (160) Here, first of all, is yet another endorsement of the odd, unargued brand of formalist determinism to which I object. More important, however, is the explicitness with which it is maintained in this passage that a source of that determinism is the view that the fictional objects and events in a film and the ways in which they appear to a viewer are the results of the *"structural activity"* of the *languagelike elements* that are said to make up a film's narration. Of course, this is an established motif in much film theory of a vaguely structuralist orientation, but sheer repetition has hardly made its import less elusive.

This is not the place to examine the long and unhappy history of the notion of a language of film. Its manifestations are too numerous and too diverse; its confusions are too deeply entangled. Nevertheless, I think it is possible to say enough to shake the conviction that any sort of formalist determinism is supported by the methodological premise that representation in film is fundamentally a function of structural determinants of a quasi-linguistic kind. This conviction and its would-be basis set an agenda for theory of film which excludes the sorts of film criticism and approaches to theory which I have attempted to promote.

It will be helpful, in this context, to turn to a theorist who is more self-conscious about his assumptions and arguments and who is less tendentious in his aims than MacCabe. Brian Henderson, in his book *A Critique of Film Theory*, offers a revealing summary statement of what he counts as the domain of film theory. The reader is told that it encompasses questions about "the relations between film and reality, the relations between film and narrative, and the question whether film is a language and, if so, what kind of language. Related to these questions is *the even more fundamental one of determining the basic units of film (and of film analysis) and the rules governing the combination of these units*" [italics mine].[4] Subsequently, long sections of *A Critique* are devoted to criticism of Christian Metz's attempts, in his early work, to identify "basic units of film" and their "rules of combination."[5] Throughout his book, Henderson's own seemingly a priori commitment to this type of implausible analytical atomism never wavers. His most extreme expression of this Democritean enthusiasm is found in the following passage: "Each [film theory] should provide a comprehensive model of cinematic units at all levels and of the modes of combination and interaction at each level. In short, a film theory should provide concepts, terms, and dynamic models of interaction for the analysis of cinematic parts and wholes of all kinds."[6] This reads, at first, like an invigoratingly ambitious prolegomena to a new, more objective, more scientific theory of film, until one pauses to wonder what scientific discipline could conceivably aim at such an enterprise. We would not even have the theory of the simple pendulum if physicists, in considering, for example, the grandfather clock, had demanded of themselves "dynamic models" of its various "components" at every "level" of (possible?) analysis. We probably would not have grandfather clocks. Finding fruitful and manageable questions in a given area of thought is usually at least as hard as finding answers to those questions. Symptomatically, one is hard-pressed to locate in Henderson's book a set of specific phenomena *derived from real films* which film theory is supposed to explain. Rather, it is flatly assumed from first to last that a general and largely unconstrained inquiry after "units," "rules," and "models" is well-conceived and valuable.

Naturally, the difficulty here is not that there is a lack of parts and wholes in film; everything in a film is a part and a whole of some kind for some analytical purpose. The difficulty, at least in the first instance, is that we are never informed what the cinematic units are units *of* or what general types of rules or laws of combination are supposedly at stake. Presumably, if these units and roles are to play a role within a systematic account of cinematic content (and, after all, this seems the goal), then the units are to be units of meaning (in some sense appropriate to film) and the rules are to be projective rules that determine the meaning of a "combination" from the meanings of its constituent units and the structural relations that the combination embodies. Admittedly, it is hard to be certain of even this much, because we are never given a single example of the hypothesized units or the associated rules, and we are never given any evidence that film narration comes in honest units that generate larger narrational complexes in accordance with determinate projective rules. Still, as noted, at least this construal of Henderson's remarks offers his conception a kind of theoretical role to play which he and MacCabe and a host of other kindred spirits so often deploy. Indeed, *if* the resulting conception had some substance, it might give a basis to that formalist determinism that MacCabe has been seen to favor. Limits to the expressive power of the putative film "language"—the "language" of classical film perhaps—would presumably set the limit to what such film can show. This, I think, is the idea that MacCabe has accepted.

With just this much set out, let us bypass the whole question of locating a conception of cinematic meaning which has promise of being subject to the type of theory envisaged, and let us not concern ourselves about the form that the projective laws or rules might have. (Needless to say, I believe that we are simply bypassing a hopeless morass in each case.) Rather, I want to focus upon a pair of more general assumptions which are engendered here and do their work in tandem. The first is that it *is* possible to segment a film (at least at a given "level") into visual and aural "units" whose "interaction" gives structure and content to the film as a whole. The second is that such a segmentation is epistemically prior to interpretation and forms the core of the evidential basis for whatever interpretation may ensue. It is this second assumption that provides the principal rationale for supposing that the truth of the first assumption would offer a useful foundation for film analysis and theory. Certainly from the two assumptions together, it follows that it is essential to an adequate theory of film that it provide an account of admissible modes of segmentation. Taken together, these assumptions define a kind of formalist foundationalism with respect to meaning in films. Other less "linguistic" versions are doubtlessly possible, but the present formulation encapsulates a conception that many, consciously or subliminally, have found compelling. It yields, in any case, an explicit statement of a methodological view with which I am at odds. The explicit statement permits a direct marshalling of the main grounds for repudiating this view and others of its ilk.

It is implausible to suppose that narrative, plot, or basic story line can be construed as a "level" where these assumptions fit. This point leaves open the possibility that films can be sliced along other dimensions that would yield a simple level more amenable to the project of segmentation. However, even this vague possibility seems foreclosed by suitable reflection on an example like the striking series of three shots from *The Lady from Shanghai*.[7] The shots are these: a truck pulls out in front of a car containing two men; a woman's hand presses a button; the car crashes into the truck. In viewing this segment, one has the impression that the pressing of the button causes the crash. We attribute, immediately and without conscious inference, a causal connection between the two events. If we think about segmenting this three-shot progression, two very broad possibilities arise:

(1) The onset and culmination of the accident constitute an independent segment crosscut with an unrelated segment showing the woman's action. The impression of causality is to be discounted as inadvertent and irrelevant to the content of the film.

(2) The whole series is a unified segment showing the button pressing to be a cause of the crash. If a shot of a cannon firing were followed by a shot of an explosion, we would view this pair of shots as showing cause and effect: the cannon's hitting a target would be an event in the film. In our present example, it is merely that the apparent causal connection is a good deal less familiar.

Now, how might one reach a decision between (1) and (2)? Surely, nothing in the three shots themselves—no interaction of units into which this series might be analyzed—will settle the matter. It is just this fact that initially makes (1) and (2) genuine alternatives. At the same time, this does not mean that there is no way in which the choice can be settled at all. I would contend that (2) is correct by showing how the attribution of strange causal powers to the woman is systematically integrated with her peculiar role in the surrealistic context of this unusual film. Obviously, this contention would depend upon a careful and detailed interpretation of *The Lady from Shanghai*, and it does not matter for present purposes whether the argument would be sound. The moral is that it is impossible to resolve a question of segmentation as elementary as the choice between (1) and (2) independently of a thorough analytical viewing of the total film. In this extreme but instructive case, we cannot even identify the *simpler fictional occurrences* in the film without an appeal to the widest framework that contains the problematic three shots. If this is so, then it must be a mistake to believe or hope that segmentation can be treated as prior to, and foundational for, interpretation. In general, the way in which we will be inclined to divide a stretch of film into "interacting levels and units" will rest on large problems about how narrative, narration, and associated aspects of structure are to be construed. The analytical atomism conveyed by the description of film theory given by Henderson ought to be replaced by a lively, reiterated sense of the holistic character of all interpretive work.

The considerations that underlie the general force of this example are these. In everyday perception, we often judge directly that one observed event has caused another, but the immediate perceptual data that elicit that judgment from us are substantially inadequate to give it conclusive grounds. Furthermore, we do not, upon reflection, believe otherwise: we readily grant that, in making the judgment, we have drawn upon a large and somewhat indeterminate mass of background belief about the world. The same is true when we judge that we have seen one and the same physical object at distinct times or that we have observed different stages of a single, continuous movement through space. In short, we do not imagine in any of these cases that such rudimentary and basic judgments are derived from our immediate visual experiences by means of projective rules that take features of that experience as their input. Indeed, it is implausible to suppose otherwise.

But then, why should the situation be essentially altered when what we have been "given" is a series of shots showing events that appear to be causally linked or a series that appears to show the same object or the same temporally extended movement photographed from different times and places? Here also, it is certain that the direct connections and re-identifications that we make are heavily conditioned by our preestablished beliefs about the film world, the actual world, and standing relations between the two. As in actual perception, these judgments about the content of the film will normally not be the rule-governed upshot of features depicted within the shots. Finally, if these considerations are correct—if even our rock-bottom judgments about the *identity of objects and events* within a film fail to satisfy the model of units and structural laws—then it is hard to grasp how more sophisticated judgments about filmic content and significance can reasonably be expected to satisfy the model either. The example from *The Lady from Shanghai* is useful because of the intuitive simplicity of the content in question. It thereby illustrates the hopelessness of finding some more fundamental "level" where the projective account might finally take purchase on the film. That is, the example demonstrates clearly and decisively that basic narrative events cannot, in general, be units *or* functions of units in the sense required, and once this is made salient no more simple level is to be found.

The objection that I have been sketching reflects the existence of a deep division about the relations between theory of film and film criticism, a division that is too deep, no doubt, to be settled by these brief remarks. In a passage that Henderson repeats twice in his book, he says, "film theory is, after all, a metacriticism or philosophy of criticism. It is pursued to improve film criticism through the determination of basic film categories and the identification of those assumptions about film on which any criticism is based.... [F]ilm theory itself is the continued improvement and clarification of the principles and assumptions of film criticism." [8] It is instructive to set these assertions alongside a passage from Stanley Cavell's *The World Viewed:*

> The aesthetic properties of a medium are not givens. You can no more tell what will give significance to the unique and specific aesthetic possibilities of projecting photographic images by thinking about them or seeing some, than you can tell what will give significance to the possibilities of paint by thinking about paint or looking some over. You have to think about painting, and paintings; you have to think about motion pictures. What does this "thinking about them" consist in? Whatever the useful criticism of an art consists in. [9]

Clearly, I am sympathetic to much of what Cavell here suggests. In particular, I am inclined to see theory of film not as providing the foundations for criticism, but as more or less continuous with that which is most searching, articulate, explicit, and self-reflective *within* criticism. Moreover, these alternatives are not to be represented, as they often are, as a choice between rigorous methodology and impressionistic dabbling. Rigor, in any reasonable sense, and impressionism occur on both sides. For example, we have seen something in this paper of the speciousness of the claims to rigor made in the name of various structural hypotheses. The antifoundationalist sentiments I have expressed are not meant to be justified definitively by the present discussion, but I hope to have issued effective warning that the pretensions of first philosophy are as tempting and dangerous in the study of film as they have been in other fields of thought.

As indicated earlier, I believe that film theory needs to develop a minimally adequate account of point of view in the narrative cinema.[10] More specifically, I assume that point of view in film can be specified in terms of a set of assumptions about how the viewer is epistemically situated in relation to the narrative. Or, following Gerard Genette, we could just as well say that point of view is based upon the various ways in which information about the narrative is *systematically regulated* throughout all of or large segments of the narration.[11] Just as a theory of point of view in literature explores the broader systematic relationships that can hold between an activity of fictional telling and the fictional situations that are told, so a theory of point of view in film should study fictional activities of showing and their relations to the shown. Literary theory should be more than an inventory of strategies; it should explicate the ways in which the different strategies raise different problems about what the activity of narrative comprehension can and cannot achieve. Similarly, different narrational strategies in film differ in their implications for perceptual comprehension in any of a host of ways. Since verbal telling and cinematic showing are such very different narrational procedures, the issues that get raised in each case are not at all identical. Nevertheless, a network of substantial but limited analogies exists. The importance of point of view considerations in film and literature are much the same. The forms of narration in question substantially help to define the orientation of the viewer or reader in apprehending the fictional world of the work and thereby fix some of the most general attributes that diverse narrative elements are understood to have. Further, it is not only the apprehension of matters within the narrative that can be formed or altered in this way. One's perception of film or literature as mechanisms of narrative portrayal can also be reshaped at the same time. I assume that the power of techniques of point of view to transform the reading of a novel or short story are well-known, but the extent and depth of this power in films has not been adequately appreciated. There are reasonably determinate narrational structures that underlie the kind of global shift of prospect that

I have stressed. These structures can be described and discussed in a style that makes plain their relevance to familiar issues about the quirky interplay of human perception and the world.

This approach has as its principal recommendation that such distinctions genuinely help to capture the rationale behind the works of film makers as diverse as Ford and von Sternberg, Lang and Ophuls, Renoir and Nicholas Ray. There may be other ways of stating the same or similar observations about the relevant films, but, at a minimum, these categories are not merely idling in the realm of the a priori: they accomplish straightforward and needed tasks. Also, even in their restricted generality, they serve to open up and enhance our sense of the epistemic possibilities of classical film. This can be a mixed blessing, because the implications that a broadened sense uncovers tends to lack theoretical tidiness and elegance and make the grander ambitions of theory more difficult to satisfy. Still, this situation is preferable to one in which an ambitious but too simple theory, such as MacCabe's, has swept the less predictable and more interesting possibilities out of sight from the beginning.

However, if assorted film theories have sinned in their treatment or lack of treatment of epistemic matters in film, more intuitive approaches have hardly fared better. A lot of film criticism and analysis whose theoretical concerns are negligible have been more than ready to make use of general epistemological concepts and dichotomies, impressing them in an ad hoc fashion on the films they scrutinize. It is, for instance, a cliché of film criticism to announce that a certain work deals with matters of "appearance and reality." No doubt this assessment is often enough correct, but the formula is simultaneously too weighty and too slight to characterize the questions about perception and knowledge which a reasonably sophisticated film propounds. The formula fails utterly to discriminate between the bleak investigations of cinematic manipulation in *You Only Live Once* and the more light-hearted self-consciousness about cinematic transparency in *North by Northwest*. It does nothing to help conceptualize the difference between Ophuls' delicate and distanced portrayal of Lisa's private world of fantasy in *Letter from an Unknown Woman* and von Sternberg's rendering of a public world in *The Devil Is a Woman*, whose very substance seems made of the most private fantasies of the film maker. The stereotyped characters and conclusion of *Rebel Without a Cause* are likely to be dismissed as the illusions of a simplifying social cinema unless it is noticed that the film's true closure is the expression of a cultural determinism that mocks our bland "reading" of stereotypes our social order presses upon us. The rhetorical strategies that inform these films and guide our experience of them are nuanced and complex, and an analysis of any one of them in terms of "appearance and reality" could only blunt an effort to describe the methods and issues at stake.

This stricture is or ought to be obvious, but it has apparently been less obvious that other very broad distinctions have been equally inflated and correspondingly impoverished. Talk of "first-person" and "third-person" film narration invites recurrent confusion, and the related pair, "subjective" and "objective," fares no better. It should also be clear that an opposition between "the transparency of classical narration" and "the reflexivity of modernist narration" is seriously misconceived, and that divisions of film narration into "omniscient" and "perspectival," "closed" and "open," "personal" and "impersonal," and so forth are bound to be grossly inadequate to the distinctions that fruitful film analysis requires. Admittedly, no taxonomy of point of view in film will yield a set of categories which cleanly carves up the domain of individual films, assigning to each its perfectly apt classification. Nevertheless, it is fair to expect that a minimally satisfactory account will contain categories that are enlightening when we set out to think through a film of at least moderate intricacy. This requirement entails that any such taxonomy will have to be derived from an examination of the variety of epistemic factors which comes into play when film narration provides a determinate form of perceptual access to a connected series of narrational events. These factors, taken singly and in combination, can be realized in many ways, and it is the most central of these possibilities which the classifications of the point of view I have introduced are intended to designate. I am sure that these categories need to be extended and, in some cases, revised, but the objective has been to offer a perspicuous setting for the process of reconsideration to begin.

To my mind, the chief advantage of looking at the concept of cinematic point of view is that this approach places that concept in immediate conjunction with undeniably interesting questions about what we see and how we comprehend when we watch narratives in film. Many of these questions about how we operate in apprehending film stories have, quite naturally, interested most of the best film makers as well. Their work constitutes a heritage of reflection on film which has been registered in film, and it is important to retain that heritage and value it properly. There is, I believe, no art other than the cinema which has a comparable capacity to reconstruct analytically and thereby explicate the possible modes of perceiving a localized slice of human history as an evolving field of visible significance. Classical narrative film, in particular, engenders and investigates possible modes of seeing a pattern in the events of such a history—a pattern that yields, either genuinely or speciously, "the sense of an ending." It models, in this way, our search for closure and coherence in our long-term view of things. A theory of point of view in film, as I conceive it, is a theory of these reconstructed forms of being witness to the world.

Notes

1 This article is a revised version of Chapter 10 of George Wilson's *Narration in Light* (Baltimore and London: The Johns Hopkins University Press, 1986); used by permission of the author and the publisher.

2 Colin MacCabe, "The Classic Realist Text," *Screen* 15, no. 2, 152–62, reprinted with omissions in *Realism and the Cinema*, ed. Christopher Williams (London: Routledge and Kegan Paul, 1980), 152–62. All page citations in the text are to this volume.

3 All of the films mentioned in this discussion are analyzed at length in *Narration in Light*.

4 Brian Henderson, *A Critique of Film Theory* (New York: E. P. Dutton, 1980), 3–4.

5 The relevant early work is found in Christian Metz, *Film Language: A Semiotics of the Cinema*, trans. Michael Taylor (New York: Oxford University Press, 1974).

6 Henderson, p.5.

7 I have deliberately simplified the description of this sequence from *Lady from Shanghai*. The three shots referred to constitute a part—the crucial part—of a somewhat longer series of shots. I have simplified in this way in order to avoid irrelevant complexity, and, I believe, the material that I have ignored does not affect the points that I am trying to establish. For a much longer and extremely interesting discussion of the issues raised by this specific sequence, see Edward Branigan, *Narrative Comprehension and Film* (London: Routledge, 1992), 39–56.

8 Henderson, 49.

9 Stanley Cavell, *The World Viewed* (New York: Viking Press, 1971), 31.

10 The following paragraph is excerpted, with omissions, from chapter 5 of *Narration in Light*, 99–101.

11 Gerard Genette, *Narrative Discourse*, trans. Jane E. Lewin (Ithaca: Cornell University Press, 1980), 162.

4 Towards an Ontology of the Moving Image

Noël Carroll

Introduction

The purpose of this paper is to address the longstanding question: "What is cinema?" However, as my title indicates, in the course of my attempt to answer this question, I shall reorient the inquiry somewhat, and, for reasons that will soon emerge, I will ultimately try to approximate an answer to the related but different question: "What is the nature of the moving image?"

Traditionally, cineastes, in the conversation that is sometimes referred to as *classical* film theory, have raised questions about the nature of film in the expectation that were one able to isolate the essential feature or features of cinema, then one would be in a position to know what style or stylistic choices were the most appropriate ones for the medium.[1] The underlying idea here, which we will call *essentialism*, holds that the essence of a medium, such as film, determines what style should prevail in that medium. André Bazin wrote, for example, that "The realism of cinema follows from its photographic nature."[2]

What is perhaps most peculiar about the strongest version of this brand of essentialism is that it regards artistic media as natural kinds equipped with unalterable, gene-like mechanisms that propel their destiny along one vector of stylistic development. But this presupposition is doubly wrong, because: first, artistic media are generally hospitable to multiple, nonconverging and even potentially conflictive stylistic projects (such as montage versus long-take deep focus photography); and second, artistic media are not natural kinds—they are made by humans to serve human purposes. Thus, artistic media are not unalterable. Indeed, they are frequently adapted and altered to serve stylistic purposes—exactly the opposite course of events from that which essentialism predicts.

For instance, the piano was developed at a time when composers were becoming more interested in crescendos, while it is also arguable that Beethoven's desire for a wider range of notes in the upper register influenced piano design. In such cases as these, the reach of existing keyboards did not limit style, but rather stylistic ambitions reshaped the medium. Thus, it is not, *pace* essentialism, the pre-existing shape of the medium that dictates style, but style that dictates the very structure and shape of the medium.

This is not to deny that a close look at the medium by a given artist may suggest an avenue of stylistic development. It is only to deny a central premise of essentialism, viz., that the nature of a medium *always* determines what style is appropriate to it, i.e., that the direction of influence always only goes one way—from medium to a determinate style. For not only may an artistic medium support several divergent and even "incompatible" styles, but style may determine the very shape of the medium, rather than vice-versa.

However, even if we reject the nexus between style and the medium espoused by cinematic essentialists, we still may be interested in the residual question of whether film has an essence, or a set of essential features, or a set of necessary conditions that are jointly sufficient for defining an instance of film. Such an essence, of course, would not indicate anything about which stylistic choices are appropriate; essentialism, as described above, is false. But this does not preclude the possibility that there may nevertheless be some general features of film which, among other things, might help to distinguish it from neighboring artistic media.

In what follows, I will try to identify four necessary conditions of film.

Disembodied Viewpoints

One attempt to isolate the essence of film concentrates on the photographic basis of the cinematic image. Moreover, it is argued that photographic representation is essentially different from other modes of picture making, notably painting. For whereas the relation between a painting and the object portrayed by the painting is something like resemblance, the relation between a photograph and its object is said to be identity. Bazin claimed that the photographic image—and by extension the cinematic image—re-presents the objects, persons and events that give rise to it. He writes: "The photographic image is the object itself.... It shares by virtue of the process of its becoming, the being of the model of which it is a reproduction; it is the model."[3]

Though Bazin's concept of re-presentation is somewhat obscure and though it has been subjected to criticism,[4] several contemporary philosophers, including Stanley Cavell, Roger Scruton, and Kendall Walton, have come to defend their own versions of the view, which we might call "photographic realism."[5] Since Walton's argument is the most elaborate, let me sketch his position.

When we look through a telescope or a microscope or a periscope or into one of those parking lot mirrors that enables us to look around corners, we say that we *see* the objects to which we have access by means of these devices. These devices are like prosthetic devices; they are aids to vision.[6] When I focus my opera glasses on the ballerina, I see the ballerina, rather than a representation of the ballerina. Such devices expand my visual powers; they enable me to see distant stars and microbes. In fact, these devices are not really very different from the corrective lenses that adjust our eyes for near-sightedness and, thereby, enable us to see the world aright. Analogously, photography is a prosthetic device; it enables me to see now my dead grandfather in his youth; or, if I am watching *Triumph of the Will*, it enables me to see Adolf Hitler.

Photographs are transparent—we see through them to the objects, persons and events that give rise to them. Indeed, what a photograph is a photograph of is counterfactually dependent on the objects, persons and events that cause the photograph to be. That is, if the perceptual properties of the relevant objects had been different, the photograph would have been different. In this way, photographs are like ordinary vision (where what we see is counterfactually dependent on the visible properties of the things we encounter).

However, painting is not transparent in the same way. Paintings are not counterfactually dependent on the visible properties of the objects of which they are paintings. They are dependent upon the painter's beliefs about those objects. A painting offers us a representation of an object, whereas a photographic image, and by extension a cinematic image, provides us with access to the object that gave rise to the photographic or cinematographic image in the same way that a telescope boosts our perceptual powers so that we see distant towers as if they were close by.

For the photographic realist then, a necessary condition of a genuine photographic image—and, by extension, of a cinematic image—is that we see through it to the objects that cause it; moreover, this property of transparency also marks a crucial differentia between images of photographic provenance and other sorts of pictures, like paintings. For in the case of painting, we do not literally see the object portrayed by the painting.

Yet, before we accept the putative findings that the realist offers us, we must pause to ask whether it really makes sense to say that we see through photographic and cinematic pictures. In favor of this conclusion, we are offered an analogy between photographs and film, on the one hand, and microscopes and telescopes, on the other hand. If we are willing to talk about seeing through telescopes, so the argument goes, why should we draw the line with photographs? Photography is just another prosthetic device. Indeed, can we draw the line between the lenses of the telescope and the lenses of the motion picture camera in any principled way?

I think that we can. If I look through opera glasses at a ballerina or her consort, the visual array that I receive, though magnified, is nevertheless, still *connected* to my body in the sense that I would know how to get to the place in question if I wanted to. I can orient my body to the ballerina and her consort spatially. The same point can be made about the bacteria that I see through a microscope; I can point my body roughly in its direction.

However, the same is not true with the visual array in the photograph or the cinematic image. Suppose I am watching *King Kong* and I am looking at the great wall on Skull Island. It is not the case that I can orient my body to the wall—to the spatial co-ordinates of that structure as it existed sometime in the early thirties. I do not know how to point my body either towards the wall or away from it. The space between the great wall on Skull Island as it appears on the screen and my body is discontinuous; the space of the wall, though visually available through the film, is disconnected phenomenologically from the space I live in.

Francis Sparshott calls this feature of viewing cinema alienated vision.[7] Ordinarily our sense of where we are depends on our sense of balance and our kinesthetic feelings. What we see is integrated with these cues to yield a sense of where we are situated. But if what we see on the cinema screen is a "view," then it is a disembodied view. I see a visual array, but I have no sense of where the portrayed space really is in relation to my body, whereas with such perceptual prosthetic devices such as the relevant sorts of telescopes, microscopes, periscopes, mirrors, binoculars and eye-glasses I can orient my body in the space I live in to the objects these devices have empowered me to see. Indeed, I do not speak of literally *seeing* the objects in question unless I can perspicuously relate myself spatially to them—unless I know where they are in the space I inhabit.[8]

This requirement, of course, implies that I do not literally *see* the objects that cause photographic or cinematic images. What I do see are representations, or, better yet, displays—displays whose virtual spaces are detached from the space of my experience.[9] But insofar as cinematic images are to be understood as representations or displays, they are better categorized with paintings and pictures than with telescopes and mirrors.

Photographic realism, then, is mistaken. Photographic and cinematic images cannot be presumed to be on a par with telescopes as devices through which the sight of remote things is enhanced. For authentic visual, prosthetic devices preserve a sense of the body's orientation to the objects they render accessible, whereas photographic and cinematic images present the viewer with a space that is disembodied from her perspective.

Though photographic realism's candidate for a necessary condition of cinema has been challenged, it is important to note that the way the challenge has been posed suggests another candidate, viz., that all photographic and cinematic images involve alienated visions, disembodied viewpoints or detached displays. That is, all cinematic images are such that it is vastly improbable and maybe effectively impossible that spectators, save in freak situations, typically are able to orient themselves to the real, "profilmic" spaces physically portrayed on the screen.

Nevertheless, though this is a plausible candidate as a necessary feature of film, it is not a feature that distinguishes cinema from adjacent visual media, such as painting. In order to draw that distinction, we need to introduce another necessary feature of film.

Moving Images

Even if a disembodied viewpoint is a necessary condition of film, it is not a feature that enables us to distinguish film from paintings, since paintings like Poussin's *The Triumph of David* involve a disembodied viewpoint in exactly the same way that a cinematographic restaging of that painting would. So what distinguishes a painting from a film? In order to answer that question, let us turn to an interesting suggestion proposed by Arthur Danto.

In his paper "Moving Pictures," Danto considers the relevance of movement to an essential contrast between things like film and other pictorial techniques, like painting.[10] Notice that I have said "things like film." For, as Danto's title indicates, he is not concerned narrowly with cinema, but with the wider class of motion pictures which, among other things, would also include video. Moreover, this expansion of the class of objects under consideration to motion pictures in general is, to my mind, all for the good, since I predict that in the future the history of what we now call cinema and the history of video, TV and whatever comes next will be considered to be of a piece.

That these objects are already called motion pictures gives us a clue to the role of movement in defining them. But, as Danto realizes, one must be careful about the way in which one exploits that clue. It will not do, for example, to contend, as Roman Ingarden does, that the difference between painting and film is that in films things are always happening whereas paintings, drawings, slides and so on are static.[11] For it is the case that there are films in which there is no movement, including: Oshima's *Band of Ninjas* (a film of a comic strip), Michael Snow's *One Second in Montreal* (a film of photos), and *So is This* (a film of sentences), Hollis Frampton's *Poetic Justice* (a film of a shooting script on a tabletop with a plant), Godard and Gorin's *Letter to Jane* (a film of photos), and Takahiko Iimura's *1 in 10* (a film of addition and subtraction tables).

A perhaps more widely known example of a film that is [almost] without movement is, of course, Chris Marker's *La Jetée*, a saga of science fiction time travel that is told through the projection of still photographs. Admittedly, there is one movement in *La Jetée*; however, it is easy to imagine a film like *La Jetée*, but without any movement whatsoever.

Undoubtedly, the prospect of *movies* without movement may strike some readers as oxymoronic or even self-contradictory. "What," they may ask, "is the difference between a so-called film-without-movment and a slide show?" Indeed, might not one suspect that a film-without-movement merely is a slide show mounted on celluloid for the purpose of convenience in projection?

And yet there is a profound difference between a film, without motion, of Jane Fonda's face and a slide of Jane Fonda's face. For as long as you know that what you are watching is a film, even a film of what appears to be a photograph, it is always justifiable to expect that the image *might* move. On the other hand, if you know that you are watching a slide, then it is categorically impossible that the image should move. If you know it is a slide and you understand what a slide is, then it is unreasonable—in fact, it is irrational and even downright absurd—to anticipate that the image might move.

Movement in a slide would require a miracle; movement in a film is an artistic choice and an always available technical option. Before *Band of Ninjas* concludes—i.e., up until the last image flickers by—the spectator may reasonably presume, if she knows she is watching a film, that there may be movement; but if she knows that she is watching a slide, it is absurd for her to entertain even the possibility of movement.

Moreover, this difference between slides and films can be applied generally across the board to the distinction between still pictures—paintings, drawings and so on—on the one hand, and moving pictures—videos, mutoscopes and so on—on the other hand. With still pictures, it, by definition, is conceptually absurd and even self-contradictory—a veritable category error—for someone to expect to see movement in what she knows to be a still picture, whereas it is reasonable to have an expectation of seeing movement in films not only because most films move, but because even in static films, it is possible that the subject might move up until the last reel runs out and the lights go up.

Once one has seen a static film in its entirety, it is no longer acceptable to anticipate that there will be movement in it a second time around (unless one has grounds for thinking that it has been subsequently doctored). However, on first viewing, one can never be sure that a film is completely still until it is over. This is what makes it reasonable to stay open to the possibility of movement throughout first viewings of static films. But to anticipate movement from what one knows to be a slide or a painting is conceptually confused.

Indeed, one can imagine a slide of a parade and a cinematic freeze frame of the self-same moment of the procession. The two images may be, in effect, perceptually indiscernible from each other. And yet they are metaphysically distinct. For the epistemic states that each warrants in the spectator when the spectator knows which category confronts him are different. With moving pictures, the anticipation of possible future movement is always logically permissible; with still pictures, never.

Like so many of Danto's arguments, his case for the preceding necessary condition is transcendental.[12] He arrays a set of two indiscernible objects—a film of the title page of *War and Peace* and a slide of the same leaf—before us, and he invites hypotheses to the best explanation to account for the imperceptible, yet real categorical difference between the two indiscernibilia. His own candidate is the difference between epistemic states of spectators with regard to movement when they are fully informed in each case about the status (slide versus movie) of that at which they are looking.

Thus, on the basis of this conjecture, Danto is in a position to conclude that a logically necessary condition for something x to be a moving picture is that it is reasonable or justifiable to expect to see movement in x, or, at least, it is not absurd to anticipate the possibility of movement in x. This feature of moving pictures differentiates them all as a class from still pictures, including paintings.

One putative counterexample to Danto's way of distinguishing film, and motion pictures in general from slides and still pictures in general is an artwork by Michael Snow entitled *A Casing Shelved*. This is a slide of a frontal view of industrial shelving packed with painting materials. As the slide is held on the screen, an audio tape is played on which Hollis Frampton describes what is on the shelves. His voice directs our glance and we move our eyes in search of the objects Frampton itemizes. Understood historically, the event is reflexive, making the spectator aware of her spectatorial activities and the way in which the voice guides the eye in the "sound film."

The best interpretation of *A Casing Shelved* situates it in the tradition of film history, specifically in the history of modernist or reflexive film, as a comment upon the phenomenology of spectatorship and its related structures. And this may tempt some to count *A Casing Shelved* as a film, even though such a classification contradicts the conclusion of Danto's transcendental argument. Do we have a counterexample here or not?

The grounds for considering *A Casing Shelved* to be a film are historical; we get our most accurate interpretation of the piece if we regard it as a station in the evolution of the historical conversation of reflexive film. That is, it secures its best explanation as an artistic contribution or comment to the modernist dialogue in film history. Thus, we have explanatory reasons for classifying *A Casing Shelved* along with (other?) reflexive art films. Do these explanatory considerations outweigh our categorical or transcendental reasons for discounting its candidacy as a motion picture?

I do not think they do for the simple reason that we may make the historical points we wish to make about the place of *A Casing Shelved* in the tradition of film modernism without maintaining that *A Casing Shelved* is a film. The only reason to suppose that this is not an alternative is if one assumes that the only reflexive comments that can be made about an artform are in the idiom of the medium in question. That is, for example, reflexive comments on film must be made by films, and artistic comments on the nature of painting must be made in the medium of painting.

But this is clearly false. Happenings, which are in the nature of theatrical performances, make comments on the politics of modernist painting.[13] There is no problem with artworks in one medium, like Happenings, making comments on artworks in another medium, nor is their belonging to the history of another art form paradoxical. Thus, of *A Casing Shelved*, we can concede that it is not a film, while, at the same time, we may agree that its best interpretation is as an episode in film history—i.e., as a comment (from an adjacent artistic medium) on the structure of film spectatorship.

Though Danto's conception of moving pictures has much to recommend it, it does appear to me to call for one small adjustment in order to successfully accommodate the phenomena in question. For where Danto speaks of "moving pictures," it would be more appropriate to speak of moving *images*. "Picture" seems to imply the sort of intentional visual artifact in which one recognizes the depiction of objects, persons, situations and events. But many films and videos traffic in what are called nonrepresentational or non-objective imagery. Films and videos may comprise nonrecognizable shapes and purely visual structures. This, of course, may be *moving* imagery, or, if it is static imagery, the films and videos in question nevertheless afford the possibility of movement.

X, then, is a moving image only if x possesses a disembodied viewpoint (or—to state it less anthropomorphically—only if x is a detached display), and only if it is logically justifiable to expect movement in x when the spectator of x is informed about its nature. The latter necessary condition gives us the conceptual wherewithal to differentiate films and videos from paintings and slides. But since movement is a legitimate expectation in theater, how will we differentiate the relevant sort of moving images from dramatic representations?

A Difference In Performances?[14]

Theatrical performances are detached displays insofar as we cannot orient ourselves in their space; and the viewpoint may be equally said to be dis-embodied in the sense that when we see a dramatic re-enactment of Lee's surrender at Appomatox, we receive no information about the relation between the spatial co-ordinates of our bodies and those of Appomatox, Virginia. Similarly, though there may be still works in theater—such as Douglas Dunn's performance piece *101*[15]—throughout the event it is rea-sonable for us to suppose that movement may be forthcoming. So even if we have already delivered some necessary conditions for the moving image, we have not differentiated things like films and videos from dramatic per-formances.

Earlier philosophers, such as Roman Ingarden, attempted to draw the line between theater and film by claiming that in theater the word domi-nates and the spectacle is ancillary (shades of Aristotle here?), while in film, action dominates and words serve only to enhance the comprehension of the action.[16] However, there are significant counterexamples to this view, including: *History Lessons* and *Fortini-Cani* by Jean-Marie Straub and Daniele Huillet, and *Journeys from Berlin* by Yvonne Rainer, not to mention Robert Benchley's once popular comic shorts, Burns and Allen sit-coms, and Groucho Marx's *You Bet Your Life*.

Photographic realists, in contrast, try to get at the distinction between film and theater by focussing on the performer.[17] Because of the intima-cy of the photographic lens to its subject, some, like Cavell, think of the quintessence of film acting in terms of stars, whereas stage performers are actors who take on roles. For Erwin Panofsky, stage actors interpret their roles, whereas film actors incarnate them.[18] In the case of movies, we go to see Bogart, whereas in the case of theater we go to see Paul Scofield playing or interpreting *King Lear*. But is this contrast really compelling? People go to the theater to see Baryshnikov dance and to hear Callas sing no matter what the role, just as they once flocked to see Bernhardt act. We may say "Sam Spade just *is* Bogart," but only in the sense that people once said that Gilette was Sherlock Holmes or O'Neill was the Man in the Iron Mask.

But maybe there is another way to get at the difference here. Let's begin by focussing on the difference between theatrical performances and things like film performances. We might go to a film performance tonight at seven or to a theater performance. In either case, we are likely to be seated in an auditorium, and perhaps each performance starts with a rising curtain. But whatever the similarities, there are also deep differences between a theatrical performance and a film performance.

This assertion may at first strike some philosophers as strange. For it is very common nowadays to divide the arts into those arts that involve unique objects (some paintings, some scupltures) and those that involve multiple copies of the same artwork—there are probably over a million copies of Jane Austen's *Pride and the Prejudice*. Furthermore, having distinguished some arts as multiple in some sense, philosophers frequently go on to characterize the multiple arts—like novels, plays, and movies—in terms of the type/token relation.[19] But on this account, film performances and theatrical performances don't appear very different; they are both tokens of types. Tonight's film performance is a token of *The Piano* by Jane Campion, while tonight's dramatic performance is a token of *The Frogs* by Aristophanes. So, it might be concluded that there really is no profound distinction between theatrical performances and film performances.

However, though a simple type/token distinction can be useful as far as it goes here, more needs to be said. For even if theatrical performances and film performances may both be said to be tokens, the tokens in the theatrical case are generated by interpretations whereas the tokens in the film case are generated by templates. And this, in turn, is related to a crucial aesthetic difference between the two, viz., that theatrical performances are artworks in their own right which, thereby, can be objects of artistic evaluation, while the film *performance* itself neither is an artwork nor is it susceptible to artistic assessment.

The film performance is generated from a template—standardly a film print, but it might also be a videotape or a laser disk or a computer program. These templates are tokens; each one of them can be destroyed and each one can be assigned a spatial location. But the film—say *Broken Blossoms* by D.W. Griffith—is not destroyed when any of the prints are destroyed, including the negative or master. Indeed, all the prints can be destroyed and the film will survive if a laser disk does, or if a collection of photos of all the frames does, or if a computer program of it does whether on disk, or tape or even on paper or in human memory.[20]

Moreover, to get to a token film performance tonight we require a template which itself is a token of the film type. Whereas the paint on the *Mona Lisa* is a constitutive part of the unique painting, the print on the page of my copy of the novel *The Green Knight* conveys Iris Murdoch's artwork to me. Similarly, the film performance—the projection or screening event—is a token of the type, which token conveys *Broken Blossoms*, the type, to the spectator.

The story is somewhat different and a little more complicated when it comes to plays. First, plays may have as tokens both objects and performances. That is, when considered as a literary work, a token of *Major Barbara* is a text, in the same sense in which my copy of *Emma* is a text. But considered from the viewpoint of theater, a token of *Major Barbara* is a performance which occurs at a specific place and time. Unlike the film performance, however, the theatrical performance is not generated by a template. It is generated by an interpretation. For when considered from the viewpoint of theatrical performance, the play, by Shaw, is rather like a recipe which must be filled in by other artists—such as the director, the actors, the various designers, and so on.

This interpretation is a conception of the play and it is this conception of the play that governs the performances from evening to evening. Actors may change while the interpretation stays the same. Other casts may repeat the same interpretation. For the interpretation is a type, which, in turn, generates performances which are tokens.[21] Thus, the relation of the play to its performance is mediated by an interpretation, suggesting that the interpretation can be construed as a type within a type. What gets us from the play to a performance is not a template, which is a token, but an interpretation.

One difference between the performance of a play and the performance of a film, then, is that the former is generated by an interpretation and the latter is generated by a template. Moreover, this difference is connected to another, which is perhaps more interesting, viz., that performances of plays are artworks in their own right and can be aesthetically appreciated as such, whereas performances of films and videos are not artworks, nor does it make sense to evaluate them as such. One may complain that there is a focus problem at a film performance or that the video is not tracking, but these are not artistic failures; they are mechanical or electrical failures or shortcomings with respect to routine procedures.

In theater, the play, the interpretation and the performance are each arenas of artistic achievement in their own right. Though ideally integrated, in our theatrical practices, we recognize that these represent different, separable strata of artistry. We regard the play by the playwright as an artwork, which is then interpreted like a recipe or a set of instructions by the director and others in the process of producing another artwork.[22]

But in our practices with regard to motion pictures, things stand somewhat differently. If in theater, the play-type is a recipe that the director interprets, and the recipe and the interpretation can be regarded as different though related artworks, in film both the recipe and the interpretations are constituents of the same artwork. When the writer produces a play, we appreciate it independently of what its theatrical interpreters make of it. But in the world of motion pictures, as we know it, scenarios are not read like plays and novels, but are ingredients in moving pictures (or, more accurately, moving images).

Indeed, insofar as moving picture types always involve recipes in conjunction with interpretations, they are more like what are called theatrical productions than they are like play types. Perhaps this is why movies are also called "productions." But, in any case, it should clarify why people say things like "Many actors can play Prospero and the performance will still be a performance of the play type *The Tempest*, but it would not be an instance of the movie type *To Kill A Mockingbird*, unless Gregory Peck played Atticus Finch." For Gregory Peck's performance of Atticus Finch is part of the 1962 film *To Kill A Mockingbird* because Peck's interpretation, in concert with the director Robert Mulligan's, is a nondetachable constituent of the film. Saying "No *To Kill A Mockingbird* without Gregory Peck" loses its paradoxical air when the movie type is no longer compared to the play type, but to a theatrical production. For it is not paradoxical to say: "No instance of the Burton-Gielgud production of *Hamlet* without Burton," since theatrical productions, like movie types, have interpretations (by directors, actors, etc.) as constituent parts.

Whereas film performances are generated from templates which are tokens, play performances are generated from interpretation types. Thus, whereas film performances are counterfactually dependent on certain electrical, chemical, mechanical and otherwise routine processes, play performances are counterfactually dependent upon the beliefs, intentions and judgments of people—actors, lighting experts, make-up artists, and so on. Though there is an overarching directorial interpretation of the playwright's recipe, the realization of the token performance on a given night depends on the continuous interpretation of that plan, given the special exigencies of the unique performance situation. It is because of the contribution that interpretation makes in the production of the performance that the performance warrants artistic appreciation, whereas the performance of the film warrants no artistic appreciation, since that is merely a function of the physical mechanisms engaging the template properly, or, to put the matter differently, it is an issue of running the relevant devices properly.

A successful motion picture performance—i.e., the projection or screening of a film, or the running of a video cassette—does not merit aesthetic appreciation, nor is it considered as an artwork. We do not commend projectionists as we do actors or violinists. It is true that we do complain when the film dissolves in the projector beam, but that is a technical failure, not an aesthetic one. For if it were an aesthetic failure, we might expect people to cheer when the film does not burn. But they don't. For the happy film *performance* only depends on operating the apparatus as it was designed to be operated. Since that involves no more than (often minimal) mechanical understanding and savvy, running the template through the machine is not an aesthetic accomplishment and, therefore, is not an object of artistic evaluation. On the other hand, a successful theatrical performance involves a token interpretation of an interpretation type, and inasmuch as that depends on artistic understanding and judgment, it is a suitable object of aesthetic evaluation.

Furthermore, if the argument so far is correct, then it seems fair to surmise that a major difference between motion picture (or moving image) performances and theatrical performances is that the latter are artworks and the former are not, and, in consequence, that performances of motion pictures are not objects of artistic evaluation, whereas theatrical performances are. Or, yet another way to state the conclusion is to say that, in one sense, motion pictures are not a performing art—i.e., they are not something whose performance itself is art.

This, undoubtedly, will sound like a peculiar conclusion, one that will certainly call forth counterexamples. Three come to mind immediately. First: before motors were installed in projectors, film projectionists handcranked the performance, and audiences supposedly came to prefer some projectionists over others; weren't these projectionists performers who deserved artistic appreciation? Second: the avant-garde filmmaker Harry Smith accompanied some of his film screenings by personally alternating colored gels in front of the projector lens; wasn't he a performing artist? Third, Malcolm LeGrice presented a piece called *Monster Film* in which he walked—stripped to the waist—into the projector beam (his shadow becoming progressively larger like a monster), while a crashing din sounded loudly. If *Monster Film* is a film, surely its performance was an artwork.

However, these counterexamples are not persuasive. Since the early projectionists who are cited usually are also said to have cranked the films they thought were boring in such a way that the films were comically sped up, I wonder whether their performances were actually performances of the film types that were advertised, rather than travesties or send-ups thereof—that is to say, comic routines in their own right. On the other hand, both Smith and LeGrice seem to me to be engaged in multi-media artworks in which film or film apparatus play an important role, but which cannot be thought of simply as motion pictures.

What seems so bizarre about denying that moving pictures (and/or images) are instances of the performing arts is that motion picture types are made by what we standardly think of as performing artists—actors, directors, choreographers and so on. But, it is key to note that the interpretations and the performances that these artists contribute to the motion picture type are integrated and edited into the final product as constituent parts of the moving picture type.

We do not go to see Gregory Peck's performance, but a performance of *To Kill A Mockingbird*. And while Gregory Peck's performance required artistry, the performance of *To Kill A Mockingbird* does not. It requires only the proper manipulation of the template and the apparatus. A performance of a play, contrariwise, involves the kind of talents exhibited by Gregory Peck prior to the appearance of the first template of *To Kill A Mockingbird*. That is why the performance of a play is an artistic event and the performance of a moving picture is not.

Thus, there are important differences between the performance of a motion picture and the performance of a play. Two of them are: that the play performance is generated by an interpretation, whereas the performance of the motion picture is generated by a template; and, the performance of a play is an artwork in its own right and an object of aesthetic evaluation, whereas the performance of the motion picture is neither. Moreover, the first of these contrasts helps to explain the second. For it is insofar as the performance of the motion picture is generated by engaging the template mechanically that it is not an appropriate object of artistic evaluation in the way that a performance generated by an interpretation or a set of interpretations is. These two features of film performances are enough to differentiate performances of moving images from performances of plays, and, furthermore, the two differentia under consideration apply to all films and videos, whether the film and video types are indexed as artworks or not.

Conclusion

So far we have identified four necessary conditions for the phenomena that we are calling moving images. X is a moving image 1) only if x possesses a disembodied viewpoint (or is a detached display); 2) only if it is reasonable to anticipate movement in x (on first viewing) when one knows what x is; 3) only if performance tokens of x are generated by templates; and 4) only if performance tokens of x are not artworks. Moreover, these conditions provide us with the conceptual resources to discriminate the moving image from neighboring artforms like painting and theater.

Of course, with these necessary conditions in hand, it is natural to wonder whether or not they are jointly sufficient conditions for something to be what we typically call a motion picture. I think they are not, because treated as a set of jointly sufficient conditions, they are overly inclusive. For example, the upper right hand page corners of Arlene Croce's *The Fred Astaire and Ginger Rogers Book* contains photographs of the eponymous couple dancing.[23] If you flick the pages quickly, you can animate the dancers after the fashion of a flip book. And though condition #3 above eliminates hand-made, one-of-a-kind flip books from our catch basin, the Astaire/Rogers example meets condition #3, as would any mass-produced flip book, whether it employed photographs or some other mechanically reproduced illustrations. Similarly, Muybridge photos of horses animated by the nineteenth-century device known as the zoetrope fit the formula. However, these do not seem to be the kind of phenomena that one has in mind when speaking of moving pictures in ordinary language or of moving images in slightly regimented language.

One might try to block this species of example by requiring that motion pictures (and/or images) be projected. But that would have the untoward consequence of cashiering early Edison kinetoscopes from the order of the motion picture. Obviously it will be difficult to draw any firm boundaries between motion pictures and the proto-cinematic devices that led to the invention of cinema without coming up with hard cases; indeed, we should predict problematic boundary cases exactly in this vicinity. But, in any event, it does not seem obvious to me that we can turn the four preceding necessary conditions into jointly sufficient conditions for what is commonly thought to be a motion picture without doing some violence to our everyday intuitions.[24]

Thus, the characterization of moving pictures (and images) that I have proposed is not essentialist in the philosophical sense that supposes that an essential definition of motion pictures would be comprised of necessary conditions that are jointly sufficient for picking out the extension of motion pictures. Nor is my characterization essentialist in the sense of that label used in the opening section of this essay. For the conditions I have enumerated have no implications for the stylistic directions that film and/or video should take. The preceding four conditions, it seems to me, are compatible with any motion picture style, including ones that may conflict with others. Thus, if I have indeed managed to set out four necessary conditions for moving pictures (and images), then I have also shown that, contrary to the previous tradition of film theory, it is possible to philosophize about the nature of moving images without implicitly legislating what film and video artists should and should not do.

Notes

1 For an account of the tradition of classical film theory, see Noël Carroll, *Philosophical Problems of Classical Film Theory* (Princeton: Princeton University Press, 1988).

2 André Bazin, *What Is Cinema?*, vol. 1, trans. H. Gray (Berkeley: University of California Press, 1967), 108.

3 André Bazin, *What is Cinema?*, vol. 1, 14. See also 96–7.

4 For criticism of Bazin, see Noël Carroll, "Cinematic Representation and Realism," in *Philosophical Problems of Classical Film Theory*.

5 See Stanley Cavell, *The World Viewed: Reflections on the Ontology of Film* (Cambridge: Harvard University Press, 1979); Roger Scruton, "Photography and Representation," in *The Aesthetic Understanding.* (London: Methuen, 1983); Kendall L. Walton, "Transparent Pictures: On the Nature of Photographic Realism," *Critical Inquiry*, vol. 11, no. 2 (December 1984). A similar view has been defended by Patrick Maynard in several essays including "Drawing and Shooting: Causality in Depiction," *Journal of Aesthetics and Art Criticism* 44 (1985). In "Looking Again through Photographs," Kendall Walton defends his position against Edwin Martin's "On Seeing Walton's Great-Grandfather"; both articles appear in *Critical Inquiry*, vol. 12, no. 4 (summer 1986). Two other defenders of photographic realism include: Roland Barthes, *Camera Lucida* (New York: Farrar, Straus and Giroux, 1981) and Susan Sontag, *On Photography* (New York: Farrar, Straus, and Giroux, 1977).

6 See David Lewis, "Veridical Hallucination and Prosthetic Vision," in his *Philosophical Papers*, vol. 2 (Oxford: Oxford University Press, 1986). See also E. M. Zemach, "Seeing, 'Seeing' and Feeling," *Review of Metaphysics* 23 (September 1969).

7 F. E. Sparshott, "Vision and Dream in the Cinema," *Philosophic Exchange* (summer 1971): 115.

8 Arguments against photographic realism like this one can be found in Nigel Warburton's "Seeing Through 'Seeing Through Photographs,'" *Ratio*, New Series 1 (1988) and in Gregory Currie's "Photography, Painting and Perception," *Journal of Aesthetics and Art Criticism*, vol. 49, no. 1 (winter 1991).

9 I prefer to use the term "display" here, rather than "representation," because

the latter implies an image in which we see recognizable objects, persons and situations whereas "display" allows that the subject of a cinematic view might be what is called "nonrepresentational." In this I differ from the idiom Currie favors in his "Photography, Painting and Perception."

10 Arthur Danto, "Moving Pictures," *Quarterly Review of Film Studies*, vol. 4, no. 1 (winter 1979).

11 Roman Ingarden, "On the Borderline between Literature and Painting," in his *Ontology of the Work of Art: The Musical Work, The Picture, The Architectual Work, The Film*, trans. Raymond Meyer and J.T. Goldwait (Athens, Ohio: Ohio University Press, 1989), 324–25.

12 For a discussion of Danto's use of transcendental arguments, see Noël Carroll, "Essence, Expression and History: Arthur Danto's Philosophy of Art," in *Danto and His Critics*, ed. Mark Rollins (Oxford: Blackwell, 1993).

13 For a fuller explanation of this, see Noël Carroll, "Performance," *Formations*, vol. 3, no. 1 (spring 1986).

14 This section develops some suggestions that Danto makes in "Moving Pictures," but it differs from Danto's major line of analysis of the difference between film and theater because the main line of analysis seems confused. Danto spends most of his time examining the distinction between documentaries of plays and screenplays proper, but this does not help him to isolate the difference between drama and film because the differences that Danto finds between documentaries of plays and screenplays proper turn out to be the same differences that one finds between documentaries of plays and plays. For example, both screenplays proper and plays are *about* characters and locales, not about actors and sets. Therefore, the contrast between documentaries of plays and screenplays proper does not get at what Danto wants—a distinction between screenplays proper and plays. However, despite this criticism of Danto's central argument, his more castaway asides have led me toward the analysis in this section.

15 For descriptions of this piece see Sally Banes, *Terpsichore in Sneakers* (Boston: Houghton Mifflin Company, 1980), 189; and Noël Carroll, "Douglas Dunn, 308 Broadway," *Artforum* 13 (September 1974): 86.

16 Ingarden, "On the Borderline," 328–29. See also Rudolf Arnheim, *Film As Art* (Berkeley: University of California Press, 1957), 210–30.

17 See, for example, Cavell, 27–28. Also, see Erwin Panofsky, "Style and Medium in the Motion Pictures," *Film Theory and Criticism*, eds. Gerald Mast and Marshall Cohen (New York: Oxford University Press, 1985).

18 Cavell, *World Viewed*. Panofsky, "Style and Medium."

19 Richard Wollheim seems to be responsible for popularizing the use of this distinction amongst aestheticians. See his book *Art and its Objects* (Cambridge: Cambridge University Press, 1980); see especially sections

35–38. The type/token distinction itself, of course, derives from C.S. Peirce, *Collected Papers*, vol. 4 (Cambridge, Mass.: Harvard University Press), 537.

20 If you can print the code out, then it is theoretically possible for it to be memorized, if not by one person, then by a group—like the population of China.

21 R. A. Sharpe presents an argument for regarding interpretations as types in his "Type, Token, Interpretation, and Performance" in *Mind* (1979): 437–40. Throughout this section, I have benefitted immensely from reading parts of David Zucker Saltz's unpublished manuscript *The Real Stage: Philosophical Foundations of Performance* (though, of course, Prof. Saltz is not responsible for any of my errors).

22 This is not to preclude the possibility that the playwright may also be the director of and an actor in his/her own play. Nevertheless, his role as an artist-author is different from his/her role as and artist-interpreter, whether director, or actor, or both.

23 Arlene Croce, *The Fred Astaire and Ginger Rogers Book* (New York: Vintage, 1972).

24 In "Moving Pictures," Danto tries to block flip books and the like by claiming that moving pictures in his sense possess the possibility of moving viewpoints (e.g., camera movements), while flip books do not. But I see no reason to think that flip books can't have moving viewpoints. Think of a flip book like the Astaire/Rogers example where the scene involves a camera movement. Moreover, where the image in the flip book is drawn, the artist can still convey the impression of moving closer or further away from the object depicted.

part two ▍**Genres and Tropes**

5 ■ Missing Mothers/ Desiring Daughters

Framing the Sight of Women

Naomi Scheman

> How could she—oh how could she have become a part of the picture on the screen, while her mother was still in the audience, out there, in the dark, looking on?[1]
> —Olive Higgins, *Stella Dallas*

Much feminist film theory has focused on the nature of the gaze, both that of the characters within a film and that of the spectator addressed by the film. Questions have been raised about relations of the gaze to subjectivity, to gender, and to sexuality, and about relations among those three.[2] In particular, it has been argued, most notably by Laura Mulvey, that the cinematic gaze is gendered male and characterized by the taking of the female body as the quintessential and deeply problematic object of sight. In such accounts the female gaze—and along with it female subjectivity—becomes impossible.[3]

Yet women do, of course, see movies. Furthermore, many classic Hollywood films were made with a specifically female audience in mind, clearly not addressing that audience as though it were in masculine drag. And there are movies, in particular many of the same movies, that include women characters who see in ways that are coded as distinctively female.[4] There are also specifically feminist films, made from and for an oppositional spectatorial position, and there are feminist film viewers, critics, and theorists looking at all sorts of films.[5] How shall we account for all these gazes and for the subjectivities behind them?

These issues are addressed elsewhere in feminist theory, for example, in studies of the normative maleness of the scientist, the philosopher, the artist, and the citizen. There are at least three possible responses to the recognition that women do see, desire, and know despite the compelling theoretical demonstrations of the maleness of the gaze, of desire, and of epistemic authority: one is that we do it in drag, by tapping what Freud called our innate bisexuality; the second is that we do it as socially constructed females, in ways masculinist regimes have uses for; and the third is that we, somehow, impossible as it may seem, do it in creative rebellion, as feminists.[6]

The first option is *theoretically* unproblematic, once one accepts that gender is socially constructed: the norms of maleness are learnable, and some girls and women, especially of privileged race and class, have of late been allowed or even encouraged to learn some of them, such as those governing the academic and work worlds. It is the latter two, more problematic but also more promising, options that interest me here. In particular, I am interested in looking at the second option for clues as to how the theoretically impossible third option—feminist subjectivity (or sexuality or desire or knowledge or agency)—can exist.

One possible place to start to look for oppositional consciousness is in the films Stanley Cavell discusses in *The Pursuits of Happiness*, extremely popular films that are little discussed by feminist film theorists.[7] These comedies from the thirties and forties, particularly as Cavell discusses them, seem to be counterexamples to the gaze-as-male theories. For example, though it has been argued that both the spectatorial gaze *at* a movie and the gazes of characters *within* a movie are normatively male—and, conversely, that the female gaze is absent, stigmatized, or punished—in these films women are allowed, even encouraged, to look to (and for) their heart's content.

On the narrative level, too, these films seem counterexemplary, addressing many of the same issues raised by discussions of the gaze, particularly by those twentieth century theories of narrative that see the gaze as gendered male by its placement in a male Oedipal frame.[8] In these theories, the Oedipus story is seen as the quintessential narrative, and exclusive focus on the male version stems from the widespread acceptance of an essentially Freudian account of the genesis of female sexuality as the learned foregoing of active desire. The female story cannot stand as its own narrative; rather, we have the story of how a girl comes to embody the desired goal and the reward of the male developmental quest. But the fates of the heroines of the *Pursuits of Happiness* films are as interesting and as connected to their own desires as are the fates of the heroes, and the paths to those fates are as complex and as much, if not more, the subject of the films.

Connecting the issues of the female gaze and of the female narrative is the issue of desire. As Cavell repeatedly stresses, a central theme of these films is the heroine's acknowledgment of her desire and of its true object—frequently the man from whom she mistakenly thought she needed to be divorced. The heroine's acknowledgment of her desire, and of herself as a subject of desire, is for Cavell what principally makes a marriage of equality achievable. It is in this achievement (or the creation of the grounds for the hope of it) that Cavell wants to locate the feminism of the genre: it is the "comedy of equality."[9] There is, therefore, an obvious explanation in Cavell's terms for the anomalous nature of these films: if their vision is explicitly feminist in embracing an ideal of equality, in approvingly foregrounding female desire, and in characterizing that desire as active and as actively gazing, then they would not be expected to fit an analysis based on films whose view of female desire and the female gaze is as passive, absent, or treacherous. If we accept Cavell's readings, these films provide genuine counterexamples to feminist claims of the normative masculinity of film (in general or in Hollywood).

My affection for these films, and the ways in which Cavell accounts for that affection, lead me to want to believe that his account, or something like it, is true, that there did briefly emerge a distinctively feminist sensibility in some popular Hollywood movies, one which unsurprisingly succumbed to the repressive redomestication of women in the post-war years. But, for a number of reasons, I can't quite believe it. Some version of the feminist critical theory of popular cinema does, in an odd way, apply to these movies: they are, to use a frequent phrase of Cavell's, the exceptions that prove the rule. Though they do have some claim to being considered feminist, their feminism is seriously qualified by the terms in which it is presented, by the ways in which female desire and the female gaze are framed.

The clue to my unease with Cavell's readings, with the films themselves, and with the feminism they embody is in the double state of motherlessness (neither having nor being one) that is requisite for the heroines. By exploring the absence of mothers and maternity in these comedies, I want to illuminate some features of the distinctively female, though only stuntedly feminist, gaze they depict. I will argue that such a gaze is one a masculinist world has little trouble conscripting, and that its incompatibility with maternity functions to keep it within bounds. Turning then to melodrama, which, as Cavell has argued, is the cinematic home of the mother/daughter relationship, I want to explore a different, but equally conscriptable, female gaze—the maternal.[10] Finally, I want to suggest that we can open a space for the *feminist* gaze by redrawing the lines of sight.

Missing Mothers/Desiring Daughters: Take One

Cavell explicitly acknowledges that the motherlessness of the heroines in the films he discusses poses a problem. The problem is not unique to these films: the mothers of comedic heroines are quite commonly absent—not dead or gone, but simply unremarkably nonexistent, as they are notably in *The Lady Eve* and *It Happened One Night*. Although he recognizes the importance and the depth of this odd and troubling feature of the apparent paternal parthenogenesis of romantic comedic heroines, Cavell goes on not to explain it, but to "offer three guesses about regions from which an explanation will have to be formed"—the social, the psychological or dramatic, and the mythical.[11] My sense is that to the extent that such explanations will be adequate, those very explanations undercut the laughter. The "limitations of these comedies" are, from a feminist perspective, fatal, if not to our pleasure in them, then to our taking that pleasure seriously in the ways Cavell would urge us to do. The motherlessness of the heroines is the clue to the male framing of the desiring female gazes that provide so much of that pleasure.

We can follow this clue most fruitfully by exploring Cavell's latter two regions, the psychological or dramatic and the mythical. The two are closely connected, not surprisingly, given Cavell's reliance on Freud and Freud's reliance on mythology.[12] Initially, however, Cavell's guess about the psychological or dramatic reasons for motherlessness is puzzling, since it focuses not on the absence of women's mothers but on the presence of their fathers—as though one could have only one true parent. His argument is that "there is a closeness children may bear to the parent of the opposite sex which is enabling for a daughter but crippling to a son."[13] (The "crippled sons" in a number of these films are men who are permanently attached to their mothers; they are the men the heroines mistakenly turn to in flight from their own desires.) Beyond the puzzling shift of attention from absent mothers to present fathers, there is the further puzzle about why this should be so: why should the love of a daughter for her father stand less in the way of her coming to love someone else than a son's love for his mother?

From a psychoanalytic perspective, the answer is that a girl's connection to her father is inherently more fungible—more replaceable by a substitute—than is a boy's connection to his mother.[14] The maternal connection for both males and females is the original one, the one wherein attachment is initially learned. The attachment of a girl to her father is always already a substitute; she enters into it through learning what it is to transfer love and desire from one object to another. Males are supposed to learn to shift their desire from their mothers under the threat of castration attendant upon Oedipal desires: "In boys...the complex is not simply repressed, it is literally smashed to pieces by the shock of threatened castration."[15] In the case of a girl's attachment to her father, no such destruction is either possible or necessary: it is impossible, since on Freud's view she is already castrated, and it is unnecessary, since, being both passive and secondary, her desire for her father poses no threat to her future development. What is necessary in her case is precisely that such an attachment occur, that is, that she shift her desire away from her mother.

Presumably such a shift requires some powerfully motivating forces. It also must leave some considerable residue of loss, a grief at the heart of socially acceptable femininity, which Freud barely glimpses. Cavell more than glimpses it, but he leaves it largely buried: unearthed it would dishearteningly reveal the costs, in the world Freud describes, of comedy, and challenge its definition of ending in happiness defined as marriage.

Through cooperation in the disposition of their desire girls are learning that there is a connection between the particular fungibility of female desire and the normative passivity of that desire. By defining female desire as responsive to male—in the first instance, paternal—desire, the culture inscribes "father-daughter incest [as] a culturally constructed paradigm of female desire."[16] The paradigm shapes that desire as normatively passive, as responsive to another's active desire, even if only fantasized. And, under the conditions of patriarchal control and compulsory heterosexuality,[17] a woman's desire, if it enters into consideration at all, is meant to become fungible more or less on demand. Like Sleeping Beauty, she awakens to the man who lays claim to her.

In this story female gender identity gets linked both to the question of *origins*, as the gendered self comes into existence in relation to the father, and to *sexual identity*, as that relation is learned through a reorientation of desire. That is, the two forms of self-knowledge, about one's parentage and about one's sexual identity, which Cavell argues are demanded for a (true or happy) marriage, are in Freudian terms conflated in the case of women. A woman needs on such an account to acknowledge that she came into existence as a female only in relation to the thought of her father's desire for her; that is, she needs to acknowledge him as her one true parent.

The requisite virginity of an Athena or of other women—mortal and divine—who play her role of mediating between the worlds of maternal and paternal power (for example, the modern stereotype of the spinster schoolteacher) is, I am beginning to suspect, less a matter of avoiding sex than of avoiding maternity, which, as Cavell points out in a related discussion, used to require (hetero)sexual abstinence. The difficulties women encounter today when they attempt to combine motherhood and career are rooted in part in their violating a long-standing taboo against combining the symbolically loaded power of maternity with power as constituted in the extradomestic world.[18] To be allowed to exercise that second sort of power, to act like a man, has generally meant thinking of oneself as a genetic fluke—parthenogenetically fathered and sterile.

Cavell's guess from the region of myth about the absence of heroines' mothers makes reference to this tradition: "Mythically, the absence of the mother continues the idea that the creation of the woman is the business of men; even, paradoxically, when the creation is that of the so-called new woman, the woman of equality."[19] Beyond the obvious paradox, a deeper one appears in the claim that only as fathered can a woman claim *either* public empowerment *or* feminine sexual identity. The paradox lies in the double cultural privileging of paternity—as grounding the authorities of civilization and as creating female desire. The message to a woman is clear: within the systems of male privilege neither her appropriately feminine sexual identity nor her ability to assume public power is compatible with her being her mother's daughter.

Consider the one film Cavell discusses in which the heroine does have a mother: *The Philadelphia Story*. When we first see mother and daughter together, a couple of days before Tracy's (second) wedding and just before the arrival of Dexter and the dragooned *Spy* reporters, their relationship is extremely close. We get an intimation, however, that they live that relationship in very different ways. Tracy is affectionately bossy toward her mother (and the others she approves of) and dismissively judgmental toward her father (and the others, notably Dexter, she disapproves of). Her mother is much less severe; even when she strongly disapproves of something, she tends to hold her peace (as when she admits to Dinah that it is "stinking" of Tracy not to allow her father to come to her wedding). Mother Lord's unconditional love, not only of Tracy, but notably of her philandering husband, can be taken, I think, as a model of how Tracy is supposed to learn to feel.

But if Tracy is meant to come more closely to resemble her mother, neither she nor the viewers of the film are meant to attend to that fate in those terms; in particular, neither she nor we are meant to pay much attention to Mother Lord. Rather, Tracy's education, as we are shown it, is entirely in the hands of men, who lecture her on how to be a real woman. Tracy's mother's role in her daughter's education is precisely to allow herself to be replaced, to be silent in the face of the paternal claim.

The scene in which Tracy's father asserts his claim to her affectionate attention contains, as Cavell notes, "words difficult to tolerate," especially as we know them to be overheard by Mrs. Lord: they are simply and unredeemably cruel.[20] Mr. Lord makes it clear that he considers his behavior none of his daughter's business, that far from occupying the high moral ground she takes herself to be on, she's "been speaking like a jealous woman," and, finally, that if he's been involved with another woman, it's *her* fault. The reason he gives for this accusation (one that I fear the film does not expect us to find outrageous) is that a man has a natural need—and, apparently, consequently a right—to be looked up to uncritically by a beautiful young woman, so if his daughter refuses to meet this need once her mother is no longer young and beautiful, she is guilty of his seeking to have it met elsewhere. It is, in Cavell's words, "essential to his aria that it occurs in the presence of the mother, as a kind of reclaiming of her from Tracy."[21] But it is equally and, for the narrative, more importantly, a claiming of Tracy from her mother, an assertion of his claim to her love and attention. And Tracy goes on, oblivious to the effect of her father's words on her mother (it is not clear that she knows her to have been listening), to test what he has said against how the other men around her see her and how she wants to see herself and to be seen.

What the film seems to be telling us is that a woman's happiness in marriage requires her abandonment both of her love for her mother and of the active aspects of her own sexuality. She needs to acknowledge her identity as a sexually desiring woman, and even to act in pursuit of those desires, but the structure of desire she needs to acknowledge is Oedipal. The right man is the one who, because of the nature of *his* desire for *her*, has a claim on her. In their unsuccessful attempts to escape the claims of the right man, the heroines of *The Awful Truth* and *His Girl Friday* turn, like Tracy Lord, to unsuitable substitutes, men who lack the power to make such a claim to a woman's desire, because they have not learned to turn their desire away from their mothers.

Cavell is right to note that in these films "the creation of the woman is the business of men": that this creation requires for its fictional enactment the erasure of the woman's mother confirms feminist suspicions that, like Athena from Zeus' forehead, women born of men will identify with them and will at best leave a dubious legacy of female self-realization.[22]

Missing Mothers/Desiring Daughters: Take Two

In the previous section mothers were missing and daughters were desired. Shifting the syntax, in this section mothers are missed, even if physically present, and daughters—problematically—desire. A number of films have played out versions of the tension between a woman's attachment to her mother and the demands of heterosexual love. Three pictures of this tension are drawn, from rather different angles, in *Now, Voyager, Bill of Divorcement*, and *Mildred Pierce*. The first two are melodramas, and *Mildred Pierce* is a melodrama framed by a *film noir*. In his essay "Psychoanalysis and Cinema," Cavell discusses melodrama as that genre that confronts the threats and dangers lurking in the cracks of the comedies, and he explicitly joins that discussion to the issue of women whose creation cannot be in the hands of men, whose identity is discovered elsewhere than through heterosexual love and marriage.[23] The mother/daughter connection is the most fundamental of those elsewheres.

As Geoffrey Nowell-Smith argues, melodrama is quintessentially familial, its family is patriarchal, and it addresses "the problems of adults, particularly women, in relation to their sexuality" and "the child's problems of growing into a sexual identity within the family, under the ægis of a symbolic law which the father incarnates."[24] While I agree that patriarchal power structures the familial world of melodrama, Nowell-Smith's emphasis slights the presence and dramatic importance of mothers, which is one of the distinguishing marks of the genre. For example, *Mildred Pierce* is a perfect example of his claim that "[m]elodrama enacts, often with uncanny literalness, the 'family romance' described by Freud—that is to say, the imaginary scenario played out by children in relation to their paternity, the asking and answering of the question, whose child am I (or would I like to be)?"[25] But it is essential to Veda's attempt to discover herself as Monty's daughter, as it is to her subsequent attempt to become "incestuously" involved with him, that he is her mother's lover: a Mildred who is married to Monty would be someone she could, as she desperately needs to, acknowledge as her mother.

The story Mildred tells is a mother's story. Feminist critics have discussed the framing of her story by the detective('s) story, but equally noteworthy is Veda's attempt, internal to Mildred's story, to frame it in a way that will play out her family romance.[26] Veda's attachment to Mildred is strong, and Bert is represented as weak and emotionally absent. Veda's desire to recast the facts of her own origins therefore centers on Mildred, who comes to be the target of Veda's rage when those fantasies are unfulfilled.

Veda has the opportunity to leave Mildred and to live a life of social and economic privilege, but she uses her marriage for extortion instead. Though Veda explicitly says she wants the money in order to leave Mildred, her actions make it hard to believe that she really means this, except as an expression of enraged disappointment. Instead of turning to her father at this point, Veda rebelliously "makes a spectacle" of herself, becoming not the appropriately gazed-at object of paternal and then husbandly love, but a showgirl leered at by sailors, until Mildred succumbs to Veda's fantasy and marries Monty. Having had her fantasy family put in place, Veda takes to playing out the Oedipal story, with the father she chose. But the available cultural scripts make the incest taboo inoperative and the misinterpretation of Veda's desire—by Veda herself and by

Monty—inevitable, and fatal: at the moment of Veda's taking her desire for Monty to be a desire to take him away from Mildred, she kills him, and turns for her life back to Mildred, who cannot, this time, save her.

Mildred Pierce is in part about what becomes of motherhood when mothers lack the power to fulfill their children's dreams but are still held, by their children and by themselves, responsible for that failure. The Oedipus complex is supposed to teach both girls and boys that mothers don't have this power—that boys have it themselves and that girls are to get it from men. One of its normative results is the weakening of maternal—and, more generally, female—power. In *Mildred Pierce* neither Veda nor Mildred has come to terms with this cultural demand, and they are both punished for their refusal. At the very end Mildred is "redeemed" by the power of the law, which, knowing the truth of her innocence and Veda's guilt, releases her, as it were, into Bert's protective custody, while Veda is left behind, believing that Mildred has betrayed her. The betrayal may be illusory, but the severing of the bond between them, as the price for Mildred's return to the social order, is not. As Pam Cook points out, the film further reminds us "of what women must give up for the sake of the patriarchal order": the closing shot of Mildred and Bert leaving the police station also frames two women on their knees, scrubbing the floor.[27]

As hostile as Veda is to Mildred throughout the film, the root of both her rage and her rebelliousness is her refusal to make the required shift of attachment and attention from mother to father, her continuing insistence on Mildred's power. Veda's desires are transgressive because they continue to have as their ultimate object the phallic mother, whose castration is demanded by the patriarchal order. Unlike Mother Lord, Mildred is unwilling to enact her own disempowerment. When the force of the law finally subdues her, it is too late for her daughters: one is dead and one is imprisoned for murder. The film closes, grimly, as a dark reflection of the remarriage comedies: Mildred walks off, reunited with her first husband, framed within a childless marriage.

In many ways *Now, Voyager* is a mirror image of *Mildred Pierce*. Bette Davis is trapped by her mother's imperious refusal to let her go and by the repressions that refusal has demanded and instilled. Charlotte does not, however, obediently accept her mother's picture of the world of heterosexual desire as lethally dangerous. Though she lives a life of renunciation of desire, it is with an undercurrent of stifled rebellion, played out—with obvious Freudian symbolism—in the hidden boxes she makes and the forbidden cigarettes she smokes. In this explicitly psychoanalytic version of the incompatibility of mother/daughter attachment and heterosexual desire, therapy is called on to undermine the attachment and liberate the desire. But, in the terms of the film, the results are ambiguous. Charlotte does acknowledge and express desire, but the terms of the acknowledgment and expression are given by the men in her life, and in the end she represses her desire for Jerry in favor of a maternal connection to his daughter.

Lea Jacobs argues that Dr. Jacquith's role is "outside desire, identified with the process of narrative itself": he makes it possible for Charlotte to have a story.[28] But the story she has is one in which her desire is expressed as her desirability, a framing that she continually resists, as Jacobs demonstrates through the close analysis of shots in which Charlotte attempts either to place herself at the site of enunciation or to resist being the visibly fetishized object of desire. Neither of these attempts is wholly successful, but her persistence undermines her recuperation into the system of desire defined by the narrative into which Dr. Jacquith's cure is supposed to insert her. Instead of taking her place as an object of heterosexual desire, she takes *his* place as an asexual substitute parent to Tina. Her final gesture can be read as sacrificial of her happiness for Tina's, but it can equally, and subversively, be seen as a refusal of the terms on which she was offered an entry into narrative—a positioning as the object of the male gaze and a renunciation of maternity.

What is clear is that Charlotte cannot have both a consummated heterosexual relationship and an ongoing maternal one. As she tells Jerry at the close of the film, Dr. Jacquith has let her keep Tina "on probation," and Jerry's visit is a test of her will to renounce her sexual desires in favor of her maternal ones. Jacquith's initial "cure" of Charlotte was his positioning her as an object of heterosexual desire. In the face of her resistance to being so positioned, he agreed to shift his definition for her of healthy adulthood, but he retained the power to keep sexuality and maternity separate—and to define them both.

The mothering Charlotte embraces at the end is a replication of what Jacquith provided for her; it hardly provides a point of connection to her own mother, who, like Tina's mother, Isobel, continues to be that from which daughters need to be helped to escape. Jeanne Thomas Allen, editor of the screenplay of *Now, Voyager*, notes that Edmund Goulding's treatment of Olive Higgins Prouty's novel "begins the process of 'strengthening' the male figures as father-doctors in Charlotte's rebirth, while the roles of Charlotte's sister-in-law, Lisa, and friend, Deb, are minimized. The psychological midwives of the novel are replaced by doctors, who turn the midwives into nurses."[29] Thus, there is a deep instability in the film, not only between the demands of maternity and of heterosexual desire, but, internal to each of those demands, about the locus of defining authority.

Bill of Divorcement enacts this tension between the mother/daughter relationship and heterosexual desire with an extremely odd twist. Sydney (Katharine Hepburn) and her mother, Margaret (Billie Burke), are each happily in love and about to marry. The only shadow over their happiness is the father/husband Sydney never knew and Margaret wishes to forget. Hilary (John Barrymore) has been hospitalized for what turns out to be "hereditary insanity," and his unexpected return threatens the happiness of the impending marriages—most obviously *Margaret's*. Despite her divorce, she is as moved by her ex-husband's love and need for her as she was when she married him, and her love for another seems as without force now as her lack of love for Hilary did then. It seems to her that she has no choice but to renounce the man she loves to resume a marriage defined by another man's need of her.

Hilary, however, mistook Sydney at first for her mother: she is, in appearance and in manner, more like the wife he lost. She is also, not altogether coherently, more like *him*. The combination forces *Sydney* to be the one whose marriage plans dissolve. She is the one, she says, who understands him and can make him happy, the one he really loves, and the one who bears the hereditary taint of insanity, hence the one who doesn't dare have children. She sends away both her lover and her mother—literally handing her into the arms of a new husband—and settles down at the piano with her father, accepting her fate to live with and care for a man she saw for the first time the day before, but to whom she immediately feels more connected than to her mother or her fiancé.

The father/daughter bond in *Bill of Divorcement* is hardly conducive, as in the remarriage comedies, to the daughter's acknowledgement of sexual desire and her subsequent marital happiness. Rather, it is precisely *because* she is her father's daughter that Sydney has to forego marriage: she can neither leave him nor risk bearing children, and the possibility of her going mad is too much to expect her lover to bear (as her father's madness is too much to expect her mother to bear). The film plays out too literally the fantasy of paternal parthenogenesis: Sydney takes her father instinctively as her true parent and experiences the bond with him as nonfungible.

The knowledge of being her father's daughter transforms Sydney's experience of her desire; no longer is it compatible with continued intimacy with her mother or with having children. We may not notice how, in the comedies, the daughter's marriage is made possible by her mother's invisibility, but when the roles are reversed and a *daughter* retreats into the static space outside of narrative to enable her *mother's* romantic marriage, the underlying logic becomes disconcertingly clear. The presence of her father and the knowledge of what it means to be his daughter transform Sydney's experience of her own desire. No longer is that desire compatible, as it clearly was at the start of the film, with continued intimacy with her mother or with the desire to have children. The placement of her father at the point of definition of her identity and her desire precludes both Sydney's continued closeness to her mother and the possibility of her own motherhood.

In the terms of this film it is not the closeness of the mother/daughter bond that is incompatible with the daughter's heterosexual desire and happy marraige, but how that bond is experienced under the law of the father, and the connection between heterosexuality and male power. The consequences of Sydney's acknowledgement of her father highlight the peremptory violence of the claim of the father-right, the violence a daughter needs to ignore in the name of "normal" heterosexual development. The violence that is done to the relationship between mothers and daughers—either its total erasure, as in most romantic comedies, or the painful ruptures or sacrifices characteristic of melodrama—has its roots not simply in the daughter's need to learn to love someone else. The roots lie in the way in which patriarchy demands that she learn that lesson—as a submission to male power, first in the person of her father, and as a renunciation of her belief in her mother's power and her hope for her own.

The pain mothers and daughters experience through the teaching and learning of female powerlessness are the dark underside of the laughter of the remarriage comedies. As in Shakespeare's romantic comedies, the achievement of the happy ending of marriage requires the severing of bonds between women. The pleasure many women, myself included, take in such comedies, and in their bright, bold, sexually assertive heroines, is bought at the cost of not noticing what has become of their mothers and how their very brightness is figured as eager identification with a male-defined world, a world to which their fathers hold the key.

Framing the Sight of Women
Do women as women see, or must we become "masculine" to own the gaze? Is the position of the viewer one of power or one of passivity? In "Visual Pleasure and Narrative Cinema" Laura Mulvey argues, with respect to cinematic gazes—the gaze of the characters within the film, the gaze of the camera, and the gaze of the spectators at the film—that their structures are those of masculine desire. On her analysis, the nature of this desire and the anxieties associated with it require the diversion of attention from the camera's and the spectators' gazes, through the cre-

ation and maintenance of "an illusion of Renaissance space...; the camera's look [along with the look of the audience] is disavowed in order to create a convincing world in which the spectator's surrogate [the male character with whom the male viewer identifies] can perform with verisimilitude."[30]

Christian Metz makes a similar point, although problematically without attention to gender specificity, in distinguishing between the naturalistic, gapless *story* the film presents and the *discourse* that is its telling.[31] For Metz, narrative film gratifies a desire to be "a pure, all-seeing and invisible subject, the vanishing point of the monocular perspective which cinema has taken over from painting."[32] Such a perspective is meant to be one from which the world appears as it really is, the privileged point at which the perfect Cartesian knower situates himself. Such pure subjectivity presumes a world of equally pure objectivity, a world that is both wholly independent and essentially visible.

Attention to the role of gender in the construction and articulation of specular desire reveals this fantasy as the self-contradictory fantasy of pornography: the essence of the woman is her desire, knowable only to the man, to be seduced/raped. The contradiction comes in the demand for this desire, as her essence, to exist independently of him—he is not responsible for it—but to be at the same time wholly exhausted by his ability to evoke and satisfy it. Such a fantasy, of an object of knowledge both wholly independent and wholly knowable, and the problems caused by the impossibility of its satisfaction are at the heart of epistemic modernity. Nature as "she" is required both to be absolutely independent of the knowing subject (as he acquires his authority by his hard-won independence from *her*) and to be fully revealed by his penetration. The irresolvable tension between these two demands gives rise to skepticism.

The conditions of vision and of visibility have figured centrally in epistemology since the Greeks.[33] Those conditions underwent a transformation, starting in the Renaissance, as the definitions of epistemic authority shifted. Such authority gradually came to be framed not in terms of an omniscient, omnipresent deity, for whom distance was irrelevant, nor in the embodied terms of an engaged practitioner, who moved among and interacted with the objects of knowledge.[34] Rather, epistemic authority was ceded to those who stood at the proper distance from the objects of knowledge and who had achieved the proper degree of independence from them—and from their own contingent "limitations" and "biases." The modern scientist, who has been our culture's epistemic hero, achieves this status by reliably accomplishing the normatively male tasks of separation and empowerment based on dissociation from everything maternal and, by extension, female. The male Oedipal narrative has become the template for the processes that authorize vision and whose fantasized, effortless achievement provides (one form of) cinematic pleasure.

Cavell's account of the peculiar pleasures of movies similarly takes as definitive the wish to be an unviewed viewer of the world. Cavell's account of this wish seems, however, more innocent and less political. As in his discussion throughout *The Claim of Reason* of related issues concerning the troubling of our epistemic relations to each other and to the rest of the world, both our desires and the blocks to their gratification are given as *ours*—all of ours, as inhabitants of the modern, Western world, sharers of a particular culture. For Cavell, what cinema grants us is not meant to be the power of the pornographer but respite from our complicity in the structuring of the world, "not a wish for power over creation…, but a wish not to need power, not to have to bear its burdens." The wish is granted by the total presentness to us of the world on the screen without our being present to it, neither implicated in it nor limited in our view of it by our particular placement in it.

The innocence of this wish is, I think, misleading. The wish to be an unseen seer may be a wish for a less troubled relation to reality, but that relation has been troubled in large measure by the cultural placement of epistemic authority precisely in the eyes of an unseen seer: movies grant us the opportunity not to notice the extent to which we are supposed to work at pushing the world away to view it truly. The world of the scientist doesn't contain the scientist, but his absence from it is neither innocent nor effortless. Thus, what Iago offers Othello is meant to be access to Desdemona's world as it is in itself, but what Othello gets is the view of a spy, of someone who by his own efforts is hidden from the world he views, seeing not Desdemona-in-herself but Desdemona-as-spied upon.[35] Kant may have tried to tell us that the world is always our world, but we haven't really learned it, and we go on trying to spy on it: no wonder we are lured by the promise of a world we don't have to hide behind a curtain to see. (We see it, in fact, when the curtain is pulled aside.)

The 'we' in the last paragraph is, of course, problematic, obscuring as it does questions about whose world it is and whose view of it is authorized, or troubled by the terms of that authority. Feminist film criticism has taken as a major task the theorizing of the gender specificities of the desires, among them epistemic, that cinema gratifies, as feminist philosophy has taken as one of *its* major tasks the theorizing of the gender specificities of epistemic desires, among them visual. The analysis of the desire to know, in a culture that construes knowledge in primarily visual terms, is inseparable from the analysis of the construction of visual desire and of

visual pleasure, which is in turn inseparable from the analysis of the construction of gender.

It is in this light that we need to think about the characterization of the
cinematic gaze(s) as male. As Teresa de Lauretis argues, "[t]he project of
feminist cinema...is not so much 'to make visible the invisible,' ...or to
destroy vision altogether, as to construct another (object of) vision and the
conditions of visibility for a different social subject."[36] This is, I would
say, a feminist project quite generally: to create the conditions for a transformed subject/object relation, in part by attending to, and redrawing, the
lines of sight. The revolutions of the Renaissance and the subsequent rise
of science, capitalism, and the modern state created the conditions for the
existence and hegemonic power of the unitary subject, based on its separation from and domination over the object of knowledge. The revolutions
of the objectified others (women and members of other oppressed and colonized groups—all those who have been scrutinized, stared at, anatomized,
and ogled without being authorized to return the gaze or to see each other)
will entail another transformation in what it is to know or to be known or
knowable.

The lack of authority in women's looking is not, however, reason to conclude that we do not see, nor even that patriarchy does not allow or require
that we see. The absence of the female gaze in some feminist theorizing is
problematic, not only because such theories leave out of account significant
features of the workings of masculinist power, but also because the looking that we do is a good place to seek out cracks in that power, even when
we look as dutiful daughters or self-sacrificing mothers.

In "To Be and Be Seen: The Politics of Reality," Marilyn Frye explores
both the (con)scripting of female vision and the liberatory cracks it opens
up. [37] Starting from her own view of the world as a lesbian, she is struck
by the perception that women in general, and lesbian women in particular, are *not* seen by patriarchal eyes, whether those be the eyes of men or
the eyes of women who see as men would have them see—as Virginia
Woolf's enlarging mirrors.[38] Such eyes see the activities of men, against
an invisible background of the enabling activities of women. In such a
world, lesbian women are conceptually impossible, since lesbians, Frye
argues, are defined by their seeing of women, by the fact that women draw
and hold their attention. But such attention is ontologically inadmissable;
the illusion must be maintained that there is nothing there to look at.

Mr. Lord's demand of Tracy in *The Philadelphia Story*, that she learn to
look at men in the proper way, is a demand that she reorient her attention and with it her sense of herself in the world. The attention she gives
to Mike, when she goes to the library to read his book, is a sign to him

and to us that she is capable of this learning, of becoming what she and we are told is a "real woman." Conversely, Mildred and Veda are doomed because they refuse to learn this; they can't take their eyes off each other. At the end Mildred is "saved" by having the authority of vision taken away from her: the story is no longer her melodrama, but the detective's *film noir*, and in that story she is the "redeemed" woman, marked off from Veda, who is given that genre's other female role, as "damned." As Mother Lord's and Charlotte Vale's fates illustrate, a mother may sometimes go on gazing at her daughter, provided that she remove herself from narrative space and consent by her silence to her daughter's incorporation into the realm of the fathers.

In a study of the relationships between power and the lines of sight, Michel Foucault marks modernity in part by the directing of vision toward the subjugated, a characterization that makes the normative orientation of female vision toward men anachronistic.[39] Part of the placement of such anachronistically structured female subordination in the modern world is achieved by the framing of women's vision by diffuse masculine power: neither the attentive mothers nor the adoring daughters are unseen, and they do not acquire the power that accrues to the unseen seers.[40]

Mothers, for example, are the objects of the social scientific gaze, which judges the adequacy of their mothering from behind the two-way mirror in the psychologist's playroom. The maternal gaze is not unobserved and, although it can certainly be felt as powerful by those who are its objects, it is itself closely watched to ensure that actual empowerment flows from and not to it. Similarly, the daughter who looks up first to her father then to his surrogate is herself the specular object of his defining desire.

The specular economy of patriarchy does not define women as exclusively either the seers or the seen. Rather, we are expected to be both, sometimes simultaneously: our subordination comes in the subtle directing of the allowable lines of sight. And it is along those lines that we can look for cracks, since they are the sites of tension. Frye's account, in "In and Out of Harm's Way: Arrogance and Love," of the tension between exploitation, which requires the activity of the exploited, and oppression, which would obliterate the possibility of that activity, is illuminating here.[41] Culturally normative male arrogance demands that women look, but, as Frye argues, the maintenance of phallocratic reality requires that we not be the authors of what we see. We also are to be seen, but only as the beautiful objects we can make ourselves up to resemble.

Central to the resolution of the tension between these demands— between vision and blindness and between visibility and camouflage—has been the separation of women from each other: the seers must not see the seen. In particular, the happy expression of female desire, a goal of the remarriage comedies, requires the heroine never to have known—or thoroughly to forget—that it was in a woman's eyes that she was born as female and there that she first learned desire. The women in the melodramas, who in various ways possess this knowledge, are punished for it, for their inability to keep the domains of maternity and sexuality cordoned off: they need to be taught, like Charlotte Vale, that whatever power we have is had "on probation."

It is by "reading against the grain" of these injunctions that we can begin to "construct another (object of) vision and the conditions of visibility for a different social subject."[42] We need, that is, to remember that we did not come into existence—as subject, as female, or as desiring—in Oedipal relation to our fathers. When Mulvey suggests that the gaze is available to us because we have access to our pre-Oedipal masculinity, she colludes with Freud's heterosexist erasure of the mother/daughter relationship. I have been arguing that, even for looking at classical Hollywood cinema, there is another gaze, which is not inscribed in the film or in the terms of its address but discoverable in the cracks along the lines of sight. Such a gaze may be untheorizable, but that may be in part because of the constraints of theory. We may need to look in the untheorizable gaps—such as those generated by the tension Frye describes between exploitation and oppression or between the impossibility and the actuality of lesbian desire—for examples of the activity of resistance, and learn from them without having or needing a theory that tells us how or whom we ought to see.[43]

Notes

1 Quoted in E. Ann Kaplan's "The Case of the Missing Mother: Maternal Issues in Vidor's *Stella Dallas*," *Heresies* 16 (Fall 1983): 81-85.

2 See, for example, E. Ann Kaplan, *Women and Film: Both Sides of the Camera* (New York: Methuen, 1983); Teresa de Lauretis, *Alice Doesn't: Feminism, Semiotics, Cinema* (Bloomington, Indiana: Indiana University Press, 1984).

3 Laura Mulvey, "Visual Pleasure and Narrative Cinema," *Screen* 16 (Autumn 1975): 6–18; reprinted in Bill Nichols, ed., *Movies and Methods*, vol. 2 (Berkeley and Los Angeles: University of California Press, 1985); further citations are from Nichols.

4 For an account of the issues raised by the centrality of women both in the narrative and in the address of a film genre, see Mary Ann Doane, *The Desire to Desire* (Bloomington, Indiana: Indiana University Press, 1987).

5 In addition to the works already cited, see the essays in the "Feminist

Criticism" section of Nichols' *Movies and Methods*; Michelle Citron, *et. al.*, "Women and Film: A Discussion of Feminist Aesthetics," *New German Critique* 13 (Winter 1978): 83–107; Judith Mayne, "Feminist Film Theory and Criticism," *Signs* 11 (Autumn 1985): 81–100; and Mary C. Gentile, *Film Feminisms: Theory and Practice* (Westport, Connecticut: Greenwood Press, 1985).

6 For one account of how we do this, see Laura Mulvey, "Afterthoughts on 'Visual Pleasure and Narrative Cinema' Inspired by *Duel in the Sun* (King Vidor, 1946)," *Framework* 15–17 (1981): 12–15.

7 Stanley Cavell, *The Pursuits of Happiness: The Hollywood Comedy of Remarriage* (Cambridge, Massachusetts: Harvard University Press, 1981).

8 de Lauretis, *Alice Doesn't*, 103–57.

9 Cavell, *Pursuits*, 82.

10 *The Images in Our Souls: Cavell, Psychoanalysis, and Cinema*, ed. Joseph H. Smith and William Kerrigan, *Psychiatry and the Humanities* vol. 10 (Baltimore: The Johns Hopkins University Press, 1987), 11–43.

11 Cavell, *Pursuits*, 57.

12 Cavell makes that reliance explicit in "Freud and Philosophy: A Fragment," *Critical Inquiry* 13 (Winter 1987): 386–93.

13 Cavell, *Pursuits*, 57.

14 I owe to Ronald de Sousa the application of the concept of fungibility to emotions and their objects. See "Self-Deceptive Emotions," in Amelie Rorty, ed., *Explaining Emotions* (Berkeley:University of California Press, 1980), esp. 292–94.

15 Sigmund Freud, "Some Psychical Consequences of the Anatomical Distinction between the Sexes," *The Standard Edition of the Complete Psychological Works of Sigmund Freud*, ed. and trans. James Strachey, 24 vols. (London: Hogarth Press, 1953–74) 19: 257. See also, for issues discussed in this chapter, "Female Sexuality" (vol. 21); "Femininity," in *New Introductory Lectures in Psychoanalysis* (vol. 22); and *Moses and Monotheism* (vol. 23).

16 Sandra Gilbert, "Life's Empty Pack: Notes toward a Literary Daughteronomy," *Critical Inquiry* 11 (March 1985): 355–84, 372.

17 See Adrienne Rich, "Compulsory Heterosexuality and Lesbian Existence," *Signs* 5 (Summer, 1980): 631–60.

18 For a discussion of the effects on a culture of only women's bearing the symbolic power of infant caretakers, see Dorothy Dinnerstein, *The Mermaid and the Minotaur* (New York: Harper & Row, 1976).

19 Cavell, *Pursuits*, 57.

20 Cavell, *Pursuits*, 137.

21 Cavell, *Pursuits*, 137.

22 Cavell, *Pursuits*, 57.

23 Cavell, "Psychoanalysis and Cinema: The Melodrama of the Unknown Woman," in *The Trial(s) of Psychoanalysis*, ed. Francoise Meltzer (Chicago: University of Chicago Press, 1988): 227–58.

24 Goeffrey Nowell-Smith, "Minelli and Melodrama," *Screen* 18 (Summer, 1977): 113–18; reprinted in Nichols, *Movies and Methods*.

25 Nowell-Smith, "Minelli and Melodrama," 193.

26 See Pam Cook, "Duplicity in *Mildred Pierce*," in *Women in Film Noir*, ed. E. Ann Kaplan (London: BFI Publishing, 1980), 71.

27 See Cook, "Duplicity in *Mildred Pierce*," 81, and Joyce Nelson, "*Mildred Pierce* Reconsidered," *Film Reader* 2 (1977): 65–70, reprinted in Nichols, *Movies and Methods*.

28 Lea Jacobs, "*Now, Voyager*: Some Problems of Enunciation and Sexual Difference," *Camera Obscura* 7 (Spring, 1981): 88–109, 94.

29 Jeanne Thomas Allen, "Introduction: *Now, Voyager* as Women's Film: Coming of Age Hollywood Style," in *Now, Voyager*, ed. Jeanne Thomas Allen (Madison: University of Wisconsin Press, 1984), 20.

30 Mulvey, "Visual Pleasures," 314.

31 See de Lauretis, *Alice Doesn't*, 24f–26, 78–79, 144–46.

32 Christian Metz, *The Imaginary Signifier: Psychoanalysis and the Cinema*, trans. Celia Britton, Annwyl Williams, Ben Brewster, and Alfred Guzzetti (Bloomington, Indiana: Indiana University Press, 1982).

33 For a discussion, with attention to gender, of the historical shifts in the epistemology of vision, see Evelyn Fox Keller and Christine Grontkowski, "The Mind's Eye," in *Discovering Reality: Feminist Perspectives on Epistemology, Metaphysics, Methodology, and Philosophy of Science*, eds. Sandra Harding and Merrill B. Hintikka (Dordrecht: Reidel, 1983), 207–24.

34 See Samuel Y. Edgerton, Jr., *The Renaissance Rediscovery of Linear Perspective* (New York: Basic Books, 1975), 20–21.

35 In "Othello's Doubt/Desdemona's Death: The Engendering of Scepticism," in *Power/Gender/Values*, ed. Judith Genova (Calgary: Academic Printing and Publishing, 1987), I discuss Othello as enacting the paranoia that underlies modern Western epistemology. My discussion is a response to Cavell's use of Othello to illuminate the origins of scepticism in the position of the modern knower (gender unspecified) in *The Claim of Reason* (Oxford: Oxford University Press, 1979), 481–96.

36 de Lauretis, *Alice Doesn't*, 67.

37 See Marilyn Frye, *The Politics of Reality: Essays in Feminist Theory* (Trumansburg: N.Y.: Crossing Press, 1983), 152–74.

38 Virginia Woolf, *A Room of One's Own* (New York: Harcourt, Brace, and Co., 1929), 36.

39 Michel Foucault, *Discipline and Punish*, trans. Alan Sheridan (New York:

Pantheon, 1977).

40 See Sandra Bartky, "Foucault, Femininity, and the Modernization of Patriarchal Power," in *Feminism and Foucault: Reflections on Resistance*, eds. Lee Quinby and Irene Diamond (Boston: Northeastern Univ. Press, 1988); reprinted in Bartky, *Femininity and Domination: Studies in the Phenomenology of Domination* (New York: Routledge, 1990).

41 Frye, *Politics of Reality*, 52–83.

42 de Lauretis, *Alice Doesn't*, 68.

43 This paper is a response to a number of people and events: to Stanley Cavell, who evoked my serious interest in films, to discussions with the students in a course I taught using *Pursuits* in the University of Minnesota English and Philosophy Departments in the Fall of 1984, and to several years of discussing related issues in a faculty reading group. My thanks to all, especially to my colleagues John Mowitt, Martin Roth, and Eileen Sivert. Thanks also to Marilyn Frye for helpful discussions about the value and limits of theory, and to Michael Root for conversation, encouragement, and editing advice. I received massive and invaluable editorial help from Ruth Wood, whose strenuous attempts to produce clarity have, I hope, borne fruit. My research time was supported by a Bush Sabbatical Fellowship from the University of Minnesota.

6 Failures of Marriage in *Sea of Love* (The Love of Men, the Respect of Women)

Nickolas Pappas

Somewhere among contemporary *films noir* lies a genre yet to be mapped out, in which women occupy classically male *noir* roles.[1] The films of this group bring women to the centers of their plots, as if to subvert the genre's expectations, since these women behave neither as victims nor as ornaments to a male *agon*, but as instigators of the action. These purportedly subversive films question the woman's identity and therefore, one might feel inclined to say, open their traditional themes—crime, love, the woman—to new interpretations.[2]

Fatal Attraction (Adrian Lyne, 1987) stands out in this genre, both in commercial success and notoriety; recent years have also brought *Basic Instinct, Crush, Final Analysis, The Hand that Rocks the Cradle, Shattered,* and *Single White Female.*[3] It is fair to say that a genre is forming, since these films all focus specifically on dangerous women, who are, or are suspected of being, psychotic. Like most film psychotics, they belong to no category recognized by psychiatric medicine. As Noël Carroll has observed,[4] the lunatics of psychological horror films resemble traditional monsters in that science tells us they do not exist.[5] I would add that the impossibility of film psychotics hints that madness in the movies works as an allegory of something else.[6] In the films in question, the madwomen move toward their violence because of a symbolic lack, interpreted here as the loss of a marriage.

Call this "The Case of the Unmarried Woman." I might move toward working out a taxonomy of the genre by considering its use of the home as its scene of violence. Domesticity haunts these movies, and it would seem that looking into their eruptions of violence could show from a fresh vantage point how marriage fails women. But the films skirt the subject of marital failure as insistently as they invoke it, thanks to their frequent expedient of letting the women's psychoses function as their plots' motor. Because psychosis accounts for the women's status, the failure *of* marriage calls for no investigation; it amounts only to the women's failure *at* marriage.

Take *Fatal Attraction*, which claims to invest a woman with lethal power, thereby turning women's desires for children and fidelity into enforceable demands. The premise—a man's infidelity endangers his family—promises a revision of the genre, with its shift to the home as a scene for violence. But *Fatal Attraction*'s fatuity keeps any subversion from taking place. Although the woman (Glenn Close) is established as a threat, she never becomes a subject. Lunatic enough to kill a pet rabbit for revenge, she represents not self-mastery but at best a manic unpredictability. That she stands in some way on the side of moral principle, punishing a man for his infidelity, only trivializes her psychosis. *Fatal Attraction* never turns into this woman's own film: she is almost always the intruder from well outside the family. She stages only one scene fully within their house, and that turns into the scene of her death. *Fatal Attraction* squanders the force of any surprises its premise may have offered, because it never criticizes the man's place as spectator to the drama, which also means that it does not criticize its spectators' position as men, who continue to witness this dangerous woman as one fundamentally apart from themselves.

I could as easily locate *Fatal Attraction*'s irresponsibility to its subject in its refusal to find its male protagonist (Michael Douglas) complicitous in Close's psychosis. It is striking, in fact, how often the men in these films are moral ciphers, sometimes implausibly naive (*Final Analysis*, *Shattered*), at worst guilty of peccadilloes more than expunged by the punishment the women measure out to them (*Single White Female*). Only a few films in this genre ever ask what the man's complicity might consist in; I want to use those few to discover what the genre is capable of. Two in particular, *Blue Steel* and *Sea of Love*, shift their focus from the threat the woman might pose to the marital failure that produced that threat, and identify marital failure in turn as a problem of the woman's unknownness to men. My study of these films might be philosophical, if it is, thanks to the films' orientation toward their narratives' constructions of knowledge. Though the narrative information in these films fits into traditional film conventions, it resists those conventions enough to suggest that what may seem one kind of story admits of quite another sort of telling.

Blue Steel (Kathryn Bigelow, 1990) presents a woman, Megan Turner (Jamie Lee Curtis), a police officer rather than a criminal, who nevertheless finds herself in the predicament of having the men around her consider her dangerous. Megan knows that Eugene Hunt (Ron Silver) is the killer the police are looking for, but the police won't trust her when she tells them. The work of the film becomes Megan's attempt to be acknowledged as knowledgeable. The film's narrative acquires an odd balance, to reflect the oddity of Megan's task: one-third of the way through she knows that Eugene is the killer, and spends the rest not trying to learn more, as she might in a traditional detective story, but trying to make someone else believe her. In this film the unbalanced narrative is not a directorial solecism, nor a hackneyed point (as Gary Indiana claims) about our bankrupt legal system, but a way of visualizing the woman's pursuit of an independent existence in the eyes of men.[7] *Blue Steel* establishes marriage as an issue for Megan. Her friends press her to find a husband; but she knows about the dangers in marriage, dangers represented here by domestic violence. Megan trains for confrontations with abusive husbands, and away from work faces her father's violence toward her mother. Her marriage *to* her work threatens to fail when the other policemen, standing in for husbands, remain incredulous about her story. With its restructured chronology, then, *Blue Steel* shifts the epistemic problem of crime films from that of a subject eager to know, to that of a subject already possessing the facts, herself needing to be known before the danger can be eradicated. Megan finds herself forced into the place of a spectator to her own life, captive to Eugene's manipulations. But if Megan moves into the movie's audience, we spectators enter her place: as witnesses to a staged drama, captive to the dramatist, there is nothing for us to do, any more than there is any action Megan can initiate which will wake men's trust in her. Megan's predicament feminizes our spectatorial experience. Because we know everything she knows, we participate in the passivity that can, under circumstances of disacknowledgment, accompany even complete knowledge.

This link between the woman's unacknowledged capacity for experience and the failure of her marriage suggests for me that the films of this genre can function as comments on the genre that Stanley Cavell has called the melodrama of the unknown woman.[8] *Stella Dallas*, *Gaslight*, and *Now, Voyager*, among others, depict women's claim to existence apart from marriage, and their arrival at a state of self-understanding from which they cannot tell men about their own existence.[9] To be sure, the murderous violence of the "unmarried woman" genre is one sign that these genres will not match up exactly. But the genres differ mainly in their diagnoses of the male exclusion of women. Whereas the melodramas locate exclusion in a masculine privacy that women may not enter, the films I have chosen to talk about identify a male practice aimed more aggressively against women, a police action made to keep their knowledge irrelevant to masculine concerns.

Hermetic masculine privacy finds its truest image in Max Ophuls's *Letter from an Unknown Woman* (1948). Lisa Berndle (Joan Fontaine) spends her life in love with the celebrated pianist Stefan Brand (Louis Jourdan). After one night with her he promises to see her again, but never comes for her. Years later she finds him at a concert in Vienna; he recognizes her (she thinks) and invites her to his apartment. Forgetting her husband, she goes. Brand tries to seduce her, not realizing that he has before, with the same patter he used the first time. She leaves. She writes to remind Brand of who she had been ("By the time you read this I may be dead."), and as he recalls the scenes she tells him about he is horrified, covering his face with his hands.

Brand is horrified, Cavell says, at both the sight of himself to himself and the sight of himself to her.[10] Because Lisa Berndle has a voice with which to tell him she's seen him, he finds himself turned from a desultory spectator of his experience into an unpleasant spectacle in someone else's. As in the course of psychoanalysis, the man's private ritual, here seduction, remained invisible to him until someone resisted it. In analysis the analyst permits transference to develop and then withdraws, to show the patient that what may have seemed a normally progressing relationship between them is really the patient's repetition of some earlier exchange. Brand has twice tried to fit Lisa into a particular role in his own ritual; because she arrives twice in his life, she, like the analyst, can see as a solipsistic construction what she (and he) had previously taken for conversation.[11] He therefore sees that she has seen him simulating love, acting out both parts by himself, and is horrified at having been spotted amidst his narcissism.[12] His dramaturgical powers, until now magically efficacious, turn into pomp when their secret is guessed. That is to say, because the woman has regained her subjectivity, the man can understand himself as visible to her, hence visible as an incomplete creature. The film's spectators, uneasily identified with the unknown woman, face his horrification with a discomfort that is discomfort with understanding the woman's subjectivity.

There is much in this denouement that I want to use. The woman who suddenly comes to see, and to be seen *as* one who sees; the man who, like Prospero, has hidden himself by putting on a mask.[13] The film discloses that masculine solipsism requires a repression of feminine subjectivity. The limitation of this line of thinking is that the male anxiety which initiated the repression remains self-generated, rooted in private events of infancy. The woman comes to see the man's narcissism, but that narcissism has nothing specially to do with women. Cavell interprets the man's final defeat in *Letter from an Unknown Woman* as his openness before women, when he speaks of the man's

> being seen by the woman of the letter, by the mute director, and by his (her?) camera...and seen by us, which accordingly identifies us, the audience of film, as assigning ourselves the position...of the feminine. Then it is the man's horror of us that horrifies us—the revelation, or avoidance, of ourselves in a certain way of being feminine.[14]

But solipsism threatens all relationships, not just those that include women. Is it that in marriage, actual or fantastic, solipsism poses its greatest threat? Or is marriage one context among many in which to show solipsism at work? (In which case it barely matters that these are women who come to look back at it.) Or is it that women's loss of sight, born of some other cause, has let men be solipsists around them? But then that which cannot be faced need not be connected with the woman; and that other cause still has to be addressed.

Sea of Love: The Unmarried Woman

After the melodramas, the film I find most useful to take up is *Sea of Love* (Harold Becker, 1989), which I count as a clear case of the unmarried woman. As in all this genre's films, the woman Helen (Ellen Barkin) is considered a danger to men. She might be the murderer who shoots men in their beds. We also know that marriage fails Helen: she is divorced, and her dates end in the men's deaths.

As in *Blue Steel* and in Cavell's melodramas, the men in *Sea of Love* act out fantasies of the stage. Frank Keller (Al Pacino) first appears setting a trap for criminals, in which he and other policemen pretend to be former New York Yankees. When Frank decides that the murderer is a woman, he plants a personal ad to snare her, and meets every woman who answers the ad in a carefully prepared restaurant, dramatic down to a designated audience, the two plainclothes cops at the next table.

Helen's ex-husband Terry (Michael Rooker) has his own dramaturgical powers. When he bursts into Frank's apartment near the end of the film, it becomes clear that he has been going to every man Helen slept with or dated, commanding them to simulate their sexual act with her, and shooting them as they did. Because Helen naturally is absent from that tableau, you might say that Terry stages the conditions for the possibility of her existence, a re-enactment of his loss. Frank's scenario resembles Terry's in this respect, that as long as Helen exists for him as part of his drama of entrapment, she will be a suspect to him, therefore something outside his capacity to acknowledge.

So far we are still on melodramatic ground. But *Sea of Love* interrogates the masculine complicity in this failure to communicate from a direction that the melodramas choose not to take. Where the men of the melodramas are noteworthily alone, those in *Sea of Love* seek out company. They fail to see Helen not because they have locked themselves into practices of seduction, but because their apparent seduction of the woman has been directed all along at other men. *Sea of Love* implicates its villain in repressed homosexual desire. It departs from the typical use of homosexuality as a sign of criminal insanity in Hollywood films of the last few decades, by confusing its male protagonist's motives too. Like Terry, Frank professes heterosexual desire, but expresses it in a community of men. Like Terry, he hints at homosexual fantasies, and interprets his jealousy as a relationship with other men. The film flirts with male homosexuality around Frank and his partner Sherman Touhey (John Goodman):

1. Frank meets Sherman and mentions the song, "Sea of Love," which is linked to the first killing. Sherman starts singing it and gyrating in front of a group of policemen; Frank says, "Something's got to come off," and Sherman pulls his jacket down over one shoulder.

2. Frank and Sherman phone women to set their trap. Frank says to one, "You like boys *and* girls? Me? Yeah, well…sometimes, but mainly girls."

3. One woman having a drink with Frank tells him, "If you're a printer, I've got a dick." Later Sherman asks Frank, "Could you go for a babe with a dick?" "Depends on her personality."

4. When Frank invites Helen out to dinner, he is distracted by a violinist hovering near their table. Begging off from mentioning his reason for the invitation, Frank says, "I feel like I've got the whole New York Philharmonic on my ass."[15]

Al Pacino has been associated with homosexual characters more regularly than any American actor of his age.[16] *Cruising* (William Friedkin, 1980) comes to mind first, since in it Pacino plays a policeman gone undercover to find a killer of gay men. As in *Sea of Love*, he is the bait set to catch a serial killer; here too, the murderer, given to elaborate private performances, kills men after having made them lie face down and naked. And just as *Sea of Love* will bring out Frank's similarity to Terry, *Cruising* ends with the suggestion that Pacino has committed its final murder, an act of jealousy that presupposes in him the same desires mixed together in the film's killer.

Still more like *Sea of Love* is *Dog Day Afternoon* (Sidney Lumet, 1975), whose impetus is a homosexual desire that pretends to be something else. The movie watches a stalled bank robbery in which Sonny (Pacino) had robbed the bank to pay for his lover's sex-change surgery, as if to create a woman who can be the true object of his desire. The woman-to-be of *Dog Day Afternoon* works as the offstage but necessary motor of its plot, much as Helen, a placeholder for her husband's desires and Frank's, motivates both the narrative of *Sea of Love* and its male spectator's interest, so that on all counts the pattern of desire can pretend to be aiming at its appropriate target.

Homosexual desire matters to *Sea of Love*, because it illuminates what pretends to be its opposite. Unlike *Reservoir Dogs* (Quentin Tarantino, 1992), which with a great show of knowingness lays out secretive male desire as the solution to its characters' friendships with other men, *Sea of Love* meditates on the desire for women as itself a relationship among men. Consider the policemen's pursuit of their suspect. Frank and Sherman, certain that the murderer is a woman, plan to trap her with a personal ad. Since the woman has responded to men who wrote their advertisements as poems, the police know they need a poem of their own. They cannot write one, so Frank uses the poem that his mother had written for his father in high school. Of all the implications of this episode—that the killer has been stalking men feminized enough to write poetry, or that Frank warms to the poem as if courted by his own mother—what especially merits attention is the comment on *Letter from an Unknown Woman*: like Louis Jourdan's soliloquy of seduction, the poem is a free-floating signifier of love. It snares the woman, but because it has been prepared in her absence it leaves her unknown. She is doubly unknown in *Sea of Love*, since she is being chased with bait made to catch a man. The poem complicates Jourdan's set speech in being one man's yearning call for another, instead of a man's ode to himself.

I have already identified Frank with Terry in their uses of dramaturgy. This last characteristic of the policemen's poem—that it was written to catch other men and in fact leads Frank to one—also has its analogue in Terry's dramatic opus, namely the mime he directs in other men's beds. When he tries to force Frank into this part, Terry pushes him onto his bed, makes him lie face down, and straddles his buttocks. "Show me what you did with her." His mind hardly seems to be on his ex-wife. (If anything, this simulation of anal intercourse calls to mind Terry's obsession with anality. He first appears telling a joke about anal sex; and when he comes to the police with misinformation about the murders, he refers to a black man's cornrows as "cornholes.")

Terry has been following Helen for eight months, jealously killing everyone she may have slept with. But I would not want to suggest a simplistic repression according to which Terry's jealousy contradicts his homosexuality. On the contrary, this film points to the homoeroticism of the jealousy itself. Terry is furious not because his ex-wife has betrayed him with other men, but because those other men witnessed his betrayal. His real quarrel is with them and so is his relationship; Helen the means by which he communicates with other men.[17] That species of jealousy turns up in Frank as well. For the first third of the film, he torments himself with the thought of his ex-wife Denise. But he acts out the torment not with Denise, who is never seen or heard, but with her new husband Gruber (Richard Jenkins), another policeman in Frank's squad.[18] Twice Frank taunts Gruber about Denise; when Frank finally accepts the loss of his old marriage, it is Gruber he apologizes to. Even in reconciliation, what claims to be his fight with a woman is transacted with another man.

Sea of Love: Currency of Women

If *Letter from an Unknown Woman* and *Gaslight* play out the male exclusion of women as narcissistic rituals, *Sea of Love* exposes a practice of exclusion that that model of ritual cannot accommodate. Here the ritual among men consists in exchanges for which the women are tokens. In saying so, I am appealing to the terms in which Luce Irigaray has cast male representations of women. As I have described it so far, *Sea of Love* has followed Irigaray's account of men's fear of women, and their use of women as a currency for transactions with other men. What I claim now is that *Sea of Love* takes its critique of the exclusion of the feminine beyond the scope of *Letter From an Unknown Woman*, as Irigaray takes her critique beyond Freud's vocabulary of male narcissism.[19]

For Irigaray, the problem of gender has its epistemological manifestation in a theory of woman as non-man that denies the possibility or accessibility of feminine subjectivity. Irigaray follows Freud in making the predominant characteristic of a male theory of woman its narcissism; only now, narcissism attaches itself to an entire gender.[20] In her reading of "Femininity," Irigaray diagnoses Freud's description of feminine desire as a projection of anxiety,[21] penis-envy imagined from the man's point of view:

> Woman's castration is defined as her having nothing you can see, as her *having* nothing. In her having nothing penile, in seeing that she has No Thing. Nothing *like* man. (48)

What the woman does have finds itself worked into sexual economics as a version of the male child's anus, rather than a value outside male experience.

> [Freud's] conception of the "child" proves, on analysis, to derive from *anal erotism's primacy* over what is called genital sexuality.... The

> vagina...functions like the anus, rectum, and intestines. In fact "interest in the vagina, which awakens later, is also essentially of anal-erotic origin." (74)

On Irigaray's reading of Freud, the man's private property represents "the only goods acceptable for sexual trading." (51) Sexual activity needs men for its consummation; lacking them, it searches for women interpreted into male categories. But this redirected desire will distinguish itself by its efforts to dominate:

> Anal erotism...is possessive, narcissistic, constantly reacting offensively or defensively to the demands of the other; it is aggressive toward the "object" that it tortures systematically whenever possible, that it would like to eliminate when its needs have been served. (94)

What counts in this explanation is not homosexuality itself—not any desire between men that lets its name be spoken—but the male society, borne out of such desires and practices, that masquerades as heterosexual desire. The reason that male desire for women must be given another interpretation seems to be, in Irigaray's view, that woman is not a convenient enough negative image of the man who is looking at her. The otherness of the woman is consequently denied, at most interpreted as the male subject's anxiety. The object's "possession by a 'subject,' a subject's desire to appropriate her, is yet another of [the man's] vertiginous failures.... The quest for the 'object' becomes a game of Chinese boxes. Infinitely receding." (134) What cannot be tolerated, in the male tale of woman and desire, is the sight of "*her* having other desires, of a different nature from *his* representation of the sexual and from *his* representations of sexual desire." (51)

Thanks to theories like Freud's, women fit more conveniently into the relations among men. In that case, we should expect to find three concurrent phenomena in masculine practices, which any critique of those practices ought to bring to light:

1. Women function as currency in social transactions. When it comes to women, men economize. (No one more dramatically than Terry, who re-enacts Helen's betrayal without her, defining her nature as the other half of whatever a man is doing in bed.)
2. Transactions apparently engaging women mask the masculine exchange at work behind them.
3. As a result of 1. and 2., woman's subjective experience is not permitted to count as experience.

I have argued for 2.'s appearance in *Sea of Love* by describing the film's men. Now I want to establish the credibility of this film by pointing out its acknowledgment of 1.; armed with that credibility, I will ask what *Sea of Love* has to say about what the woman sees.

The economizing of women reveals itself most unmetaphorically in social institutions which *Sea of Love* takes pains to keep in our sight. Prostitution is a blatant form that this economizing takes; the opening sequence of credits, which shows Times Square, prostitutes, and porn theaters advertising "Women"—a sequence that otherwise does nothing for the film's action—emblematizes the plot's moving force if we read the film's characters as I have been doing.[22] But marriage, more central to the social economy, is also a transaction between men. Leave aside Terry's own marriage, and Frank's, both doomed to fail in the way that any ritual does when denied its desire. Any wedding could make the same point; for the marriage contract "is drawn up between the father and the husband...with virginity being figured as a value over and above the dowry.... *Two men* will come to an agreement whereby the woman passes from one 'house' to another and joins another 'family circle'."(122) *Sea of Love* calls on wedding negotiations to forward each step of the policemen's dramatic trap. When Frank first goes to his superior officer with his plan for staging simulated first dates, the lieutenant assumes that Frank wants a woman. "Let me fix you up with my sister-in-law"; he describes her marriageable attractions. The second time Frank brings him the scheme the lieutenant approves it, but again stands in for the bride's father with his warning, "You will not have intercourse with [the women]." He needs to preserve the suspects' virginity for the plan to work.

Then there is a literal wedding, Sherman's daughter's, to which Sherman invites Frank; at this wedding Frank gets his idea about trapping the murderous woman. He tells Sherman, "How we catch her," and sketches the plan of baiting the woman. "Bingo. She's dropped." Frank's train of thought moves from the wedding to another plan hatched between men for disposing of a threatening woman.[23]

Sea of Love: What the Woman Sees

The woman will continue shuttling between men only if she loses the power to transact exchanges of her own. Call that power the ability to *witness* the transaction.

> Subjectivity denied to woman: indisputably this provides the financial backing for every irreducible constitution as an object: of representation, of discourse, of desire. Once imagine that the woman imagines and the object loses its fixed, obsessional character. (133)

The male fantasy or drama of subjecthood calls for the repression of woman's imagination, one of the acts of which may be seeing the man's dramatization for what it is.

Sea of Love reiterates questions of who sees and what is seen. While trying to ask Helen to move in with him, Frank assures her that she is incapable of vision. "If you live with a cop.... There's you, what you see—which is nothing—and what we see." Helen will have to accept the fact of her blindness before Frank lets her into his house. (In the future marriage between them, Helen may take Frank Keller's name and come to be called Helen Keller.) The most important question is whether the film underwrites this blinding of the woman, or whether her gaze achieves authoritative standing, as the witness to male narcissism.[24] For whom does the spectacle of this film exist?

Sea of Love begins by presupposing a male gaze. Its action opens in a bedroom with the sounds of intercourse. The camera finds a man's buttocks, then glides up his back to his head, in shots too close for the audience to tell what is underneath him. He pants, "Oh, baby. OK? Is this OK?" Unremarkable enough dialogue, given what he appears to be doing. Unremarkable, too, that we have not seen the woman yet, for the conventions of sex on film dictate that its viewer wait before seeing the consummation. Even explicitly pornographic film occasionally slows its action into rudimentary exposition. But to call these opening moments of *Sea of Love* a tease is to recognize that their spectator is male and heterosexual. Hence we may expect that the spectacles to follow similarly exist for the eyes of a man.

The scene's resolution into a murder problematizes this expectation. The next shot after the man's head should be the sight of a woman; so the logic of sexual narrative tells the male spectator that what he does see next, a gun aimed at the man, is part of a woman. The act of love turns out to have been an act of violence—which means that violence and love have thus far been sensually indistinguishable, and further that a woman may have stood there in the position of power. In case the scene ends too briefly to establish these suspicions; we get a second killing, which, while revealing nothing more about the murderer, adds the information that the murdered men have been shot while writhing in bed alone. Whoever killed them therefore caught them in the ridiculous act of solo intercourse, a weak moment, not so much because their bodies are exposed, but because their solitariness is. To be confronted as a coupler without the other partner present is to be seen as an incomplete being.

Of course, one appears in exactly the same way during all intercourse—from the other's point of view, any person in intercourse is performing half an act. But normally the woman is not thought to watch. If she should ever see the male fantasy of self-sufficiency, all the pretense will be over. Hence the special anxiety in these scenes. If a woman is watching, she sees through the man's dramatic fantasy of having a woman with him, hence sees through the gender's narcissistic fantasy; at the same time, because the murderer sees what the spectators do, the male spectators themselves run the risk of watching as women watch, hence being feminized. If, on the other hand, the killer/witness is a man, he is only participating in the continuing construction of the imaginary woman.

Now the *expectation* of a male gaze becomes the *wish* for one, and the resolution of the story initially seems a relief. When Terry bursts into Frank's apartment, we know the viewer had been a man all along. Learning that Terry was the audience to those scenes of solitary love is easier to bear than the alternative. "Better than the gaze of the other, which is necessarily threatening because of its different viewpoint, is the subject's self-observation, the protective and reflexive extension of his 'own' gaze." (81)

That is one reading of the resolution: *Sea of Love* returns to business as usual in its manipulation of male spectators' anxieties. The gaze it assumes remains masculine, from the opening titillation to the final relief that no woman had been present at the murders. However, this argument overlooks the instability of any such relief. As I understand *Sea of Love*, it does not re-establish the male gaze so much as force it to look at itself, whether by blocking what the man's eye wants to see, or showing it a perverted version of itself.

In the first place, if *Sea of Love* harps on the question of whether the woman has seen something, it just as emphatically leaves open the question of whether she has *been* seen. The economical use of woman calls for her availability to the masculine world as much as it does her inability to enter that world; and the camera of this film takes pains to block the masculine view of the woman. When *Sea of Love* does not refuse to show a woman, it frustrates the viewer's expectations about her appearance. Frank's ex-wife Denise amounts to no more than a buzz of telephone voice. Helen makes much of the feminine home she shares with her mother and daughter; but the mother gets only a minute of movie time, the daughter nothing.

The woman who really matters here is, of course, the one who kills. The camera teases most blatantly during the murder scenes, always stopping just short of revealing the killer's body. But there is a parallel scene of withholding in this film, which like the murder scene twice keeps itself secret, and then the third time reveals its mysteries. I mean the recurring shots of the corridor outside Frank's apartment. After Frank's first night with Helen, his doorbell rings while he is in the shower. He comes to the door to see the elevator closing. After his second time with Helen, he comes home to hear someone at the end of the hall. Frank goes to the corridor window but only finds pigeons. The third time he hears someone unknown in the hall, he says, "Helen?", confirming what his guess had been all along. The gaze titillated by the dark corridor's end is an eye straining after the woman, but it is an eye which, according to the camera's announcement, will not always get its way. Once Helen has been established as the possible killer, she is the presupposed and unrepresented body that lurks beyond the camera's reach ["at/as back to the scene of representation which she props up by not/without knowing it" (345)], the suppressed sight that retains power by resisting the anxious look.

I am saying that calling this film another exemplification of the masculine gaze oversimplifies its treatment of that gaze. Rather than follow the demands of its genre's narratives, *Sea of Love* resists them. Here we might discover its philosophical interest; for the film's refusal to let its woman be a killer frustrates the same complex of expectations by which she has become the token in a man's game. The frustration of the camera's powers further gives her the power to be known and acknowledged. By means of the latter especially, a reversal that finds a dramatic character eluding the conventions of stagecraft, *Sea of Love* enters into conversation with the long tradition of dramatic works that use characterization as a figure for subjectivity. An obvious forebear is *Gaslight* (George Cukor, 1944), in which Ingrid Bergman's rediscovery of her power within marriage is signaled by her "Lady Macbeth" soliloquy. But I find traces of the process at work as far back as certain plays of Aristophanes (*Wasps*, *Frogs*, *Thesmophoriazusae*), whose heroes overcome and escape their stultifying social existence by refusing to stay in the game of dramatic impersonation. Since, as I would further claim, those Aristophanic plays form the ground against which Plato develops his anti-tragic screed, *Sea of Love* belongs unambiguously to a history of dramatic works that ask philosophically how the dramas that happen offstage might function to cover over an excluded voice.

I cannot argue for all those points here. I will content myself with indicating a way in which *Sea of Love* ultimately resolves itself into an image of Helen's acknowledgment by Frank. Beginning with Terry's violent entry into Frank's apartment, the film's denouement is best read as Frank's acceptance of Helen's knowledge about him. I say this because the scenes in this last section treat his meeting with Terry as a revelation for Frank. First he is humiliated before Helen in the police station; then we see him some time later, in a bar with Sherman; finally there is a reconciliation between Frank and Helen. The last two clearly entail that there had been something revelatory about the scene with Terry. Frank's conversation with Sherman is penitential, marked by his abstinence from alcohol and his confession to having mistreated Helen. Just before Terry burst into his apartment, Frank had been interrogating Helen, as if certain that she was the murderer; so it took whatever he saw in the course of that scene to bring him to Sherman's confessional. What is more, the confession to Sherman—a resolution between men of a problem with women—no longer does the trick for Frank, but needs to be followed up by his conversation with Helen. We might reasonably ask when Frank has come to acknowledge Helen's power of sight.

The men's confrontation is determined on both sides, because their scenarios for trapping Helen have led them, as if by accident, to each other. (I take the look of accident about their meeting—Frank was really after the killer woman, Terry after his ex-wife—to point up the repressed wish that brought them together.) Once Terry reveals himself to be the object of Frank's obsession, Frank can recognize the homoeroticism latent in his own romance with Helen. The distance between *Sea of Love* and *Letter from an Unknown Woman* shows itself in the requirement that Frank meet his man before he can see his narcissistic ritual for what it is. Given this meeting of men, which forces the issue of the impossibility of male desire, Frank is ready to acknowledge what the men see in the melodramas, that a woman has witnessed his histrionics. He not only realizes the excessiveness in his interrogation of Helen—an excess of fury that did not belong in that scene, because it had been tailored to fit another relationship—but also that she has witnessed her exclusion from this male relationship. She spotted the excess in his arrest-play by virtue of knowing what she had and hadn't done with the murdered men (slept with one, she says, and dated the others). By virtue of having witnessed her own sexual activity, she has put herself in a position to know that Frank's tirade of suspicion was really about someone else.

When Helen's reaction to Frank becomes, in retrospect, the epistemological center of the film, the gaze directed at that spectacle loses its masculinity. Meanwhile, the fight between Frank and Terry acts out a *crisis* of masculinity, for Frank because he sees who has all along stood waiting in his romance of pursuit, and for the male spectator as well, because *he* sees that the pornography he glimpsed in the three murders thus far has all along been male pornography, a secret shared among Terry, the murder victims, and the men in the audience.

In that case, the greater relief (greater than the relief that no woman watched the scenes of half-intercourse) comes of recognizing that Helen had held a reliable perspective on Frank's antics, i.e. of accepting the feminine persona in our experience of the rest of the film. In the world of *Sea of Love*, the crisis of masculinity displays itself in the manly emblems that

Frank and Terry fight with: guns, dumbbell, police trophy. The struggle stages itself domestically, as if over a woman, but these men are wrestling over which one will get to claim our vision of him. Which makes us, as eyes, their women and prize, waiting out the fight, but this time from the distance of detachment and disbelief.

Notes

1 The films may be called revivals of or tributes to *film noir*. They are all reinterpreted versions of older evocations of the outlaw. This category includes *Bad Influence*, *Bad Lieutenant*, *Cape Fear* (1991), *D.O.A.* (1988), *Masquerade*, *Tough Guys Don't Dance*, and *Unlawful Entry*, perhaps such varieties as *Married to the Mob* and *Miami Blues*, or parodies like *Love at Large* and *Reservoir Dogs*.

2 A substantially different version of this paper, "A *Sea of Love* Among Men," appeared in *Film Criticism* 14 (1990): 14–26. Some of the discussion of *Sea of Love* has remained the same, but few conclusions have. I owe thanks to Cynthia Freeland for her editorial help, and particular thanks to Tamsin Lorraine, for her comments on my use of Irigaray.

3 Other films in or near this group include *Thelma and Louise*, *Presumed Innocent*, and *Silence of the Lambs*.

4 Noël Carroll, "Horror," delivered at the American Philosophical Association, December 1992.

5 T. J. Ross has specifically argued this point about the psychosis of Catherine Deneuve in Polanski's *Repulsion* (a film that belongs in the genre I am sketching): "Polanski, *Repulsion*, and the New Mythology," in *Focus on the Horror Film*, eds. Roy Huss and T. J. Ross (Englewood Cliffs: Prentice-Hall, 1972), 152–61.

6 This mention of horror suggests yet another guise for the genre, namely what I call the horror of the unmarried woman. I hope to show on another occasion that *Bram Stoker's Dracula* (Francis Ford Coppola, 1992) instantiates this genre, by conceiving virginity as a kind of necessary condition for becoming a vampire.

7 "Pretty Near Dark," *Village Voice* 35 (June 19, 1990), 73–76.

8 The rest of this section owes much to Cavell's work, especially "Psychoanalysis and Cinema: The Melodrama of the Unknown Woman," in *The Trial(s) of Psychoanalysis*, ed. Francoise Meltzer (Chicago: University of Chicago Press, 1988), 227–58; "Ugly Duckling, Funny Butterfly: Bette Davis and *Now, Voyager*," *Critical Inquiry* 16 (1990): 213–47, and "Naught Orators: Negation of Voice in *Gaslight*", in *Languages of the Unsayable*, eds. Sanford Budick and Wolfgang Iser (New York: Columbia University Press,

1989), 340–77.

9 Cavell, "Psychoanalysis and Cinema," 233.

10 Cavell, "Psychoanalysis and Cinema," 256.

11 For a comical treatment of this predicament, see Preston Sturges's *The Lady Eve* (1941).

12 The men in these melodramas are distinguished from their counterparts in other genres chiefly by virtue of their solipsism. Take Cary Grant in *The Philadelphia Story* and Charles Boyer in *Gaslight*: both have a nearly magical power over events; both undermine the woman's sureness of her own perceptions; both moralize about her suspicions; both test her memory. They differ in their capacity to overcome their epistemic solitude.

13 It is striking how many men in these melodramas, as in the films I discuss, function as directors. I imagine the Shakespearian model for these men to be either Prospero or his degraded counterparts, such as the Lord in the opening to *The Taming of the Shrew* (a play which might fit among these cases of unmarried women), or Ulysses in *Troilus and Cressida* (itself a study of the exchange-value of women).

Two more recent films, which I consider cousins to *Sea of Love* and *Blue Steel*—*Honeymoon in Vegas* and *Mad Dog and Glory*—foreground their heroes' histrionics: Nicolas Cage dresses as Elvis and swoops out of an airplane in the former, while Bill Murray in the latter struts through his fantasy of being a comedian. These films also center around two men's use of a woman as the means of exchange between them, which locates them specifically in the genre that contains *Sea of Love*.

14 Cavell, "Psychoanalysis and Cinema," 256.

15 I am grateful to Sonya Jones for reminding me of this line.

16 Cynthia Freeland has pointed out to me that Michael Rooker is the lead in *Henry: Portrait of a Serial Killer*, which broadcasts its homosexual subtext.

17 *Shattered* (Wolfgang Petersen, 1991) takes the narcissism of male jealousy to its limit. An amnesiac, his face reconstructed after an accident, learns that his wife had been unfaithful to him until just *before* the accident. Hectic with jealousy, he tracks down this other man, but finds that *he* is the other man, now inserted into the (murdered) husband's place. His jealousy finds relief only when he stares into a dead version of his own face.

18 In the TV cut, scenes were added that did show Denise (Lorraine Bracco).

19 I will rely on the analysis as outlined in Luce Irigaray, *Speculum of the Other Woman*, trans. Gillian C. Gill (Ithaca: Cornell University Press, 1985). All page numbers in the text refer to this work.

20 "We can assume that any theory of the subject has always been appropriated by 'the masculine'" (133).

21 See 50–53, and the subsection "'Woman Is a Woman as a Result of a Certain

Lack of Characteristics'" (112–29).

22 See "The Vanity of a Commodity" (113–15).

23 Nor is there any coincidence in this being a policeman's daughter's wedding. Frank's closest relationship to marriage exists within the police department: he repeatedly calls the arrival of his twentieth year in police work "my anniversary."

24 Both may be the case. The important move of an analysis like Irigaray's is that she exposes the narcissism of male desire while simultaneously pointing out where that narcissism leads itself into crisis. The breakdown of the male gaze therefore signifies not something praiseworthy about the film, but the instability of the very pattern of desire that it is endeavoring to put forward. On the implications of penis-envy—"You men can see nothing, can know nothing of this; can neither discover nor recognize yourselves in this."—see p. 50. Cf. pp. 232–33, which suggest that theorizing woman as non-man renders her inaccessible to theory, since there will be no theory of the accidental. (This is only one of the points at which I am indebted to Tamsin Lorraine.)

7 ▌ Realist Horror

Cynthia A. Freeland

A Chicago man steals corpses and skins them to make himself a suit. A drifter from Texas confesses to 600 murders. A Milwaukee man cannibalizes and has sex with the corpses of numerous boys he has killed.

These sketches illustrate realist horror narratives.[1] They begin in the newspapers but move swiftly to Hollywood contracts and major motion pictures.[2] It is no news that art imitates life: Mary Shelley's monster was born out of Galvani's experiments on the publicly displayed bodies of executed criminals, and nineteenth-century newspapers inspired the more chilling episodes in Dickens, Poe, and Dostoyevsky.[3] But the ties between fact and fiction have become increasingly intricate and ramified. The fiction of *The Silence of the Lambs*, based partly on facts about real corpse-stealer Ed Gein, permeated media coverage of the arrest of cannibalistic serial killer Jeffrey Dahmer, and publicity over Dahmer's arrest in its turn threatened the box-office take and opening date of the horror film *Body Parts*.

What is it to engage in a philosophical examination of realist horror? An important precedent in the western tradition is the ancient Greek debate about tragedy. Plato faulted tragedy because it (like horror) appeals to the audience's baser instincts, obscuring truth and showcasing scenes of overwhelming terror and violence. Aristotle defended tragedies as worthy *representations* with a distinct cognitive status, and he described a positive aspect, *katharsis*, of our emotional reactions of pity and terror to such representations.

I am not the first to observe a parallel between tragedy and horror. Noël Carroll's recent *The Philosophy of Horror* brings horror into the western aesthetic tradition by supplying a framework that recalls Aristotle's defense of tragedy in the *Poetics*.[4] In this paper I want to show that such a classical approach will not work for realist horror. I argue this by illustrating how little it can say about a key example, *Henry: Portrait of a Serial Killer.* Realist horror requires us to think in new ways about the moral assessment of films precisely because of its realism—or rather, because of what we may call its postmodern reweaving of the relation between reality and art. Later, I focus further on this reweaving and propose my own alternative to the classical approach, to ground a more fruitful and subtle discussion of moral issues raised by realist horror.

The Classical Approach

Plato attacked tragic poetry for confusing people who took it to be more vivid than reality itself. It was crucial for Aristotle to show that we recognize and evaluate tragedies as imitations (*mimeseis*), in which plot *represents* action and characters *represent* people. Carroll's *The Philosophy of Horror*, like Aristotle's *Poetics*, examines a genre that seems to rely upon our direct, problematic interest in fearful violence. Again like Aristotle, Carroll argues that this genre evokes a distinct aesthetic response built upon a somewhat distanced intellectual interest in plot. We enjoy tracking the suspenseful narrative, and so we put up with the revulsion that Carroll calls "art-horror."[5] Art-horror is a distanced emotional response to a representation: though monsters in horror are repellent and scary, they do not threaten us directly, and we are protected by knowing they are in fact impossible. They fascinate us because they violate our conceptual categories, arousing in us a strong desire to know something unknowable.

This theoretical defense of horror fails to work for the entire subgenre of realist horror because it depends crucially upon the fictitious nature of the monsters at the center of horror. Carroll defines a monster as "any being not believed to exist according to contemporary science." This requirement is essential to keeping the emphasis on narrative or plot and to preserving the particular aesthetic response Carroll approves, art-horror. He seems to see in the psychotic killer a sort of falling away from an essence of horrific monstrousness. So he is forced to discount a film like *Psycho* as horror, for example, because the monster in it is naturalized: "He is a schizophrenic, a type of being that science countenances." (38)

Yet realist horror is a prevalent and important subgenre of horror that deserves consideration. *Psycho* and *Peeping Tom*, both released in 1960, initiated a significant shift in the horror genre. They chillingly depicted "ordinary" men who were unable to connect with the reality around them.[6] Due to traumas of childhood and sexual repression, so the story went, they become mad slashers. This scenario has become formulaic in numerous subsequent variations; and the subgenre became the dominant form of horror in the 1980s.[7]

To see the limitations of Carroll's Aristotelian or classical approach to horror, I want to look in some detail at one example, *Henry: Portrait of a Serial Killer* (1990, prod. 1986, John McNaughton), a movie loosely based on the story of real serial murderer Henry Lee Lucas.[8] *Henry* is exceptionally interesting—and also disturbing—for its realism of style and amoral viewpoint. It violates the usual rules of both the horror genre in general and the slasher in particular.[9] It offers no audience identification figure, nor does its plot depict any righting of wrongs. As a horror movie, though, this film succeeds by creating terror and unease, both promising and withholding the spectacle of violence.

Henry flouts horror-movie conventions for suspenseful narrative. Its opening scenes show an array of corpses accompanied by an eerie sound track, intercut with scenes of a young man who, by implication, is the multiple murderer Henry, talking to a waitress in a late night diner. The film sets up the viewer to expect him to attack her, but nothing happens. Next Henry follows a woman home from a shopping mall. Tension rises almost unbearably, but at the last moment as she arrives at home a man greets her, and Henry drives away. Even when Henry finally does kill, the film again flouts conventions by withholding the spectacle of the murder. Henry picks up a hitchhiker carrying a guitar, and returns home later carrying her guitar. Or, in a long shot, we see a woman let Henry into her house with his exterminator's equipment. The audience is set up to expect to enter the house and witness a murder. Instead, the film cuts to a shot of a living room. A slow and impersonal pan reveals the woman, naked, dead. A third killing happens so fast and is so obscured that it barely has time to register. Henry snaps the necks of two prostitutes in his car and then goes with his friend Otis to buy a hamburger.

The plot of *Henry* seems flat and random. Certain events occur when Becky, the sister of Henry's roommate Otis, moves into their small Chicago apartment and disrupts their somewhat repressed homosexual partnership. Victimized by incest, Becky has sought refuge with her brother who also proves abusive. A parole violator and drug pusher, he repeatedly kisses Becky and demands to see her breasts, as her father had. Becky tries to normalize the household by getting a regular job and fixing meals, but her efforts fail. (At one point the film cuts from the corpse of the woman Henry has exterminated to a shot of a fish Becky is vigorously cleaning in the kitchen sink.)

Otis and Henry had met in prison, and when Becky asks Otis what

Henry was in for, he at first refuses to say. "What did he do, kill his mama?" she asks. "Yes, he killed his mama with a baseball bat," Otis replies, as if it's a joke. Later Becky pursues the subject with intense fascination. In the only scene in the film that tells us anything about Henry, the facts remain hazy. Henry says that he did kill his mother, he stabbed her to death. He tells Becky, "Daddy used to drive a truck before he got his legs cut off. My mama was a whore. But I don't fault her for that. She made me watch, she beat me, made me wear a dress and watch." Becky responds by confiding that she too was abused, by her father, then says gushingly "I feel like I know you, have known you for a long time." Henry says, summing up, that yeah, he shot his mother on his fourteenth birthday. "Shot her?" Becky asks, "I thought you stabbed her." "Oh yeah," he says.

From this point on the intensity of the killings in the film escalates. After a fight during a drug deal Otis comments, "I'd like to kill somebody." Henry subsequently takes him out for sport to shoot a young man who stops to help with their car. Again. it's all over in a flash. Next Henry murders a pawn shop owner after an argument over the purchase of a television. He turns murder into a science, explaining to Otis how you must vary the method each time, switch guns so as not to be caught, etc. Henry remarks, "It's either you or them. Open your eyes, look at the world, Otis. You or them, you know what I mean."

The stage is now set for two especially gruesome final killing scenes. First there is the killing of a suburban family. In a long shot the killers are shown approaching a house at night. Then the scene switches to a grainy, tilted home video version of the family's murder. It soon emerges that we are watching this footage alongside the killers who are reviewing it afterwards on their living room sofa, as recorded by their stolen camcorder. Point of view and real time are wrenched in a disconcerting way, with contradictory effects. On the one hand, the scene distances viewers and makes the murders seem less awful. The effect is as if we were just watching something on TV. The people in the family are already dead, depersonalized, not individuals. On the other hand, the amateur camera also makes the murders seem more real: things happen unexpectedly, everything seems unplanned and awkward. The viewpoint is not standard, and the murders are not cleanly centered for our observation.

The most graphic and bloody of the murders in *Henry* is Henry's murder of Otis, whom he has caught raping Becky. Henry blinds Otis and then stabs him while lying atop his body in an orgiastic, sexualized attack. Henry chops up Otis's body and loads it into large garbage bags which he packs into suitcases and dumps in the river. He leaves town with Becky, who looks at him and says "I love you Henry." "I guess I love you too," he says. The car radio plays the song, "Loving you was my mistake." They stop for the night at a motel room and get ready for bed. Becky looks up trustingly at Henry who says it's time to turn in. The next morning we see Henry shaving with a straight razor, getting dressed and leaving the motel room—alone. He piles suitcases into the car, and later stops along the road to set a suitcase along the berm. In close-up we see blood seeping through the soft-sided case. That's it, she's dead. Inevitable. Henry drives on in his beat-up old brown Chevy. The movie ends.

Henry is an example of realist horror: based on a real serial murderer, it features a possible, realistic monster. But the classical account of horror modeled on Aristotle's defense of tragedy will not work for this movie. Carroll makes these central claims about the subject matter and construction of horror films. First, horror concerns monsters. Though they may seem possible, they are not real. Our central interest in horror is cognitive, learning about the monster who violates our conceptual categories. And so, second, horror films can be described and assessed mainly in terms of their plots. Our reaction to such narratives is the aesthetic response of art-horror, a revulsion contained by our knowledge that the monster is fictitious, rather than a direct interest in realistic spectacles of violence. But Carroll's central claims are violated by realist horror, where monsters and plots function differently from the way they do in classical horror. Let me comment further by reexamining these two key features, monster and plot, in *Henry*.

First, in realist horror like *Henry*, the monster is a true-to-life rather than supernatural being. Henry *is* a monster. Like many movie monsters, he seems all-powerful, unpredictable, and a source of hideous violence. His approach to his fellow humans is loathesome. He is nevertheless a possible being; he is based upon a real Death Row killer, Henry Lee Lucas. Of course, we do not believe in watching the movie that this monster threatens us, and yet monsters like him do threaten us—there are men who kill others randomly on the streets, in stores, and in their homes. What is monstrous about both versions of Henry is not simply the deeds done but the attitudes, the flatness: "It all seemed fun to start with," Henry Lucas says. "I should have my tail kicked for that. I just didn't have any willpower."[10] He is talking here about confessing, not about the murders themselves.

Other instances of realist horror also feature a realistic or possible monster. It is common for us to regard contemporary serial killers and other "heroes" of realist horror films as monsters. Jeffrey Dahmer or Ed Gein, as much as "Buffalo Bill" or Hannibal Lecter, are horrific, loathesome, disgusting creatures that skin, eat, or have sex with corpses, and kill without remorse. Our interest in killers like Henry Lucas or Dahmer, the basis on which they quickly achieve a certain celebrity status, seems to amount simply to a basic fascination with the sheer fact of their monstrousness. This fascination may even acquire an erotic edge; films like *Henry* or *The Silence of the Lambs* work to generate such an allure. The brilliant and charming Hannibal Lecter engages in an intensely intimate relationship with young FBI agent Clarice Starling in *The Silence of the Lambs*. Henry is chivalrous to Becky, and she responds by eroticizing him. The film conspires in this, as the camera lingers on the good-looking young actor, Michael Rooker, who plays Henry. He is treated iconographically as a Marlon Brando/James Dean angry young rebel, complete with pout, mumbles, short curly hair, square jaw, and white T-shirt. What is most striking is that Becky begins to eroticize Henry just when she learns he's a killer; but isn't this the source of our fascination, too? Henry/Rooker's assimilation to the angry young rebel category is heightened by the film's promotional materials that feature him scowling at himself in a mirror. (Indeed, when I watched the film on video, there were advertisements featuring the dark young man in a white T-shirt at the end of the tape, in "Henry" posters and T-shirts.) The case of Ted Bundy being played by Mark Harmon in the TV movie *A Deliberate Stranger* is another example of this phenomenon; Jeffrey Dahmer and the Menendez brothers acquired groupies during their trials.[11]

Again *contra* Carroll, our fascination with such monsters persists in the face of a basic frustration of our desire to understand or explain them. If the monster is given any motives at all, they are formulaic sexual ones. But such clichéd horror film explanations are similarly trotted out in news accounts of real cases:

> In sado-sexual killings, "the payoff is erection and orgasm," said forensic psychiatrist Park Dietz of Newport Beach, California. The highly popular "slasher" and horror movies incessantly exploit precisely that combination. On the screen, "the baby sitter starts to take off her bra," Dietz said, "which makes the kid in the audience get sexually excited. Then Jason comes in and decapitates her."[12]

Similarly, *Henry* provides a standard and clichéd psycho film explanation. When Henry was a child his mother, who had a lot of lovers, symbolically castrated him by forcing him to wear a dress while watching her have sex. However, the fact that there are three different versions of this story marks it as a generic explanation and undermines its authenticity.

From the allure of the real-life monster, I move to explore the second key feature of *Henry*, its displacement of interest from plot onto spectacle. *Henry* is not a narrative of discovery; rather, it moves the viewer through a gradually intensified spectacle into climax and denouement. *Henry* shocks and announces its gory nature by its opening graphic sequence of nude corpses. But it reveals spectacle slowly, and the scenes that depict killings play with the viewer's emotions in non-standard ways. When Henry and Otis kill the man in the TV pawn shop, while the murder is vicious and gruesome, it is rather comically cross-cut with one of Becky washing the hair of a large Chicago matron spouting racist slogans. After this murder the spectacles begin to crescendo through the murder of the family to climax in the particularly intense, brutal and sexualized murder of Otis. Finally as a diminuendo or anticlimax, restoring symmetry with the opening sequences, *Henry* ends after implying the off-screen murder of Becky.

Realist horror, whether fictive or factual, like *Henry*, typically showcases the spectacular nature of monstrous violence. Realist horror is like other film genres that rely chiefly upon spectacle (for example the musical or hard-core pornography film[13]) in these genres, plot serves to bridge together the "real thing" the film promises to deliver. Although *The Silence of the Lambs* offers many conventional plot elements, it too allows spectacle a major role. The movie highlights the skinned bodies of Buffalo Bill's victims and the bizarreness of his underground den and moth fetish. In the outer story, Lecter is an even greater master of spectacle, operating with a Nietzschean aesthetic all his own. We witness one of his grotesque aesthetic acts (almost a piece of performance art itself) when he orchestrates the murder of his two guards as part of a seamless whole that includes his drawings of Clarice with a lamb, a dinner of rare lamb chops, and Bach's *Goldberg Variations*. The murder is not simply bloody (it is that) but it is artistically arranged, with one body stretched on high as a disemboweled angel and another man's face skinned off to provide Lecter's own disguise. Significantly the director Demme conspires with Lecter by setting the audience up to see and share the expectations of the local police who have been duped by Lecter, just as it offers the audience the killer's view of Starling when he tracks her with his night-vision glasses.

An emphasis on the spectacle of random violence rather than plot in realist horror would lead philosophers from Plato and Aristotle to Noël Carroll to downgrade this genre. Plato categorized our drive toward violent spectacle as lowest among his rank-ordering of human desires,[14] and in the *Poetics* Aristotle argued that spectacle is the "least artistic" of tragedy's six parts."[15] Carroll follows Aristotle in emphasizing plot, which again, like Aristotle, he sees as the focus of our cognitive interests in horror— hence as having greater legitimacy than a "mere" interest in spectacle. In other words, in this tradition, realist horror has little merit aesthetically and would no doubt have to be condemned as morally perverse.

Against this classical approach I have several things to say. First, I think realist horror is a subgenre of horror. But such films rely crucially upon the realism of their horror, the possibility of their monsters, the showcasing of gruesome spectacle, and (at least in the case of *Henry*) the flat randomness of their structure. And second, realist horror films *can* be good movies. That is, they can be well-made constructions or representations that effectively carry out their aims of evoking suspense and horror. I would cite *Henry* or *The Texas Chain Saw Massacre* as examples; *The Silence of the Lambs* won many Oscars, including Best Motion Picture. Realist horror forces us to attend to the very problem of moral perverseness that Carroll wants to avoid: that we are somehow attracted to monsters and to the horrific spectacle itself. The orchestrated representation of violence evokes an ambivalent thrill as we react to realistic depictions of horrific events we know to be possible.[16] I find standard critiques of our direct interest in such monsters and spectacles both simplistic and naive. We need room for a subtler sort of moral assessment. The intricacy of interconnections between the news and film plots necessitates more reflection upon the representational character of violence in realist horror, and it also calls for the use of a different strategy than the classical approach.

An Alternative Strategy

I have described two key features of realist horror, the fascination of the realistic monster and the foregrounding of gruesome spectacle over plot, that prevent this genre from neatly fitting within a classical theory like Carroll's. As I use the term, a classical theory, like Aristotle's in the *Poetics*, has three elements. We first understand there is a clear relation between art and reality: artworks imitate or represent reality. Second, we describe the construction of such imitations, focusing on plot and narrative. Aristotle discerned key patterns that involve a hero, an action, a mistake or *hamartia*, a downfall, and a denouement or unwinding. Carroll similarly describes variations in horror plot patterns. And third, in a classical theory we describe the aesthetic/emotional reactions that such representations aim at producing or evoking. Both Aristotle and Carroll argue that such reactions are unproblematic or unperverse.

Now, I contend that realist horror problematizes the classical approach by thwarting the initial assumption that we can draw a clear distinction between artistic imitations and reality. Realist horror must be understood as a particularly postmodern phenomenon. I mean by this several things. In the immediacy of transmission of the news and in the growing world of infotainment, realistic elements from news stories are easily, commonly, and quickly integrated into new feature film plots. Conversely, fictitious characters (like Hannibal Lecter) are alluded to in presenting or describing real ones (like Jeffrey Dahmer). In addition, realist horror can present violent spectacles with an uncanny immediacy right before our eyes, with the immediacy that the camera also allows on our nightly news. Let me say more about the postmodern aspects of realist horror in relation to each of the three key elements I just identified for classical theories.

First, most significantly, there is an increasingly intricate interweaving between fiction and reality about monsters. Numerous film characters (like Henry) are based on real killers, and there are also docudrama films about real killers (like Ted Bundy), and re-created "reality TV" shows enacting deeds of real killers (like George Hennard). In addition, real killers in the news (like Jeffrey Dahmer) may be described in terms of fictional killers (Hannibal Lecter), or they may have been inspired by fictional killers. John Hinckley, Jr. committed his crime after obsessively identifying with film character Travis Bickle in *Taxi Driver*. Bickle's character was modeled on real attempted assassin Arthur Bremer, who was himself inspired by the film character Alex in *A Clockwork Orange*. Hinckley corresponded with serial killer Ted Bundy (before his execution)—subject of his own TV movie, *Deliberate Stranger* (1986) where he was played by *People* magazine's "Sexiest Man Alive," Mark Harmon.[17] Other real killers or slashers in the news (the Menendez brothers, Lorena Bobbitt) become celebrities in trials that construct them in the media as alternative types of fictional characters (abused victims or vengeful villains).

Second, as news and reality interweave, there is a diminishing role for the constructedness of plot. Plots in realist horror, like stories on the nightly news, are dominated by the three r's: random, reductive, repetitious. Both are about gruesome acts, spectacle, and aftermath, more than about action, downfall, motives, mistakes, and justice. And so, third, it is inappropriate to speak here of any specifically aesthetic or distanced reaction of art-horror. Instead, like the news, realist horror evokes real, albeit paradoxical, reactions: at the same time it is both emotionally flattening (familiar, formulaic, and predictable in showcasing violence), and disturbing (immediate, real, gruesome, random).

I want to move away from talk about the aesthetico-emotional responses of *katharsis*, or art-horror, to seek a subtler and more nuanced moral assessment of realist horror films. I propose a method of *ideological critique*. I am interested in asking these sorts of questions: how do realist horror narratives operate as a discourse that creates knowledge and power? Whose interests do they serve? Ideological critique interprets film texts by identifying how they represent existing power relations so as to naturalize them.[18] Such readings can register contradictions between surface and deeper messages, so can offer more complexity than the moral psychological condemnation of realist horror as perverse. I mean that a good ideological reading can enable the critic to question and resist what she sees as problematic moral messages of films.

This strategy has pitfalls, because the critic may seem to assume a superior stance by identifying encoded relations of dominance that standard audiences are unable to discern (and of course, the critic is prey to her own ideological biases). So a potential limitation of this kind of reading is that it seems to downplay the audience's ability to construct readings against the grain of the film. I want to be careful in my position, then, as a critic diagnosing ideologies, because I recognize that audiences may resist or even subvert ideological messages of realist horror. Horror is an innovative film genre where new directors get their start and new film techniques are developed. Horror movie audiences can be surprisingly sophisticated and critical, exhibiting loud and oddball reactions to scenes in movies—including reactions that deconstruct apparently intended messages or highlight horror's peculiar forms of humor.[19]

There is no particular map for ideological critique; it is more like a possible guide to use in studying a film genre. As I use it, it reflects my own concern with issues that are especially likely to be raised in realist horror. These typically concern gender, since so much of realist horror involves male violence against women, but there also may be issues about violence in general as it relates to social class, race, urban alienation, etc. Focusing on the examples I have mentioned so far, I can identify two particular sorts of morally problematic messages typically conveyed in realist horror, related to what I have called the key features of this genre, the monster and the spectacle.

Monsters in Realist Horror

Some argue that the only way to deconstruct or undo the damaging myths of fascination of monstrous killers is to argue, persuasively and rationally, that they are not extraordinary or monstrous, and deserve no particular attention.[20] My response here is somewhat Baudrillardian or cynical: it seems simply too late or impossible to undo the kinds of mechanisms that currently exist for making such figures famous, for portraying Bundy for instance by the "sexiest man alive," as *People* magazine once dubbed Mark Harmon, or for instant hysterical recreations of disasters at Waco or Killeen. So if rational resistance has become impossible in the society of spectacle, than the alternative is to understand that we/the masses are enjoying spectacle as hyperbolic charade. We have begun to take the spectacle to extreme forms that make it deconstruct itself when we make the repulsive one-eyed short and dumpy Henry Lucas into the handsome Brandoesque Michael Rooker, or the cannibal Lecter into the fascinating genius-villain played by Anthony Hopkins in an Oscar-winning performance. As I have argued above, *Henry* glamorizes and eroticizes its central figure at the same time that it raises for the audience real and disturbing issues about our fascination with him and with this spectacle. So also, *The Silence of the Lambs* unleashed an unusual amount of ordinary on-the-street discussion about the legitimacy or strangeness of a cannibalistic serial killer being so fascinating, smart, and sympathetic. What is more interesting, perhaps, is the possibility that we can become aware of how a heroizing treatment of these monstrous characters reveals the ugly converse of the tradition of the American male hero as a macho loner who is rebellious, misunderstood, and unable to communicate except by violence. When even Arnold Schwarzzeneger begins to parody himself, as he did in *Last Action Hero*, something interesting is happening.

Though feminist critics have attacked horror films for linking violence against the female body with male spectatorial pleasure, a more insidiously troublesome feature of realist horror is to target and victimize viewers by playing on the fascination of the monster so as to eroticize him.[21] This is equally true in the presentation of real cases (Dahmer, the Menendez brothers, Bundy) and fictive ones like Henry or Hannibal Lecter. In particular, a film like *Henry* eroticizes the killer by linking him to traditional Hollywood film heroes like James Dean and Marlon Brando. Of course, from Gary Cooper to Clint Eastwood this hero has been strong, potentially violent, inept at communicating, independent, etc. Significantly, although many real life serial killers (like Dahmer) prey on young men or boys, this sort of killer has not been made the focus of major films, presumably because he violates the clichéd association between potent maleness and heterosexuality. In other words, realist horror creates links between the dark side of male traits (violence, uncontrolled sexuality) and the heroic side (power, independence, etc.).

This means that realist horror legitimizes patriarchal privilege through the stereotyped and naturalized representation of male violence against women. These cultural narratives treat male violence as an inevitable concomitant of normal male sexuality:

> At a minimum, Dietz said, two conditions are necessary to produce a sexual serial killer: a psychopathic personality and a highly developed sadistic tendency. The former is in ample supply. According to studies done for NIMH, about one in 20 urban males is psychopathic—that is,

lacking normal inhibitory feelings of guilt or remorse and operating outside familiar social or moral constraints.[22]

In realist horror, male sexuality is a ticking time bomb, a natural force that
must be released and will seek its outlet in violence if it is frustrated or
repressed. Since women, and usually the monster's mother (as in *Henry*,
Psycho, *Silent Madness*, or real-life accounts of criminals like John
Hinckley), are scapegoated as sources of this repression, they are shown
somehow to deserve the violence they evoke. The net effect is that we
simply accept as a natural and inevitable reality that there will be vast
amounts of male violence against women.[23]

Nevertheless, I believe that the formulaic depictions of violent male sexuality in realist horror can come to be seen *as* just that, formulas. Many
prominent examples of contemporary horror employ self-parody and
bizarre humor, recognizing and poking fun at the audience's participation
in the formulas of the genre (including gender stereotypes). Consider
changes that occurred in the sequel to *The Texas Chain Saw Massacre*.
Both Part I and its successor are framed by a grim announcement that
"this film is based on a true story"; but the realism of *Chain Saw I* has
vanished by version II to be replaced by hyperbolic violence, violence as
excess. Key scenes in this film play with the sex/slash formula in hilarious ways. The unforgettably frightening Leatherface from the first *Chain
Saw* has here become a rather pitiful younger sibling who gets a crush on
the heroine and is teased about it by his brother. When Leatherface first
moves to attack Stretch he becomes mesmerized by her long naked legs
in a scene that blatantly parodies the notion of buzzsaw as phallic substitute. The point is driven home (as if it needed to be) when the patriarch
of the cannibalistic family tells his son sternly "Sex or the saw, son, you
have to choose."

Films like *Henry* or *The Silence of the Lambs* may actually lead audience
members to question their own fascination with the monstrousness of the
serial killer and to query associated icons of male heroism. This is a tricky
point to demonstrate. Realist horror films may undercut the standard
Psycho explanation that scapegoats women, particularly mothers, for male
violence. I have suggested that something like this occurs in *Henry*, a film
that relies upon but simultaneously empties out the formula "he did it
because of his mother." Similarly, *The Silence of the Lambs* contrasts one
stereotyped psycho killer whom the FBI can explain ("Buffalo Bill") with
another whom they cannot begin to fathom. Although many news accounts
struggled to attribute to Luby's mass-murderer George Hennard a motive
stemming from his rejection by local women, others looked beyond this
to discuss the man's work history, war record, and access to guns.[24]

Spectacle in Realist Horror

As I argued above, realist horror highlights spectacle over plot, and this means that one ideological effect of such narratives is to perpetuate a climate of fear and random violence where anyone is a potential victim. Paradoxically these films send out the comforting message that we are safe because the violence is, at the moment, striking someone else. The emphasis on pessimism and powerlessness in realist horror also obscures the truth about factors that produce a climate of violence: racism; inequities in education, health care, social and economic status, and political power; urban blight and flight; drug use; and gun laws. So instead of the horror prompting action and resistance, it works to produce passivity and legitimize current social arrangements. Realist horror even furthers a conservative agenda pushing for increased police patrolling, stricter jail sentences, more use of the death penalty, etc. Realist horror narratives may showcase the frightening spectacle precisely in order to invoke images of safety by offering structures of explanation and power that champion traditional forces of law, criminal justice, and medicine (especially psychiatry). This is the route typically pursued by so-called "reality television" shows, most of which revel in the horrific spectacle for some minutes before offering up a happy resolution: the man who put a nail into his heart with a nailgun is saved by the hospital team; the Hawaiian radio broadcaster during the hurricane gets married over the air to provide everyone a reason to celebrate after the disaster; the "Top Cops" arrest the cop-killing drug-dealers (delivering a few gratuitous punches in a shockingly racist sequence in reenactment), etc. In other words, in the face of domestic violence, marriage is redeemed as salvational; in the face of health care inequities the emergency teams are celebrated; in the face of racist Los Angeles cops we see that the black offenders (in reenactment) really are scary and violent scum, etc.[25]

But there is more to be said about this specularization of gruesome violence. Again, what is going on involves a blurring, even inversion, of the classical relation between *mimesis* and reality—simulations of violence can precede and come to define reality (this is Baudrillard's notion of the hyperreal[26]). There does seem to be a sense in which the spectacle is hyperreal—the depiction of violence sets the standard for the reality. For example, it is common for survivors of real disasters to exhibit flattened responses and to describe the reality by comparing it to television or movie disasters, as in this news account of the scene in Killeen, Texas after the Luby's massacre:

> DPS spokesman Mike Cox said after the attack that the cafeteria looked like a slaughterhouse or a scene from a movie.
>
> "There are bodies scattered throughout the entire cafeteria," Cox said,

"the floor is covered with broken glass, bullet holes, bullet fragments, blood."

"It's almost a surrealistic, nightmarish-looking scene. You think you are on a TV set. You have to remind yourself this is the real thing."[27]

The spokesman here can almost be seen as anticipating the inevitable reenactment soon to be shown (as it was indeed shown) on *America's Most Wanted*. Americans watched virtually the entire Persian Gulf War on live television, and we could see the television movie about David Koresh in Waco right in the same week the apocalyptic fire there ended the long cult standoff.

Of course, it is tempting to stop after pronouncing a negative verdict about this increasing dominance of the spectacle, or making the critical points I made just above. This supposes that audiences are seduced and perhaps controlled or victimized by the increasing spectacles of violence offered by the modern entertainment industry, with as the result an obscene sort of flattening that equates all experiences and produces indifference, as even horrific disasters like Chernobyl or the Challenger explosion become, in Baudrillard's terms, "mere holograms or simulacra."[28] Nevertheless, I again want to insist that as members of the masses, we bear some responsibility for our participation in the specularization of violence. I think that realist horror, by its very hyperbolic excess, may actively encourage the audience in its critical awareness of its own interest in spectacle. Recall that *Henry*, for example, is a particularly self-reflexive movie that forces viewers into the viewpoint of the murderers themselves as we become spectators, alongside Henry and Otis, watching their video-recorded home movies of murders. This naturally prompts audience unrest and questions, so I do not think it is sufficient to analyze it as an exercise in ideological control. Much the same is true, I would argue, of *The Silence of the Lambs*, which problematically encourages the audience to sympathize with brilliant serial killer Hannibal Lecter. Other realist horror films allude to the use of surveillance devices in our culture to problematize the spectacle of violence. For example, in *Menace II Society* the character O-Dog is criticized for repeatedly watching and screening a videotape that recorded his murder of a Korean store owner.

The realist horror film may also be seen to use random, formulaic, or recycled, self-referential plots to challenge conservative, patriarchal social agendas. Despite the fact that the monsters in realist horror are typically men who exercise hideous violence against women, they are also men who do not participate in the traditional patriarchal order (law, politics, the working world, medicine, religion, morality, etc.). In *Texas Chain Saw Massacre II* the Dennis Hopper Texas Ranger character who would formerly have saved the damsel in distress proves to be just as looney and dangerous as the cannibal family itself. Many horror films depict psychiatrists in particular (the very psychiatrists who try to naturalize the monsters) as cartoon characters. *The Silence of the Lambs* is particularly interesting in this regard because it shows an expert psychiatrist who is also a cannibalistic serial killer but who resists the FBI's expert profiles; the fact that the audience cheers Lecter on at the end has as much to do with their desire to buck the system (the officious jail psychiatrist, the stern uncaring male ranks of the FBI), as with the sheer desire for spectacle. Similarly the psychotic assassin Lear in *In the Line of Fire* is clearly shown to be a product of our government, specifically the CIA's, training in assassination. The film blithely depicts a situation in which key government agencies withhold secrets and engage in subversive power plays against one another. Films like *Henry*, *The Texas Chain Saw Massacre* and *Menace II Society* actually do portray conditions of everyday violence in our culture; drifters living in poverty, jobless farmers, racist matrons in beauty shops, Iowa farm girls who are victims of incest, bums mugging one another in city parks, racist policemen, children raised in a drug culture, etc.

Conclusion

Realist horror is like ancient tragedy in that it presents horrific events and features an element of problematic spectacle; these are in each case set within a broader context of somewhat regimented representational devices. The similarity is strong enough to have tempted philosophers to build upon it in fashioning a theory of horror that may work as a defense of the genre. But I have argued that a classical approach to realist horror does not work, for various reasons. Realist horror showcases spectacle, downplays plot, and plays upon serious confusions between representations of fiction and of reality. I do not believe that my task as a philosopher of film is to defend the genre of realist horror. Instead I want to describe it and comment upon its appeal. My own strategy of reading this genre involves me, admittedly, in a sort of tension: ideological critique focuses on problematic ways in which realist horror films create discourses of knowledge and power, serving conservative and patriarchal interests, and it is likely to produce a critical view of realist horror. But I have also tried to foreground the horror and mass media audience's ability to produce subversive interpretations, acknowledging that viewers do indeed have a significant power and interpretive role in reading, and resisting, realist horror films.

Notes

1   I am grateful to Noël Carroll, Anne Jaap Jacobson, Doug Kellner, Justin Leiber, and Tom Wartenberg for comments on earlier versions, and to Doug Ischar, Lynn Randolph, and Bill Simon for watching and discussing *Henry* with me.

2   See Lisa W. Foderaro, "Crimes of Passion, Deals of a Lifetime," *New York Times*, 10 February, 1991, 6E.

3   See Anne Mellor, *Mary Shelley: Her Life, Her Fiction, Her Monsters* (New York: Methuen, 1988), 98–100, 105–106; and Thomas Boyle, *Black Swine in the Sewers of Hempstead: Beneath the Surface of Victorian Sensationalism* (New York: Viking, 1989).

4   Noël Carroll, *The Philosophy of Horror, or Paradoxes of the Heart* (New York and London: Routledge, 1990).

5   "Art horror" is a complex aesthetic and emotional response; see Carroll, *Philosophy of Horror*, 179–82.

6   There are rare female counterparts in 60s films, for example, Roman Polanski's *Repulsion* (1965).

7   The prevalence of realist horror featuring psycho killers is confirmed and analyzed in several recent studies. See James B. Twitchell, *Dreadful Pleasures: An Anatomy of Modern Horror*, (New York and Oxford: Oxford University Press, 1985); Andrew Tudor, *Monsters and Mad Scientists: A Cultural History of the Horror Movie* (London: Basil Blackwell, 1989).

8   Michael Graczyk, "Odyssey of Henry Lee Lucas," *Houston Chronicle*, 15 August, 1993, 5D.

9   Carol Clover has shown that slashers usually do obey a certain moral code in *Men, Women, and Chain Saws: Gender in the Modern Horror Film* (Princeton: Princeton University Press, 1992).

10 Graczyk, "Odyssey," 5D.

11 "Potential Dahmer jurors asked if they can handle gory details," *Houston Chronicle*, 29 January, 1992, 3A; "Menendez Mania," *Houston Chronicle*, 13 October, 1993, 3D.

12 See Curt Suplee, "Serial killers may be closer to normal than we'd like to believe," *Washington Post*; reprinted in *Houston Chronicle*, 7 August, 1991, 12A.

13 See Linda Williams, *Hard Core: Power, Pleasure, and the "Frenzy of the Visible,"* (Berkeley: University of California Press, 1989), 131–34.

14 Plato, *Republic* X, 439e–40a.

15 Aristotle, *Poetics* 6, 50b16–17.

16 For a similar objection see Robert Solomon, Review of Noël Carroll's *The Philosophy of Horror, Or Paradoxes of the Heart*, in *Philosophy and Literature* 16 (1992): 163–73 (with reply by Carroll).

17 On Hinckley see James W. Clarke, *On Being Mad or Merely Angry: John W. Hinckley, Jr., and Other Dangerous People* (Princeton: Princeton University Press, 1990).

18 An example of an ideological analysis of horror is offered in Michael Ryan's and Douglas Kellner's *Camera Politica: The Politics and Ideology of Contemporary Hollywood Film* (Bloomington, Indiana: Indiana University Press, 1988).

19 For example, Kellner and Ryan are critical of a female bondage scene in *Cat People* that they interpret as a backlash against feminism, but when I saw this movie in New York, the audience hooted at the scene and "saw right through it" to the male fantasy lurking barely below its surface.

20 Mary Lou Dietz, "Killing Sequentially: Expanding the Parameters of the Conceptualization of Serial and Mass Killers," paper presented at the First International Conference on "Serial and Mass Murder... Theory, Research, and Policy," April 3–5, 1992, University of Windsor, Windsor, Canada.

21 See Tania Modleski, "The Terror of Pleasure: The Contemporary Horror Film and Postmodern Theory," in Tania Modleski, ed., *Studies in Entertainment: Critical Approaches to Mass Culture* (Bloomington, Indiana: University of Indiana Press, 1986), 155–66; and Linda Williams, "When the Woman Looks," in Mary Ann Doane, Patricia Mellencamp and Linda Williams, eds., *Re-Vision: Essays in Feminist Film Criticism* (Los Angeles, California: American Film Institute Monograph Series, University Publications of America, Frederick MD., 1984), 83–99.

22 Suplee, "Serial Killers," 12A.

23 See for example R. Emerson Dobash and Russell Dobash, *Violence Against Wives: A Case Against the Patriarchy* (New York: The Free Press, 1979).

24 Jim Phillips, "Killeen quiet, but questions are disquieting," *Austin American-Statesman*, 18 October, 1991, A1.

25 My paper "Ordinary Horror," (unpublished, 1993) discusses these shows.

26 Jean Baudrillard, "The Precession of Simulacra," in Baudrillard, *Simulations*, trans. Paul Foss and Paul Patton (New York: Semiotext(e), 1983).

27 Cindy Rugeley, "22 slain, 20 hurt as gunman opens fire in cafeteria," *Houston Chronicle*, 17 October, 1991, 16A.

28 Douglas Kellner, *Jean Baudrillard: From Marxism to Postmodernism and Beyond* (Stanford, California: Stanford University Press, 1989), 209.

8 ▌ Black Cupids, White Desires

Reading the Representation of Racial Difference in *Casablanca* and *Ghost*

Robert Gooding-Williams

What can be said about the representation of racial difference in *Casablanca*? Some fifty years after the film's release, the standard answer to this question is that *Casablanca* marks a defining moment in the history of Hollywood's representation of black characters. Thomas Cripps, for example, writes that "of all the films following the *Gone with the Wind* thaw in racial depictions *Casablanca* (Howard Koch, 1942) reached the widest audience and probably had the strongest impact within the limits of liberal faith."[1] For Cripps, the gist of *Casablanca*'s racial liberalism was its representation of Sam (Dooley Wilson) as Rick's friend and equal, and its related repudiation of traditional racial stereotypes. More recently, Aljean Harmetz has written that the "role of Sam in *Casablanca* was one of a handful in the early 1940s in which an African-American was allowed some dignity."[2] For both Cripps and Harmetz, *Casablanca* belongs to a moment in the history of Hollywood film in which demeaning depictions of blacks have begun to give way to representations that, since they do not mock and insult black characters, can be said to recognize in blacks a human worth on par with that of whites.

In this chapter, I question Cripps's and Harmetz's reading of the representation of race in *Casablanca* and in particular their suggestion that in breaking with established norms of racial representation, *Casablanca* affirms black dignity and equality at the expense of received racial stereotypes. For despite its apparent liberalism, *Casablanca* recodes racial difference. What Cripps and Harmetz see as a movement *away* from black stereotypes and *towards* a vision of black equality, I interpret as a revaluation of racial difference that re-inscribes racial subordination. Sam, though his actions manifest none of the personality characteristics that typically had been assigned to blacks—e.g., foolishness, dim-wittedness, sexual expressivity, laziness, etc.—functions in his relation to whites as a figure for at least one of the these characteristics, namely sexual expressivity. Sam's figurative relation to sexual expressivity is more allegorical than symbolic, because he largely represents this characteristic without exhibiting a personality that is manifestly sexual.[3] By positioning Sam as a figure for sexual expressivity, *Casablanca* recycles racial stereotypes and reinscribes racial subordination.

Sam appears as a figure for sexual expressivity because he plays the role of the mythical Cupid, a character who facilitates and sustains the erotic relationships between other characters—in this case *Casablanca*'s white male and white female protagonists (Rick and Ilsa). The cinematic casting of black characters as cupid figures is hardly unique to *Casablanca*; it is evident, for example, in John Ford's classic 1962 western, *The Man Who Shot Liberty Valance*, as well as in a number of more recent commercial films, including *Something Wild* (1986), *Ghost* (1990), *Passion Fish* (1992), and *The Crying Game* (1992). Here, I will focus on *Ghost* in connection to my reading of *Casablanca*, because it further develops the idea of a black cupid figure who represents sexual expressivity while lacking it as a personality trait. Loosely based on Shakespeare's *Macbeth*, *Ghost* is about the effort of a dead but "legitimate" white American patriarch and capitalist to defend his realm against the designs of an "illegitimate" usurper.[4] The black cupid in this movie is Oda Mae Brown (Whoopi Goldberg), and her primary role in the film is to mediate the romance between *Ghost*'s two white lovers, the dead patriarch Sam Wheat (Patrick Swayze) and his beloved fiancée, Molly (Demi Moore).[5] In discussing *Casablanca* and *Ghost*, I will highlight both films' ambivalence about the value to "white civilization" of black sexuality.

Black Cupid/Black Song: The Case of *Casablanca*
Love Triangles and Outlaw Heroes

My reading of *Casablanca* draws its inspiration from two treatments of the film I have found provocative. The first of these is Umberto Eco's "*Casablanca*: Cult Movies and Intertextual Collage"; the second is Robert Ray's interpretation of *Casablanca* in his *A Certain Tendency of the Hollywood Cinema*.[6]

Of particular interest in Eco's essay is his emphasis on the Rick/Ilsa/Victor love triangle. Eco is right, of course, to stress the significance of this unhappy trio. Yet he makes no note of the connections between the Rick/Ilsa/Victor triangle and at least three other erotically charged trian-

gles that shape the plot of the film. First, there is the threesome consisting of Rick, Renault and Strasser; here, Renault is in the middle, especially in the film's early scenes in which we see that, though he is drawn
to the romantic hero, antifascist, and sentimentalist he senses in Rick, his
ultimate allegiance is to the power personified by Major Strasser. A second trio consists of Ferrari, Sam, and Rick. In this triangle, Sam occupies
the middle position as an employee who, because of his heartfelt loyalty to
Rick, refuses Ferrari's seductive bid to double his wage. (Despite his claim
that he neither buys nor sells human beings, Rick has, by the end of the
film, "sold" Sam to Ferrari!) Finally, the triangle consisting of Rick, Ilsa,
and Sam is the one in which Sam appears primarily in the role of a black
cupid who mediates Rick's and Ilsa's romantic love.

Though the primary focus of this essay will be the Rick/Sam/Ilsa triangle, a complete reading of *Casablanca* would attend to all of the trios
mentioned above, as well as to the fact that by the end of *Casablanca* these
four trios have been dramatically resolved into three pairs or couples
(Victor/Ilsa, Rick/Renault, and Ferrari/Sam).[7] It is inevitable, moreover,
that my discussion of the Rick/Sam/Ilsa triangle refer at least implicitly
to *Casablanca*'s three other threesomes, since each threesome is intelligible only in relation to the others. Still, my decision to emphasize the Rick/
Sam/Ilsa triangle is a deliberate one that is intended to complicate current discussions of the representation of love-triangles that foreground
gender and sexuality but not race.[8]

My reading of the Rick/Sam/Ilsa triangle has as its point of departure
Robert Ray's claim that *Casablanca* "reincarnates in Rick and Laszlo the
outlaw hero-official hero opposition," an opposition that, he contends,
appears repeatedly in the films of Hollywood's classic period. According to
Ray, the outlaw hero distrusts civilization, lives outside the law, and obeys
a private code of justice and morality. The official hero, on the other hand,
firmly adheres to the law and, unlike the outlaw hero, wholeheartedly
embraces the norms of civilization, especially marriage. In *Casablanca*, Rick
is the quintessential outlaw hero—an unmarried Robin Hood, "operating
outside of a corrupt legal system in the name of some higher, private
notion of justice…. Like Robin…Rick robbed from the rich to give to the
poor, manipulating his own roulette wheel to provide refugees with money
for exit visas." Victor, however, is married, and, like the typical official
hero, insists on the sanctity of legal rules. "The movie's basic premise,"
writes Ray, "was the basic neutrality of the 'frontier' town Casablanca, an
abstract principle that Laszlo repeatedly asserted. 'You won't dare to inter-
fere with me here,' he warned Strasser."[9]

Ray's characterization of Rick as an outlaw hero is useful for my purposes, because it helps bring into view the specificity of Sam's significance as a cupid figure who mediates Rick's and Ilsa's love. Developing Ray's reading in a direction in which he only hints, I shall in what follows attempt to elucidate the connection between Sam's role as a cupid figure and Rick's status as an outlaw. My discussion begins with a consideration of *Casablanca*'s "Paris flashback" sequence.

Lovers' Desires, Cupid's Song

Drunk in his saloon and awaiting Ilsa's appearance, Rick insists that Sam play "As Time Goes By." "You played it for her and you can play it for me," says Rick. "If she can stand it, I can. Play it!" As Sam begins to play "As Time Goes By," the camera closes in on Rick and the scene dissolves. The next image we see depicts Paris in the spring. A shot of the Arc de Triomphe is followed by one of Rick and Ilsa driving along the boulevard.

Sam's singing introduces the Paris flashback. When, during the flashback, we first see Sam with Rick and Ilsa, Sam is playing "As Time Goes By" while Rick displays the same detachment and romantic gallantry we saw him show when he and Ilsa were alone in his Paris apartment. (The screenplay tells us that "his manner is wry, but not the bitter wryness we have seen in Casablanca.") Despite the advent of the Nazis, the private sphere of Rick's life seems to him harmonious and secure as he anticipates marrying Ilsa. But Ilsa has discovered that Victor is alive, that he has escaped from a concentration camp, and so she does not show up for their meeting. Left to leave without her, Rick feels betrayed and, we later discover, does not permit Sam to sing "As Time Goes By" anymore. Catching him unawares, the play of political events has drawn Ilsa away from Rick, thus spoiling his happiness.

In Rick's nostalgic vision, the world of the Paris flashback is a picture of carefree romantic desire and of the Parisian locales Rick associates with that desire. Sam appears in this world simply in order to sing and bear witness to Rick's and Ilsa's romance; his *raison d'etre*, here, is to envision their romance as having an immutable value tied to the "fundamental" things (moonlight and love song, hearts filled with passion, jealousy, and hate, woman needing man, man needing his mate, etc.) that apply as time goes by. Cheerful and devoted servant that he is, Sam serves Rick and Ilsa by singing a song that represents their love as possessing a self-sufficient and timeless perfection, eternally and everywhere "the same old story." His narrative function is to *reify* Rick's and Ilsa's love, to make it into an object that each of them invokes to conjure up feelings of romance when one of them is absent.[10] Playing the piano and singing "As Time Goes By," Sam labors on the raw material of heterosexual desire, transforming it into a commodity fetish that each of the white lovers appropriates as a sort of erotic surplus value, an erogenous good that he creates, that they consume, and for which he seems to receive no compensation.[11]

Sam is a black cupid, a black producer of erotic value. Cast in a role that ties him essentially to heterosexual desire, he is, in part, the personification of a familiar racial stereotype that equates blackness with potent sexuality.[12] Here, however, we must be careful, since Sam's tie to sexuality is, primarily, a tie to a sexuality belonging to others. So far as he sings the song of Rick's and Ilsa's love, Sam appears as an asexual and desireless subject, not as a black epitome of sexual expressivity. Servant Sam, one might say, produces and carries the baggage of Rick's and Ilsa's desire, yet displays no desire of his own while he does his work. Still, the shadow of a stereotype equating blackness with potent sexuality haunts Sam's presence, if only because that presence helps mark the difference between Rick's outlaw hero and Victor's official hero. By providing Rick a black servant who devotedly sings his master's love song, *Casablanca* invests Rick with a romantic allure that the civilized Victor lacks, thus representing him as the proper and inevitable object of Ilsa's desire. Echoing the traditional stereotype, Sam's presence connotes Rick's access to a charismatic sexuality—an implicitly black sexuality—that no official hero could possibly possess.[13]

At only one juncture in the development of *Casablanca*'s plot are we permitted to imagine that Sam could possibly become the agent of his own desire. The scene I have in mind transpires just a few moments before the Paris flashback sequence. With Sam looking compassionately at Rick, who is getting more and more drunk as he awaits Ilsa's arrival, the following exchange occurs:

> Sam: Boss, let's get out of here.
> Rick: No, sir. I'm waiting for a lady.
> Sam: Please, boss, let's go. Ain't nothin' but trouble for you here.
> Rick: She's coming back. I know she's coming back.
> Sam: We'll take the car and drive all night. We'll get drunk. We'll go fishing and stay away until she's gone.
> Rick: Shut up and go home, will you?
> Sam: No, sir. I'm staying right here.

Worried that Ilsa is no good for Rick, for a brief moment Sam redefines the love-triangle which he, Rick, and Ilsa compose. He appears, suddenly, not as the singing muse of Rick's and Ilsa's romance, but as offering Rick a promising alternative to confronting his lover. Sam would take Rick away from Ilsa, and from the pain she has caused him. Together, he suggests, he and his boss should steal away into the night and lose themselves in the revelry of drunken driving and fishing. Posing more as Dionysus than as cupid, Sam appears here as Ilsa's rival, a potential carouser who would seduce Rick to exchange the pain and "trouble" that Rick's "lady" is bound to bring him for the nighttime delights of a romp with his servant. For a brief moment, Sam exhibits a personality that explicitly manifests the power of sexual self-expression. The homoerotic connotations of this scenario strike a familiar chord, as they immediately recall the canonical story of Huck and Jim on the lam, running away from women and from civilization, and enjoying on their raft what Leslie Fiedler describes as a "sacred marriage of males."[14] Rick, we know, resists Sam's seduction, and only a few moments later demands that Sam revert to the role of a black cupid, insisting that Sam "play it!" Refusing to become the object of Sam's desire, Rick will nostalgically consume his own desire, which Sam has made into a song.

Rick's nostalgia is for a past of heterosexual bliss on the margins of civilization. Refusing Sam's temptation to lose himself in a black night of drunkenness, he still longs for a time when, with Sam at his side, he, Rick, possessed a charisma that made him irresistible to Ilsa. This time, a time gone by, Rick's nostalgia paints in the image of a prelapsarian flawlessness that historical time, the time of human history and politics, can only ruin. Read allegorically—and there is much in *Casablanca* that invites us to read it this way—this edenic time is the idealized time of America's pre-war isolationism, a time when, we are asked to believe, America had excepted itself from the trials and traumas of the European civilization Victor Laszlo represents. Part of what distinguished pre-war America, *Casablanca* suggests, was the benefit it derived from its "innocent" exploitation of blacks; the allure that Rick acquires through his association with Sam is, allegorically, the allure that America acquires through the presence of erotically productive and entertaining black folk. It is essential, of course, that blacks' connection to eros remain subject to white control, which is simply to say that Sam, in Rick's Eden—though he can be a cupid who labors on and lends his blackness to the eros of others—is forbidden to personify a Dionysus who *enacts* a desire for Rick that Rick might never master. Here, the nostalgia of the outlaw is precise in its ambivalent attitude towards the "blackened" sexuality it craves: picturing a heteroerotic happiness on the margins of civilization, Rick will never quite imagine himself lost and helpless in the heart of a homoerotic darkness.[15]

Ilsa's Plot, Rick's Revenge

It is Ilsa, of course, who bursts the bubble. After she departs Rick becomes a bitter man. His Eden destroyed, he takes refuge in his isolation, keeping his distance from the political realities about him and insisting adamantly that he won't "stick his neck out for nobody." Ilsa gets it right when, having come to Rick's cafe in order to force him to give her the letters of transit, she tells him "You want to feel sorry for yourself, don't you? With so much at stake, all you can think of is your own feeling. One woman has hurt you, and you take revenge on the whole world."

The sequence of action following Ilsa's remarks is *Casablanca*'s most consequential turning point. When Ilsa left Rick she initiated a story line that was at odds with Rick's intention that he, she, and Sam run away together. When Ilsa comes to Rick's cafe looking for the letters of transit, she takes the initiative again, attempting again to force the story in a direction that opposes Rick's will. After scolding Rick for feeling sorry for himself she reveals a revolver and says that she will shoot him if he does not hand over the letters. Rick, ready now to resign everything, tells Ilsa, "Go ahead and shoot. You'll be doing me a favor." He then walks towards her until, reaching her, she drops her right hand, which is holding the revolver. According to the screenplay, Ilsa is "hysterical," and now says to Rick, "Richard, I tried to stay away. I thought I would never see you again, that you were out of my life. The day you left Paris, if you knew what I went through! If you knew how much I loved you, how much I still love you." At this point Rick takes Ilsa in his arms and kisses her passionately. Just a few moments after this most romantic crescendo, Ilsa tells Rick why she kept her marriage a secret and why she went to Victor without saying anything to Rick. Rick, listening attentively, responds that her story is "still a story without an ending." But now that she has given up her will to enact her own story, Ilsa rejoins that "you'll have to do the thinking for both of us, for all of us." With Ilsa's head cradled in his arms, Rick confidently replies, "All right, I will."

This pivotal scene conflates *Casablanca*'s most compelling representation of expressed heterosexual desire with Ilsa's decision to submit to Rick's will and, hence, his narrative authority. Relinquishing her effort to plot a course of action that will free Victor from the clutches of the Nazis, Ilsa cedes to Rick the right and the power to complete their story, which is "still...without an ending." As we well know, the plot that Rick invents—which involves sending Ilsa off with Victor—is no less a surprise to Ilsa than it is to anyone seeing *Casablanca* for the first time. Donning the air of self-sacrificial nobility ("I'm no good at being noble Ilsa..."), Rick avenges the pain Ilsa caused him by insisting that she endure the pain of renunciation, even though she has told him that she can't run away from him again. (Rick continues to enact the spirit of revenge—for Nietzsche "the will's ill will against time" and here an ill will against historical time—even after he hands over the letters of transit.) By subjecting Ilsa to the painful consequences of the plot he produces, Rick in effect punishes her, doing to her what she did to him and forcing himself to relinquish the dangerous happiness of being close to a woman who might challenge his will again. Where previously Ilsa's assertion of her will caused Rick to suffer, now Rick's assertion of his will causes Ilsa to suffer. Either way of course, Rick and, allegorically, America suffers the destruction of an isolated paradise. Still, it matters to Rick that he, and not Ilsa, chart the way out of Eden. Allegorically, if America is to enter the war and thus embrace the drama of European history and politics, then America must enjoy an autonomy that *Casablanca* represents simultaneously as the patriarchal triumph of a white man's will and the passionate expression of white heterosexual desires.[16]

Rick's Plot, Sam's Fate

Rick's plot, the plot that brings *Casablanca* to an end, also has consequences for Sam. Just as, according to Rick, Ilsa will become a part of Victor's work, Sam will become a part of Ferrari's work.[17] At the point at which Rick decides to send Ilsa away with Victor, Sam's role as a black producer of erotic value (a black cupid) becomes obsolete. Sam need no longer be available to sing the song that expresses Rick's most passionate heterosexual desire, because Rick has deliberately renounced that desire once and for all (something he has not done before Ilsa appears in Casablanca).[18]

Working for Ferrari, Sam will be a profit-making economic asset. Viewers of *Casablanca* tend to see Sam's change of employers as a loss for him, if only because the film represents this change as echoing one of America's persistent myths about the impact of the Civil War on the lives of southern blacks. Compared to the suave and refined Rick whose relation to his servant, Sam, seems always genteel—as, according to the myth, the relations between antebellum masters and their slaves were supposed to have been—the disreputable Ferrari, Casablanca's leading black marketeer, resembles a carpetbagger. Sam is worse off than before, because he is prey to the economic exploitation of a capitalist who will show him none of the kindness and consideration shown by his former master. Like *Gone with the Wind*, *Casablanca* encourages the belief that, in the wake of war, a precious way of life in which black Americans found happiness through subservience has given way to a cruel and callous existence in which their new masters will treat them as nothing but economic instruments.

But what distinguishes the "indignity" of sheer economic exploitation from the "dignity" that, Cripps and Harmetz suggest, Sam possesses in his relationship to Rick? If the presence of this dignity seems self-evident, or to connote some sort of racial liberalism, it is because Sam's role as a cupid figure is tied to a vision of a prelapsarian American paradise that— before the second World War? before the Civil War?—remained some- how untouched by the vicissitudes of human history. But what is Sam's role within that vision? It is to enable the flow of others' desires, to func- tion as the obstructionless medium through which these desires achieve romantic expression. In paradise Sam is exploited as an erotic if not an economic tool. Supposing that he lacks dignity in the one capacity, why maintain that he possesses it in the other?

To be sure, Sam fits neither the stereotype of the black simpleton nor that of the sexual black male. Still, *Casablanca* recodes racial difference not by creating a new kind of racial stereotype, but by depriving its only black character of a distinctive personal identity. Excepting his momen- tary appearance as a Dionysian seducer, Sam seems little more than an impersonal abstraction, a cupid-like but desireless conduit for the height- ened expression of white erotic energies. Singing a song that celebrates Rick's and Ilsa's love, he appears as a figure for white sexual expressivity, thus representing it as something black. Sam subserves this expressivity by becoming its black voice and face. Playing the deferential role of white desire's devoted minstrel, he epitomizes the subordination of black bodies to white ends.

Black Cupid/Black Body: The Case of *Ghost*
Good White Guys and Bad Ones

Broker, home renovator, and future husband to Molly, Sam Wheat fits perfectly the mold of the official hero. Sam embraces the legal institutions of marriage and property ownership, and in contrast to his friend Carl, obeys the laws which regulate his professional activities. Sam's only appar- ent fault is his inability to express directly his feelings for Molly, to say "I love you." After he is killed by Carl's henchman Willie Lopez, Sam becomes a ghost who dedicates himself to protecting Molly and to sabo- taging Willie's and Carl's criminal activities. In effect, Sam becomes an outlaw hero, operating outside of a corrupt social order in the name of justice and right.

Because he is a ghost, Sam cannot realize his aims without the assis- tance of a living human being, someone whose body he can use to make his will effective in the world. The person to whom he turns for this purpose is Oda Mae Brown, a black woman whose body becomes his instrument. Sam W.'s relationship to Oda Mae parallels Carl's relationship to Willie. In both cases a white capitalist patriarch uses a nonwhite ghetto dweller (Willie is a brown-skinned Puerto Rican) as a means to achieve his ends.

Because he is a good white patriarch, Sam attempts to instill in Oda Mae a moral sense that she apparently lacks (as when he demands that she give the "blood money" she has retrieved to a nun's charity). Carl, on the other hand, since he is a bad white patriarch, turns Willie into a thief and a murderer. In *Ghost*, dark-skinned, nonwhite individuals become physical and moral putty in the hands of their white patrons. The bad white guy uses his "darky" to disrupt a social order based on law and morality; the good white guy responds to this evil by finding a "darky" of his own to help him restore that order.

Molly, Oda Mae, and the Male Gaze

With Sam Wheat dead, Molly falls victim to the nefarious scheming of Carl and Willie. One could even say that her plight functions synecdochically to represent the social chaos produced by Carl's criminal plotting. Carl's effort to seduce Molly suggests that his ultimate aim is to usurp Sam's place in her life and to make what was once Sam's world his own. Sam's struggle against Carl and Willie focuses on Molly, because it is her liability to danger that most alarms him when he, her protective and legitimate patriarch, is cast from her world. Sam's desire to protect Molly is not distinguishable from his desire to set aright a social order in which she has been exposed suddenly to the actions and desires of the wrong men. In order to destroy the illegitimate patriarch and his sidekick Willie, Sam must save Molly; in order to save Molly, he must destroy Willie and Carl.

Molly's exposure to danger is the pivot around which the plot of *Ghost* revolves. Echoing *The Birth of a Nation* no less than *Macbeth*, *Ghost* interprets social chaos as baring an innocent white woman to a predatory evil.[19] Recalling the Gus chase sequence in *The Birth of a Nation*, *Ghost* at once racializes and sexualizes Molly's availability to danger in a scene in which her image becomes the voyeuristic object of Willie Lopez's gaze. Willie comes to Molly's apartment in order to steal the notebook he was attempting to steal when he killed Sam. While he is still there, Molly returns from a walk, enters her bedroom, and begins to undress. Unbeknownst to her, Willie lasciviously leers at her reflection in a mirror, thus enjoying the image of her partially unclad body. Though Molly's body has been represented as desirable and as appropriately surrendering itself to Sam's gaze and passion previously (in a highly stylized sequence in which Sam and Molly make love in their apartment), it appears in this scene as a desirable object that has been wrongfully exposed to the rapacious gaze of a possible rapist.[20] Here, as in *The Birth of a Nation*, the picture of a white woman falling prey to the dangerous desire of a dark man appears as a symptom of social disorder. And here, as in the earlier film, a good white man finds that there do exist black folk—in *The Birth of a Nation*, the so-called "good souls"—whom he can effectively enlist in his efforts to make the world safe for white women.

Oda Mae, of course, is the good soul who comes to Sam Wheat's assistance. She is, moreover, a woman, though one who never becomes the object of the heteroerotic gaze Sam and Willie personify when they look at Molly. Portrayed as loving when attributed to Sam, and as threatening when attributed to Willie, this gaze always appears in *Ghost* in tandem with the representation of Molly as an erotic spectacle. When, in other words, a film spectator sees Sam, Willie, or Carl seeing Molly as sexually desirable, he or she (the spectator) finds that he or she has been invited to enjoy the sight of Molly's body framed and represented as a sexually appealing visual exhibit. Oda Mae, in contrast, never appears in *Ghost* as a sexually attractive object of male desire. When, for example, she is in bed, where Sam is attempting to persuade her to help him contact Molly, and where we might expect to see her in something like the scanty, open shirt that Molly wears late at night when she and Sam make love, Oda Mae is dressed in dingy looking, buttoned-up pajama longjohns. In general, her attire consists of heavy looking and sometimes gaudy outfits that cover her entire body and that contrast sharply with the trim and short-sleeved look Molly favors. Sam's good soul appears neither to him nor to any spectator watching *Ghost* as an erotic spectacle.

Of course, Oda Mae could not have appeared as an erotic spectacle without jeopardizing her role as cupid figure. Like Sam singing the song of Rick's and Ilsa's love, Oda Mae, when helping Sam protect Molly, projects an asexual appearance. In Oda Mae's case, this appearance requires not simply that she not be the agent of her own desire but that she not be the potential object of Sam's desire. Oda Mae is convincing in her role as a cupid figure because her body functions as an obstructionless medium through which Sam's will and love can make their way to Molly. Had Oda Mae been represented as an erotic spectacle and hence as a possible object of Sam's heteroerotic desire, her body would have appeared not as a medium through which Sam's passionate and protective love could easily reach Molly, but as a threatening distraction that could displace Molly's body as the object of that love. In order to be maximally effective in her role as a cupid-figure, Oda Mae had to be depicted as having a body that was erotically neutral, both as subject and object.[21]

Passing: Black Woman as White Man

Oda Mae most vividly and dramatically illustrates her significance as a cupid-figure in a sequence of scenes that transpires near the end of *Ghost*.

In her provocative reading of this sequence, Tania Modleski asserts that Oda Mae "stands in for the body of the white *male*...."[22] Rather late in the movie, Sam Wheat expresses his desire to be alive again in order to touch Molly "just once more." Molly responds, "Me too." According to Modleski's interpretation of what follows, "Oda Mae offers up her body for the purpose, and Sam enters into it. The camera shows a closeup of the black woman's hands as they reach out to take those of the white woman, and then it cuts to a shot not of Oda Mae, but of Sam, who, in taking over her body has obliterated her presence entirely.... This sequence, in which Goldberg turns *into* a man may be seen as a kind of logical extension of all her comedic roles, for which she is always coded in the comedies as more masculine than feminine."[23]

The rhetoric of Modleski's analysis suggests three distinct readings of the sequence she describes, none of which at first glance is consistent with the others: either Oda Mae's body displaces Sam's, or Sam's displaces Oda Mae's, or, somehow, her body turns into and "becomes" his. Though inconsistent with the others, each reading is helpful, as each points to an important aspect of what has transpired.

Yes, Oda Mae should be seen as displacing Sam's body, because Sam has, according to the script, become a bodiless ghost. She stands in for his body, precisely to the extent that she permits him to use her body in place of his own. Recall, however, that earlier in the movie a black ghost uses Oda Mae's body in a similar way, but without her permission, when he enters it in order to speak to his wife. When this happens, the only body the viewer sees is Oda Mae's/Whoopi Goldberg's. We are not, in other words, provided an image of the black male ghost's body *in the place of* Oda Mae's body. One of the metaphysical implications of this scene is that if a ghost inhabits the body of a medium, it inhabits a body other than one it occupied before dying. This implication makes sense precisely to the extent that we assume, as this film asks, that a ghost's pre-death body is no longer available to be occupied. When the black male ghost exits Oda Mae's body, she is angry because he has used her without her consent. Later in the film when Oda Mae offers her body to Sam, we are again asked to assume that he needs her body because his body is not available.

What sense does it make to claim with Modleski that Sam, when he takes over Oda Mae's body, obliterates her presence, thus displacing her? On this view, Oda Mae's body ceases to be present when Sam enters it. But were this true, her body would not be serving the purpose for which she offered it: it would not be working as a medium that enabled Sam to touch his former lover. It seems clear, furthermore, that the sequence that follows is intelligible only if one assumes Oda Mae's body is working in this way. Although Modleski's view is false we should not dismiss it because it points to a significant feature of the sequence it describes, namely, that the cut from black and white hands to the figure of Sam substitutes the *image* of Sam's body for the *image* of Oda Mae's body. This substitution leaves intact the viewer's beliefs that Oda Mae's body (and not Sam's body) is present and that Sam and Molly are using Oda Mae's body for their purposes. One image displaces and obliterates the other.

Modleski's claim that Oda Mae has turned into a man is her attempt to make sense of this displacement. The claim is misleading, however, because it suggests that Oda Mae's body has actually become that of a man. But the metaphysics of the situation preclude this, since the only bodies present in the room, both before and after the substitution of images, are Oda Mae's and Molly's female bodies. A male ghost is present, but not a male body. There is no denying, of course, that Oda Mae's black female body, following the substitution of images, appears to be something that it is not, namely: a white male body. But this is only to say that the effect of this substitution is a state of affairs in which a black female body is made to pass as a white male one.

Oda Mae's racial and gender passing cannot be understood on the model of traditional racial passing, as if it were the product of her intention to hide her real racial and gender identities. Rather her passing is the product of a director's decision to represent her body by means of an image that conceals its identity. No doubt this decision was essential to evoking the crescendo of heterosexual romantic feeling which the picture of Sam and Molly, holding each other one last time, was designed to inspire. Had the image of Sam's body not replaced that of Oda Mae, the possibility of such a crescendo would have been undermined by the homoerotic picture of Oda Mae embracing Molly and acting as the agent of her own desire.

Conclusion: The Paradox of the Black Cupid

Sam Wheat's only apparent fault is his inability to convey to Molly his feelings for her. After he dies, the plot of *Ghost* dramatizes this inability as a metaphysical dilemma of vaguely Cartesian resonance: how can the love/desire of a pure mind/spirit become effective in a world of material things? Drawing on the hackneyed representation of white men as people who have trouble expressing their emotions, *Ghost* allegorically represents Sam's struggle to communicate his feelings in the wake of his death as his effort to cope with the mind/body problem. Sam solves the problem by finding in the black body of Oda Mae the means by which he can express and render tangible his thoughts, his desires, and, above all else, his love for Molly. (For Sam, Oda Mae is the functional equivalent of Descartes's pineal gland.)

By becoming the vehicle by which Sam's love acts in the world to protect Molly, Oda Mae becomes a producer of erotic value. The erotic value she produces is not an erogenous good that, like Sam the piano player's "As Time Goes By," stimulates romantic desire, but, strangely, *the asexual and desireless receptivity of her own body*. By portraying Oda Mae as asexual, *Ghost* avoids the Jezebel stereotype that characterizes black women as sexually potent and arousing, and so disarms the suspicion that Sam, when he enters Oda Mae's body, wants to be there to enjoy *her* sexuality.[24] Further, by having Oda Mae pass as Sam when she is embracing Molly, this movie blocks the perception of Oda Mae as a subject of erotic desire. Still, Oda Mae's body retains an erotic value for Sam, since he needs its unarousing and desireless receptivity to touch Molly, and thus to express physically his love for her.

Although Sam is not aroused by Oda Mae's body, the fact that he enters it has sexual connotations that *Ghost* would less easily accommodate if Oda Mae were a man. Female gender makes a difference here, because the homoeroticism of a man entering another man's body, like the homoeroticism that is hidden when Sam uses Oda Mae to touch Molly, would disrupt a storyline the end of which is heterosexual fulfillment. (The disruption here would be similar to that in *Casablanca* caused by Sam's effort to seduce Rick.) It is significant, moreover, that Oda Mae is at once female *and* black, since Sam's use of her body recalls a long and brutal history of white men's sexual exploitation of black women's bodies. When Sam enters Oda Mae, he need not pass as something other than a white patriarch, since the recollection of this history is less likely to upset a predominantly white filmgoing audience than is the suggestion of interracial homosexuality.

Because Oda Mae's body has an erotic value for Sam, her presence in *Ghost*, like that of Sam in *Casablanca*, remains haunted by a cultural stereotype equating blackness with potent sexuality. In *Casablanca*, a song sung by a black body—Sam's song—appears as a magical fetish that has the power to stimulate feelings of romance. In *Ghost*, a black body itself—Oda Mae's body—appears as a fetish whose special magic is its power to solve Sam's mind/body problem. Oda Mae's body enables Sam to express and render palpable a love that he left unexpressed and unknown to Molly during his life. The romantic and erotic magic of her body is so powerful that Sam even learns to say "I love you," leaving no doubt that, were he alive, he would be a better, more expressive lover.

By affiliating himself with blackness, Sam acquires a sexual expressivity that he previously lacked. Paradoxically, the blackness producing this expressivity—the magical blackness of Oda Mae's body—appears neither as a subject nor as an object of erotic desire. Oda Mae's body harbors erotic magic, even though there is nothing sexually expressive about her. Both erotic and not erotic, she personifies an ambiguity that is perhaps essential to the figure of the black cupid. Wanting and wanting-to-control black desire, a culture that equates blackness with potent sexuality will tend to produce in this figure the duplicitous image of its ambivalent wish both to possess and to repress a mythical black sexual magic.[25] Possession will seem desirable, when whites construct themselves as distant from their bodies, as passionless, or as lacking in romantic charisma. Repression will seem desirable when the black magic they seek seems to threaten white civilization. The figure of the black cupid will be the subject of endless narrative retakes, so long as whites fetishize black sexuality as a black magic that white civilization lacks.[26]

Notes

1 Thomas Cripps, *Slow Fade to Black* (New York: Oxford University Press, 1977), 370.

2 Aljean Harmetz, *Round Up The Usual Suspects* (New York: Hyperion, 1992), 141. Harlan Lebo expresses a similar point of view in his *Casablanca: Behind the Scenes* (New York: Simon and Schuster, 1992), 87–88. He writes: "As a result of the studio's willingness to let Wilson play Sam's character as originally written, the actor portrayed one of the few nondegrading black roles in any film (other than all-black productions) made in Hollywood to that time."

3 Here, I am indebted to Hans-Georg Gadamer's discussion of the traditional distinction between the symbolic and the allegorical image: "Thus one might sum up...the symbolic, as what is inwardly and essentially significant being contrasted with the external and artificial significance of allegory." (See *Truth and Method* (New York: Crossroad, 1982), 67). By proposing that Sam's relation to sexual expressivity resembles allegory, I suggest that he represents the power of sexual self-expression without displaying a personality that is intrinsically or "inwardly" characterized by the expression of sexual desire.

4 The film even provides an explicit allusion to Shakespeare's play when Sam tells Carl that he and Molly will attend the theater on what turns out to be the evening that Sam is murdered: the play Molly wishes to see is *Macbeth*.

5 Not all black cupids exhibit the "asexual" personalities we tend to observe in Sam and Oda Mae. (Consider, for example, the black cupid appearing in

Passion Fish.) Thus, my readings of *Casablanca* and *Ghost* are not intended to be exhaustive of the black cupids "genre." Even less so are they intended to do justice to the many ways in which blacks get portrayed in the contemporary Hollywood cinema. Neither, finally, are they meant to address the attempts by black film makers to challenge the representation of black sexuality in "white" films. [On the designation of some films as "white," see K. A. Appiah, "'No Bad Nigger': Blacks as the Ethical Principle in the Movies," in *Media Spectacles* (New York: Routledge, 1993), 79. On the attempts of some black film makers to thematize and disrupt Hollywood's construction of black sexuality, see the essays by Henry Louis Gates, Jr., bell hooks, and Jacquie Jones in *Black American Cinema*, ed. Manthia Diawara (New York: Routledge, 1993).] For a briefer discussion of *Casablanca* and *Ghost* that treats both films in the context of a general discussion of racial ideology, see my "Look! A Negro" in *Reading Rodney King/Reading Urban Uprising*, ed. Robert Gooding-Williams (New York: Routledge, 1993), 160–63.

6   Eco's essay appears in his *Travels in Hyperreality* (New York: Harcourt, Brace, Jovanovich, 1983). The full citation for Ray's book is *A Certain Tendency of the Hollywood Cinema 1930–1980* (Princeton: Princeton University Press, 1985).

7   Rick kills Strasser and ends up with Louis. He also sends Ilsa off with Victor, and arranges for Sam to work for Ferrari.

8   See, for example, Eve Sedgwick, *Between Men* (New York: Columbia University Press, 1985).

9   See Ray, *A Certain Tendency*, 101–102.

10 Rick has Sam serve this function when, just before the "Paris flashback," he asks him to sing "As Time Goes By." Ilsa does the same, during her first conversation with Sam at Rick's. "Play it once Sam," she says, "for old time's sake."

11 Here, of course, I mean to invoke Marx's famous analysis of commodity fetishism in the first volume of *Das Kapital*.

12 See, for example, Frantz Fanon's discussion in Chapter 6 of *Black Skin, White Masks*, trans. Charles Markmann (New York: Grove Press, 1967). See also Robert Miles, *Racism* (New York: Routledge, 1989), 27–28.

13 Cameron Bailey addresses related issues in his "Nigger/Lover: The Thin Sheen of Race in 'Something Wild'," *Screen* 29 (1988): 28–40.

14 See Leslie Fiedler's "Come Back to the Raft Ag'in, Huck Honey," in his *An End to Innocence* (Boston: Beacon, 1955), 148. Ray (107–108) and Harmetz (350) also discuss the connection between *Casablanca* and *Huck Finn*.

15 Rick's homophobia, which is implicit in his resistance to Sam's seduction, appears explicitly when he rebuffs Sasha (the Russian bartender) who kisses

Rick after the latter has helped one of Louis's potential victims win at the gambling table. According to Harlan Lebo, Carl Schaefer, the head of Warner Bros. Research Department, insisted that the representation of Rick's aversion to Sasha's kiss be handled delicately—in the interest of international relations! (See Lebo, *Casablanca*, 115.)

16 See Doris Sommer, *Foundational Fictions: The National Romances of Latin America* (Berkeley: University of California Press, 1991), 30–51, for a significant theoretical discussion of the ways in which erotic and political plots can function as allegories of each other. For a hilarious and heavily sexualized reading/re-imagining of the scene I've been discussing, see Robert Coover, *A Night at the Movies* (New York: Linden Press, 1987), 156–87.

17 Rick tells Ilsa that she is a part of Victor's work in the famous "airport" scene that concludes *Casablanca*. Earlier in the movie, Rick makes arrangements to have Sam go to work for Ferrari.

18 Rick's renunciation of heterosexual desire need not be read as a renunciation of desire *per se*. Much has been made, in fact, of the homoerotic connotations suggested by his beginning to have a "beautiful friendship" with Louis. From my perspective, it is significant that, after ditching Ilsa, Rick chooses to run off with Louis, and not with Sam.

19 In *The Birth of a Nation*, Reconstruction appears as a cause of social chaos and anarchy in the post-Civil War South. This reading of Reconstruction is quite questionable, and, according to Manthia Diawara, has been contested by African-American spectators. See Manthia Diawara, "Black Spectatorship: Problems of Identification and Resistance," *Screen* 29 (1988), 67–70.

20 Here, and in what follows, I am drawing on Laura Mulvey's well-known and influential analysis of the male gaze in her "Visual Pleasure and Narrative Cinema." See Laura Mulvey, *Visual and Other Pleasures* (Bloomington: Indiana University Press, 1989), 14–26. I am also addressing the question of interracial sexuality and sexual looking, described as "one of the most difficult questions raised by African-American history and literature" by Jane Gaines in "White Privilege and Looking Relations," in *Issues in Feminist Film Criticism*, ed. Patricia Erens (Bloomington: Indiana University Press, 1990), 208.

21 *Passion Fish* has a female "black cupid" who mediates the relationship between a white heterosexual couple. By providing her a black male lover, and by suggesting, at one point, that the white male member of this heterosexual couple could be sexually interested in her, the film undermines the perception of her as a cupid figure, which perception it has otherwise helped to produce.

22 See Tania Modleski, *Feminism Without Women* (New York: Routledge, 1991), 132.

23 Modleski, *Feminism Without Women*, 132.

24 For a brief discussion of the "Jezebel" stereotype, see K. Sue Jewell, *From Mammy to Miss America and Beyond* (New York: Routledge, 1993), 46–7.

25 The ambivalence implicit in the white desire to have access to while controlling and repressing "black sexuality" has deep roots in American popular culture. A useful point of departure for thinking about this issue is David Roediger's *The Wages of Whiteness: Race and the Making of the American Working Class* (New York: Verso, 1991). See, on the same theme, Eric Lott's "Love and Theft: The Racial Unconscious of Blackface Minstrelsy," *Representations* 39 (1992): 23–50.

26 A retake is the recycling of a character or character-type from one story to another. For my attempt to use this idea in the context of developing and applying a notion of racial ideology, see my "Look, a Negro!"

I wish to thank Cynthia Freeland, Amy Kaplan, Karen Sanchez-Eppler, Thomas Wartenberg, and Werner Sollers for their comments on an earlier draft of this paper.

9 An Unlikely Couple

The Significance of Difference in *White Palace*

Thomas E. Wartenberg

Perhaps the central contribution by a loose collection of European theorists grouped together under the name "postmodern" is the valorization of difference. At least since the Enlightenment, Western philosophic thought has been dominated by what is now claimed to be an illicit universalization of the norms of a particular social group—that of white European upper-class Christian males—and the claim that all departures from those norms were deficiencies. The hope guiding the Enlightenment was to create a rational culture through the actual universalization of those norms. Although there have always been critics of this Enlightenment vision, only recently have the terms of the debate changed. On the current intellectual scene, it is the defenders of the Enlightenment who are struggling to show that their vision is not corrupted by a failure to acknowledge difference.

I raise the issue of difference because I see it as a question that has been addressed in a number of films I refer to as "unlikely couple films." There are many unlikely couple films that span many different genres, including such well-known films as Chaplin's *City Lights*, Capra's *It Happened One Night*, Kramer's *Guess Who's Coming to Dinner*, and Fassbinder's *Ali: Fear Eats the Soul*. Each film depicts the attempt to form a romantic couple across a social difference, be it class, religion, ethnicity, sexual orientation, etc. By focusing on the difficulties and advantages of these socially-differentiated couples, the films present their assessment of the significance of these differences for society.

In questioning the significance of difference, these films attempt to resolve a fundamental social tension. By raising the question of what import social difference plays in the formation of a couple, the films attempt to mediate two central beliefs held by members of our culture: that individuality is fundamental and that a person's membership in a social group determines his or her life prospects in a fundamental way.

In this chapter, I shall look at the contradictions in the attempt of one recent film, *White Palace* (Luis Mandoki, 1990), to present a conception of social difference. I choose this film because, unlike many unlikely couple films, *White Palace* presents social difference as something that cannot simply be overcome or erased.[1] Initially, the film articulates a position amenable to postmodernism by showing that, despite the presence of a number of social differences, its central couple is not really unlikely. It asserts that the two "unlikely" partners in this couple are really well suited to one another, for they allow each other to achieve a more authentic life. However, the film's ending betrays its own point of view on social difference. Although ambiguous between an interpretation that asserts the superiority of working-class values and one that asserts the impossibility of shedding one's original class position, the ending contradicts the film's earlier assertion about the significance of difference.

What exactly does it mean to call a couple *unlikely?* Only within societies in which a person's membership in a specific social group determines how she or he will be treated are there unlikely couples, for the claim that a couple is unlikely reflects a judgment that the social identity of the partners is inappropriate. Within American society in the 1950s a couple composed of an African-American and a European-American was an example of a couple that bridged two distinct social groups. Since many Americans thought the "mixing of races" inappropriate, such a couple would have qualified as unlikely because it embodied social difference. But equally unlikely, at the time, was a couple composed of two men or two women, for the assumption of heterosexuality dictated that only a man and a woman could form a couple. The unlikeliness of a couple is not simply that its partners come from two different social groups, although that will generally be the case. In regard to sexual orientation, the fact that the two partners come from the same group makes the couple unlikely because the prevailing norms favor cross-group couples. The unlikeliness of a couple stems from its violation of the prevailing norms of that society or group that specify the appropriate groups from which partners may come.

To qualify as an unlikely couple film, the unlikeliness of the couple must be a central narrative focus. Such films show how the partners' membership in different social groups functions as an obstacle to the formation of the couple. There are different types of obstacles to the formation of unlikely couples. For example, the outright banning of the couple by a powerful social figure such as a father or a king is one type of hindrance. But such barriers may also be more internal and psychological, as when one of the partners is not fully able to accept the other as a partner because of that individual's social difference. In unlikely couple films, the unlikeliness of the couple is not simply a sociological fact about its composition but a central narrative feature that focuses attention on the significance of social difference.

If unlikely couple films require the presence of an obstacle to the couple's formation—thus explicitly linking the social characteristics of the two partners to their narratives—they also include an opposing narrative tendency, one that supports the formation of the couple, namely the romantic attraction between the two partners. In some cases, the desire between the two partners is not predicated on the social difference between them, giving credence to the old saw that "love is blind;" in other cases, the desire is itself implicated in society's assessment of social difference, as when the "otherness of the other" is seen as sexually alluring. In these films, romantic love is generally depicted as antithetical to social difference, as a counter-tendency to the attribution of significance to difference. Insofar as the films favor the overcoming of difference, love is the social force they recognize as antagonistic to a hierarchically structured society.[2]

With these considerations in mind, I turn to *White Palace* in order to show the film's contradictory presentation of unlikeliness. The central claim of *White Palace* is that the unlikeliness of its couple is a positive factor for the two partners, since it frees them from the dominance of restrictive social norms and expectations and thereby contributes to their living more authentically. But despite this interesting and innovative presentation of the role that social difference can play in the lives of human beings, *White Palace* succumbs to a stereotypical understanding of social difference. Especially in its ending, the film retreats from its own conception of social difference. In exploring the nature of this retreat, I will also gesture to some general conclusions about its significance.

White Palace places the tension between attraction and unlikeliness primarily within the consciousness of its male protagonist, Max Baron (James Spader). Max is torn between a desire to satisfy his social group's judgment of the appropriate extent of his unlikely relationship with Nora Baker (Susan Sarandon) and the fact that Nora provides him with an important source of intimacy and support that allows him to live in fuller accord with his own desires. More specifically, the issue is the judgment by Max's nouveau riche Jewish friends that Nora—an older, working-class "shiksa"—is not a fit partner for the young advertising executive. This threatens to predominate over his own experience of her as providing him with access to a fuller and more adequate sense of himself and a deeper experience of human life.

As this brief summary shows, there are a number of social differences between Max and Nora that qualify them as an unlikely couple. The first difference is their economic class. Max is a yuppie, living in a swanky and elegant apartment complex. He makes a lot of money as an ad-man, a fact we become aware of during the title sequence of the film as we see Max driving home from work in his new Volvo, with a number of identical, dry-cleaned and pressed suits. Nora, on the other hand, is a waitress at a fast-food joint, the White Palace from which the film takes its title. The economic difference between Max and Nora is made even more visible by the fact that she lives in a ramshackle house in a "bad" section of town.

The second social category that separates Max from Nora is age. Although a widower at 27, Max is still young enough to be viewed as a good catch by the members of his group and society at large. At 41, on the other hand, Nora is viewed as no longer young—i.e. desirable. This means that there is something inappropriate about the age distribution in this couple, a fact registered, for example, when Max's mother remarks upon first meeting Nora, "She's no spring chicken." The assumption behind such a comment is that there is something questionable in the fact that a young and highly eligible young man like Max would choose to have a relationship with a woman Nora's age.

The age difference between Max and Nora constitutes a social difference between them because of certain gender stereotypes. A couple in which the ages were reversed—one composed of a 41-year-old male and a 27-year-old female—would not be seen by many viewers as violating social norms. Only because such viewers see a 41-year-old woman no longer as desirable as a 27-year-old male is such a couple deemed inappropriate.[3]

The final social difference between Max and Nora is their religion. Max is Jewish and Nora is an ex-Catholic. This difference is actually more complex than conveyed by this simple statement. Nora is a lapsed Catholic for whom religion is not important. And although religion *per se* does not play a significant role in Max's life, his Jewishness is significant because of how his social milieu is constituted.

The religious difference between Max and Nora is really a synecdoche for a more general difference in the role that other people play in their lives. On the one hand, Nora is presented as someone whose relationships with other human beings are rather insignificant. The only people that she has any relationships with are the bartender in the bar where Max encounters her, a black co-worker with whom she rides the bus, and a sister from whom she has been estranged for years. This means, among other things, that Nora has no social group whose view of the couple could function as an obstacle to its formation. Only Max's social group is allowed to judge the relationship. This manner of representing Nora allows the film to hedge on how Nora's class identity will impact their relationship. In fact, because Nora is presented as essentially an asocial individual without any significant ties to other human beings, the question of what it is to be a working-class woman is raised in terms that already compromise the film's ability to answer that question.

Max, on the other hand, leads a life fundamentally shaped by his membership in a social group whose central members are young men his age, Jewish, and professional. This social group functions as a clan that treats people who are not of the same socio-economic status as outsiders, people who somehow don't belong.[4] As a result, Max's membership in this clan is an obstacle to his relationship with Nora, since she is prohibited from merging into its familiarity (in the literal sense). Max therefore experiences a tension between his relationship with Nora and the role that this social group had played in his life.

The barrier to Max's evolving relationship with Nora stems from the judgment of this group. From the point of view of the nouveau riche Jewish yuppies who compose Max's reference group, Nora is an inappropriate partner for him. In making this judgment, the group uses Nora's structural social characteristics—her class, religion, and (gendered) age—to form a stereotypical understanding of what she can mean to Max. Employing the stereotype of the older, non-Jewish, working-class woman as sexually available and knowledgeable, the clan believes it is able to understand the appropriate terms for Max's relationship since the basis of their relationship must be sex.[5] Women like her, the clan assumes, are fine for affairs, sexual dalliances; however, it is a serious mistake to bring them home, to treat them as appropriate partners for long-term relationships.

The attitude towards women exemplified by the members of Max's clan is a familiar one in which women are divided into two mutually exclusive categories. There are a number of dichotomies that can be used to register this distinction: bad girl/good girl; whore/virgin; girlfriend/wife; dumb blonde/brunette. Whatever the specific terms used to designate the dichotomy, women in the former group are seen as sexually exciting, but not fit to be men's permanent companions; women in the latter group lack sexual allure, but are what men must settle for in their domestic lives. So while Max's association with Nora is understandable, indeed enviable, so long as it is kept within the appropriate limits—a purely sexual relationship that is not "serious"—Max's own absorption in the relationship challenges his group's sense of the appropriate limits to that relationship.

This aspect of *White Palace*'s representational strategy displaces class differences among women onto differences in their sexuality. That is, the film's use of the bad girl/good girl scheme presents class differences among women as differences in their sexual natures, for bad girls are working-class women and good girls, women of Max's class. By using this strategy of displacement, the film is able to both address and conceal class differences, since class is present in the form of women's sexual stereotypes, and is thereby obscured.

But *White Palace* doesn't simply employ this dichotomous scheme of women's sexual stereotypes; it subjects it to critical scrutiny by showing that, contrary to the stereotype, Nora is really appropriate for Max. Using sexuality as a means for interrogating social difference, the film problematizes the assumption that knowledge of a person's structural social characteristics—her class, race, gender, age—are sufficient for understanding the grounds of her connection to another human being. The film asserts that, social characteristics notwithstanding, indeed, precisely because of them, Nora is not merely an appropriate partner for Max, but Max is lucky to have found her.[6] *White Palace* thus raises the question of how two individuals with such different structural social characteristics could come to form a couple.

Given its use of the stereotype that differences between Max and Nora make them inappropriate partners, *White Palace* has to work to get its audience to view them as really appropriate. One factor that works in favor of the audience's belief that Nora and Max are really well-suited is casting of the two characters, for the audience's awareness of James Spader and Susan Sarandon makes it anticipate their romantic involvement. The audience's experience of the film involves an interplay between the narrative level on which the characters are simply determined as fictional and its awareness that the actors who are playing these roles are the film's stars. It is not just that they are stars, however, for it is precisely these two stars—both of whom had established identities as sexually intriguing in their previous films—that makes the audience anticipate their sexual union. While James Spader had just established himself as a lead actor through his role as the sensitive but damaged videographer in *Sex, Lies, and Videotape*, Susan Sarandon had acquired a persona as the older, sexual initiator of men in such films as *Bull Durham*. Playing on these roles, the film sets up an anticipation of a similar relationship between the stars in this film. The non-transparency of the film actor marks an important way in which

Hollywood cinema differs from other art forms, for the audience's awareness of the identity of the actors never becomes fully transparent or, to be more precise, is always something that can emerge into its awareness, thus allowing for a tension between character and actor that is not possible in, say, a novel.[7]

But this anticipation of the formation of the Max-Nora couple does not explain why the audience comes to believe that Nora is really suitable for Max. Indeed, the audience's desire for the development of a sexual relationship between the two characters may rely on the same stereotyped understanding of women of Nora's type that Max's clan exhibits. We therefore need to search further to understand how the audience comes to think of Max and Nora as suitable mates and not just sexual partners.

Although the neatness/messiness dichotomy is not a specifically *social* difference, it is another dichotomized difference that separates Max from Nora. This difference plays an important role in getting the audience to accept the appropriateness of the Max-Nora couple, for the film claims that judging appropriateness on the basis of an apparent—in both senses of that word—difference is a mistake, for appearances may conceal a deeper level at which there is real compatibility.

From the first scene in which he appears Max is depicted as fanatically, even obsessively neat. As he comes home from work and enters his apartment, he stops twice to rearrange the nap on his expensive and tasteful Persian rug, making sure that no thread is misplaced. He places his freshly cleaned suits in the closet, allowing the audience to see multiple identical suits all hung neatly in two rows. There is nothing in his apartment that is out of its place, no trace of an item whose presence is not explicitly controlled and ordered.

In contrast to this, Nora's slovenliness seems almost a caricature. When Max first enters her house, it is strewn with all sorts of refuse, looking more like an abandoned shack than a person's home. Using a subjective shot, the film allows the audience to experience for itself the disarray that confronts Max as he enters her home. It really does look, as the saying goes, like a hurricane had hit, and Max's queasy reaction to what he sees parallels that of the audience. The film stresses the importance of this dichotomy by having Max pick up a half-eaten sandwich during his first sexual encounter with Nora, thereby emphasizing the problem that her messiness portends.

Considering only the level of appearance, and thinking about the difference between Max and Nora's neatness as a symbol for their compatibility, one would judge them to be deeply incompatible. Max's need for order would conflict with Nora's seeming lack of concern with it, making them unsuitable partners. There is even an incident early in their relationship that initially seems to support such an interpretation. One evening, Max arrives at Nora's house for dinner with a present for her. She is very excited and hurries to unwrap it only to find that Max has bought her a dustbuster, as if her lack of one were responsible for the messiness of her home. Nora's response is to throw Max out, telling him that flowers and perfume are appropriate presents, but a dustbuster is not. This scene could support an interpretation of the neatness issue as a sign of Max and Nora's incompatibility, for it would show Nora as not willing to meet Max's demand that she clean up her house. The only problem is that, as he leaves the house, Max—and the audience—notice that Nora has already cleaned the kitchen and prepared a table, complete with candles and flowers, for their romantic dinner together. Nora's messiness is, in some sense, a choice that she has made.

The significance of this detail emerges in the course of the film, as the audience comes to see that Max's compulsive neatness and Nora's equally compulsive messiness are not simply personal character traits that divide them from each other. Specifically, the film uses the issue of neatness as a metaphor for the question of what makes two people appropriate for one another. Its answer is that there may a deep connection between two individuals who seem to all appearances to be highly inappropriate and, hence, an unlikely couple. Because the exaggerated behaviors of both Nora and Max in regard to neatness/messiness are actually different responses to a similar event in their lives, this *difference* between them *is actually a source of connection, rather than a barrier to their union.* Prior to their encounter, both had suffered the loss of a significant member of their immediate families—Max's wife Janey had died in a car accident while Nora's son Jimmy had died as the result of substance abuse. For both of them, this loss was catastrophic in that it made them unable to continue living their lives in the same way that they had previously. Max's response was to seek to control his experience more completely, as if that would keep him from suffering; hence, his obsessive neatness. Nora's loss of a sense of purpose in her life, on the other hand, caused her not to care about what she did or how she kept her house; as a result, she appears slovenly.

By showing that the apparent difference between Max and Nora actually conceals a deeper commonality between them, the film asks its audience to realize that this difference, rather than a sign of Max and Nora's incompatibility, is actually the appearance of a common experience that allows them to share something they cannot share with others. Their common experience of loss provides the grounds for their attraction to each other at a level that goes beneath the surface characteristics that keep them apart. Instead of seeing human life as fully comprehensible in terms of a set of social categories—as do Max's friends—*White Palace* requires its audience to see that a similar experience underlies and cuts across the social categories that divide Max and Nora. While this might tempt one to see the film as relying on the idea of an essential commonality of human experience more basic than social distinctions, such an interpretation is not necessary. It is enough to say that the film posits a source of connection in the individual biographies of these two human beings that is not reducible to a common social category. Precisely because they share the experience of loss, Max and Nora are more similar than their different appearances would lead one to expect. They each have become detached from certain social expectations and patterns that Max's clan takes to be the ultimate standards of human life and experience.

In fact, when the viewer judges neatness to be a barrier to their relationship, she or he employs the very mode of judgment the film criticizes. The film counters the assumption made by Max's clan that it is able to understand the basis of the relationship by means of Nora's class, age, and religion. It presents their relationship as based on a shared experience of loss, an experience that will not let them settle for the same surface satisfactions that drive Max's peers. The film thus asserts that an individual's specific experiences are important sources of connection with others.

But the film goes on to suggest something else, namely, that the social differences between Max and Nora allow them to attain the special relationship they have with one another. Each is unable to be seen for what she or he is by members of his or her own class. The film suggests that the working-class men in the bar Nora frequents see her as simply a waitress looking for company—a sexually available older woman. The women we hear pursuing Max through his answering machine see him as quite a catch—as a male with all the social characteristics they deem necessary for a partner. For both Max and Nora, such possible partners are limiting, for they keep the relationship within a set of acceptable social parameters. Only by going outside of their respective groups, the film suggests, can they find another human being with whom to share their deepest concerns and experiences.

But the central aspect of Max and Nora's relationship that the film asks us to view as appropriate is their sexual relationship. The most notorious scene in the film, the one in which Max and Nora's sexual relationship begins, shows Nora seducing the sleeping Max. Prior to this, Max had repeatedly turned down Nora's attempts to initiate sex. Nora ignores his rebuffs and begins to fellate him after he has fallen asleep on her couch. While it may seem remarkable to claim that the sexual relationship resulting from this seduction makes Nora a suitable partner for Max, this is precisely what *White Palace* asserts. But to see why this makes sense, we need to look in some detail at the film's identification of Nora with Marilyn Monroe, for it is through this identification that *White Palace* makes its point.

From the moment that Nora is presented to the audience as more than a worker in a hamburger joint, her identification with Marilyn is emphasized. When Nora runs into Max in a bar, she asks him whether people tell him that he looks like Tony Curtis. While this may seem like a rather bizarre association since James Spader bears no resemblance to Curtis, the key to its meaning becomes clear when Nora proceeds to quote a line of Monroe's from *Some Like It Hot* (Billy Wilder, 1959):

> I had a wonderful dream. I was sorting your shells and mixing your cocktails and when I woke up, I wanted to swim right back to you.

Nora is thinking of Curtis as he appeared in that film and placing herself in the role of Monroe, an identity the film continues to stress once we see Nora's home adorned with pictures of Monroe. (Upon entering her house and noticing those pictures, Max's initial response is to ask, "What exactly is there between you and Marilyn Monroe?" She answers, "Oh, she's just so fucked up and glamorous, and losing and fighting all the time, losing and fighting." It remains for us to see how this response applies to Nora herself.) So in order to understand Nora's view of her relationship to Max as well as her relationship to Monroe, we need to turn to *Some Like It Hot*.

The relevant aspect of *Some Like It Hot* is the development of a romantic relationship between Sugar Cane (Marilyn Monroe) and Joe (Tony Curtis). Joe, a womanizing saxophone player, hides from some gangsters by disguising himself as Josephine, a female saxophone player, and joining an all-woman band. In the band, he meets Sugar Cane, a character in the dumb blonde tradition, who is vulnerable to seduction by womanizers like him.[8] The category dumb blonde, you will recall, signifies a woman who, because of her social characteristics and appearance, is seen as available to men for the satisfaction of their sexual desires. The film claims there is more to Sugar than this cliché, for underneath the dumb blonde image there is a deeper reality: the ability of a human being to triumph over pain and loss. Sugar remains a caring and vulnerable human being despite repeated desertion by the saxophonists with whom she had become involved. The film presents the appearance of the sexually available dumb blonde as obscuring the presence of a caring human being. In a film in which male characters are constantly disguising themselves, and thus not appearing to be what they are, the question of what lies behind these appearances is repeatedly raised. *Some Like It Hot* asks us to accept its perception of a deeper reality to this dumb blonde than her appearance suggests.

To seduce Sugar, Joe invents a character for himself that is intended to satisfy Sugar's desire to find a rich husband, but that also highlights the difficulty human beings experience in overcoming the loss of a loved one. Joe poses as a multi-millionaire who talks like Cary Grant and is supposed to be heir to the Shell Oil fortune—"Shell Jr.," Sugar calls him. Joe is able to seduce Sugar by claiming that Shell Jr. is impotent, unable to be aroused by a woman as a result of the accidental death of his fiancée. Posing as a multimillionaire on a yacht that is not his own, Joe sets up Sugar to try to cure him of his love-caused disability.

As in *White Palace*, the film presents a morally questionable seduction. The film expects its audience to vicariously enjoy Joe's seduction of Sugar. For this to be possible, the audience has to accept, at least partially, the idea that Sugar is a dumb blonde, thus invoking the idea of the attractive, but older working-class woman as both sexually exciting and a suitable object for male manipulation. In part, the outlandishness of the seduction story that Sugar swallows allows the audience to feel morally and intellectually superior to her as well as to enjoy her role in her victimization. Such a view is reinforced by the fact that it is Marilyn who plays Sugar, for this is part of her image as well. This spoof repeats the dumb blonde tradition that it seeks to criticize.

However, the success of Joe's seduction of Sugar is a pyrrhic victory, for the dumb blonde wins the heart of her would-be seducer, a result the anticipation of which also contributes to the audience's enjoyment of her apparent victimization. The very quality that allows Sugar/Marilyn—once again, the actor intrudes her presence—to be seduced by the duplicitous Joe/Josephine/Shell Jr./Curtis is an important virtue that will save Joe from his own superficiality in regard to women, thus enabling him to live a fuller life.

The result of Sugar's attentions is, not surprisingly, Joe's arousal; but, contrary to his intentions, he also falls in love with her. Her innocence and vulnerability, the very qualities that allow her to be such an easy target for seduction, become the reasons for Joe's attachment to her. Joe is caught by the net of his own seduction. Sugar's willingness to be trapped makes Joe see beyond her sexy appearance to her kind heart. And this entails that the stereotyped image of the dumb blonde is not adequate to the reality of Sugar/Marilyn.[9]

Some Like It Hot, then, is a film that explores the stereotype of certain women as suitable objects of male manipulation. It asserts that there is more to these women than the stereotype of the bad girl acknowledges, for they are able to help men escape from logics of desire that keep them from true intimacy. Joe's desire, ruled by a logic of conquest, as well as the invented desire of Shell Jr., ruled by a logic of frozen withdrawal, are both rendered inoperative by Sugar's ministrations. The serious point made by the film's comic antics is that these male logics of desire are inadequate.

White Palace asks to be seen as a version of *Some Like It Hot*. Indeed, since Nora is viewing her own action through the narrative of *Some Like It Hot*, her seduction of the sleeping Max is not simply the act of an over-aggressive, sexually available woman who sees in Max the opportunity to satisfy her own desire. Unlike the women of his social class who see him simply as a good catch, Nora understands the logic of Max's desire. By seeing Max as Shell Jr., Nora is able to understand that Janey's death has functioned analogously to the fictive death of Shell Jr.'s girlfriend, trapping Max in a frozen withdrawal from his own sexual desire. Identifying herself with Marilyn/Sugar, Nora sees herself as able to thaw Max, to allow him to reexperience his sexual desire, to return to a life in which sexuality plays an important role. But unlike *Some Like It Hot*, *White Palace* explores the full range of effects that such a death can have on a person by associating Max's lack of desire with his entire world. In seducing Max, Nora is acting with a vision of what he really needs, a vision that requires her to dismiss his rejection of her sexual come-ons. In return for this, she expects that, analogous to Joe/Josephine/Shell Jr., Max will come to see her as a fit partner.

Common to *Some Like It Hot* and *White Palace* is the suggestion that a full sexual experience can undermine the dominance of the social stereotypes in terms of which human beings tend to live their lives. It is the force of this sexual experience that binds Max to Nora, that overturns his sense of life as within his control, that allows him to experience himself beyond the categories of his social group's understanding.[10]

By using a character's understanding of a film to allow her to move beyond a superficial understanding of another character, *White Palace* asserts that Hollywood films, so often judged superficial, can play an important role in people's lives by providing them with new and insightful ways of understanding other human beings that go beyond the stereotyped ways in which people interact with one another. In making this claim, *White Palace* is challenging the usual opposition between entertainment and art, between pleasure and significance, asserting that, just as in the cases of Nora and Marilyn, an appealing surface should not be mistaken for a lack of depth. While overtly critiquing the male view of attractive working-class women as superficial and dumb, the film also criticizes the elitist view of Hollywood film that equates its attractiveness with a lack of depth.[11]

Even though the audience comes to believe Nora is an appropriate partner for Max because she allows him to live more authentically, Max himself does not initially share this view. Using Hegelian terms, the point is that, although Nora is *in herself* the appropriate partner for Max, Max needs to come to realize this *for himself*. At this point, we observing viewers make a judgment about her appropriateness that Max has not yet been able to achieve. The rest of the film portrays the experiences that bring Max to this realization for himself. But first, the film depicts Max's own ambivalence about Nora, his inability to accept her. Only after she decides that she cannot continue in the relationship and leaves St. Louis in order to be free of it, does Max come to share the film's own understanding of her significance for him, to see for himself what Nora really means to him.

The dawning on Max of Nora's true significance comes at a party given by Heidi Solomon, one of the women in his social group whom the film has repeatedly invoked as an example of the socially acceptable partner for him. Heidi is an attractive Jewish yuppie, the embodiment of all the values of Max's clan: sophisticated, beautiful, artistic, wealthy. Nonetheless, at her party, Max looks around at his friends and sees them with eyes from which the spectacles of social appropriateness have been removed. He begins by asking, "How do you know who's right for each other?" and continues by pointing out the reality of his friends' lives. He mentions the divorces that have occurred and how one couple repeatedly bad-mouths one another. Social acceptability, it seems, is not a guarantee of genuine appropriateness. He rises from the couch upon which he has been sitting and, to the consternation of the other guests, inspects Heidi's dustbuster, exclaiming, "There's no dust in it!" The climax of Max's public reflections on appropriateness invokes the dustbuster scene with Nora discussed earlier. The audience is now asked to see the dustbuster as a symbol of the emptiness of the lives of those in Max's clan, just as it was earlier asked to see Nora's messiness as something other than it appeared. Max now sees neatness as a sign of spiritual emptiness, and realizes that Nora is the appropriate partner for him. All that remains is for the film to engineer a reconciliation between Max and Nora, for he has now had an experience that qualifies him to be her partner.

Ironically, in presenting Max's reunion with Nora, *White Palace* undermines its own assertion that social difference can allow partners in a couple to experience themselves more authentically. This is so despite the ambiguity in the film's ending. Both of the ways in which the ending can be interpreted deny the film's earlier affirmation of social difference as a positive force in the couple. In providing narrative closure to the story of Max and Nora's unlikely couple, *White Palace* undermines its own portrayal of that relationship as an affirmation of social difference.

The most natural interpretation of the ending of *White Palace* sees the reunion of Max and Nora as privileging working-class values. On this view, Max's reconciliation with Nora is secured by his total repudiation of his social context—that of his mother and his friends. The setting of the film's ending shows Max in a context that is totally determined by Nora's values: in New York (thus extracting Max from the web of social relationships that he had in St. Louis), living in a run-down apartment with a view of garbage (thus rejecting his compulsive neatness), and hoping to work as a teacher (picking up the career he had previously given up for reasons never clarified, but at least no longer in advertising, that profession most concerned with appearances rather than reality). Max's construction of this context through a simple inversion of his own values breaks down Nora's resistance to resuming their relationship. This Prince Charming gets his Cinderella by repudiating the princely life he has been living.

On this interpretation, the ending valorizes one term of each of the social divisions that had separated Max and Nora (except age). Rather than showing Max trying to find a way of overcoming his need to live a life that is acceptable to his friends, the film portrays Max as simplifying his life by cutting off all social ties other than the one he has with Nora, thus turning his own life into a replica of hers. In so doing, the film asserts that every aspect of Nora's working-class way of life is superior to the yuppie lives of Max's friends.

By having Max embody the subordinate category of each of these dichotomies, the film adopts a simplistic view of social difference. Rather than subverting the hold of such oppositional categories on thought and judgment and seeking to show Max attempting to forge a life in touch with the deep level of human experience he found through his relationship with Nora, *White Palace* subverts its own sense of social difference as affirming. Instead, it opts for the more usual Hollywood view that presents working-class life as superior to the artifice of upper-class life.

Max's inversion of his own life is as inadequate a means of living a life as his earlier acceptance of his friends' judgments of appropriateness. In rejecting the values of his previous social group, Max rejects not only the sort of superficial snobbery that characterized that group, but also aspects of his own life that had previously mattered a great deal to him. This point is brought home by the film's use of musical taste as a class marker. Early in the film, when Max is driving her home from the bar, Nora asks him what music is playing. He responds by characterizing the opera to which they are listening as the most beautiful music in the world, exhibiting for the first time a strong emotional attachment to something. Only in relation to this music does Max reveal himself to be a human being with deep feelings; all the rest of his life is an attempt to keep those feelings in check. Nora responds to his explanation by asking him if he has any Oak Ridge Boys, thereby establishing musical taste as a class marker: the upper-class, sophisticated Max is an aficionado of opera, while the working-class waitress likes country music. At that point, although we perceive Nora's lack of sophistication as an obstacle to the relationship, we also enjoy her refusal to be intimidated by dominant cultural values. No hushed respect here.

But when Max approaches Nora in the final scene, having given up his home, his job, and his family in order to be with her, to show her that he has changed and no longer accepts the values of his clan, he asks her if she has any Oak Ridge Boys (this being a clever response to her request that he order). The message is that he is now a fit partner for her because he has rejected the "high" art of opera and is ready to be a fan of the "low" art of country music, and it initiates the vulgar final shots of the film in which Max symbolically screws Nora on a table in the deli where she works.

This choice on Max's part shows that the film has undermined its own earlier espousal of social difference as a positive force in human life. Despite its sensitive portrayal of the basis of human connection in the early parts of the film, *White Palace* reverts here to a simple dichotomous scheme. Rejecting opera for country music is simply not an appropriate way to resolve the tension between high and low, any more than rejecting art cinema is an appropriate response to the tension between it and Hollywood films. It is just the flip side of the value scheme that Max had previously accepted, one that validates the high at the expense of the low. What is required is a way of seeing both high and low as possible sources of valuable experience, that is to say, a rejection of the dichotomous scheme of social valuation itself.[12]

In making this claim, I have stressed the class terms in which this narrative can be read. But the film does not simply make its point in terms of class: the class difference between Max and Nora is represented as a difference in their religions. That is, the yuppie Max is Jewish and the working-class Nora is not. The parallel in their class and religious differences means that the film is able to use religion as a code for class difference. But this also means that the film's ending is anti-Semitic in its rejection of Judaism in favor of Nora's lapsed Catholicism.[13]

The second interpretation of Max's reunion with Nora emphasizes the significance of Max's mother, Edith. Edith plays an ongoing but relatively minor role in the film. We first see her when she and Max visit the grave of Max's wife the day after his first sexual encounter with Nora. During this scene, Edith's behavior embarrasses Max. Upset that Janey's grave has not been maintained in the manner for which they had paid, she falls to her knees and starts pulling up weeds despite Max's repeated assurance that he will take care of it. Once this inappropriate and embarrassing behavior is seen as characteristic of Edith, his attempt to live in the domesticated world of St. Louis yuppies takes on a different significance: instead of simply being his social milieu, that world becomes a space of retreat from the embarrassing features of his mother's world.

This sense is reinforced by his mother's actions during the ill-fated Thanksgiving dinner that sparks Nora's decision to break off her relationship with Max. Max picks up his mother at a house that seems more like Nora's than his own fancy apartment. Edith brings with her a noodle dish, as if she were arriving at a potluck instead of an immaculately prepared dinner. When she spills something, she screams, causing everyone to look at her. Despite calm assurances by her hosts, she continues to apologize and finally falls to her knees yet again, attempting to clean up the mess she has made. As the camera moves to Nora, we hear Edith telling Max, who has come to her side, that she didn't mean to embarrass him in front of his friends, as if that were a regular occurrence for which he regularly upbraided her.

This subplot establishes Edith as the ultimate source of Max's sense of social embarrassment and his desperate need to appear socially appropriate to his friends. He is ashamed of his mother because she is loud and clearly not of the same social class as the parents of his yuppie friends, the Horowitzes. (Although it is tempting to read Max's reaction as a case of Jewish self-hatred, it is class and not Jewishness that is the focus here.) Max's persistent sense of Nora as embarrassing to him and his inability to fully accept her is rooted in his relationship to his mother, and his coming to accept Nora should also be an acceptance of his mother, a working-class Jewish woman, and—finally and most importantly—an acceptance of himself as working-class.

Interpreted in this manner, the film's depiction of Max's reunion with Nora, rather than reinforcing its own conception of unlikeliness, reverts to a more stereotyped conception, employing an inversion of the Cinderella story. While Cinderella is elevated to her appropriate class status by the mediation of Prince Charming, Max is declassed through Nora's actions. *White Palace* sends its upstart young male back to the class from which he has come. The message that this portion of the film conveys is that social differences cannot be bridged, that one must return to the class from which one came.

Distinguishing a person's actual class from their inherited class allows one to categorize Max as having two different class statuses. While he is currently a member of the upper-class, he comes from the working-class. There is thus a disparity between his acquired wealth as an advertising executive and his inherited social class. From this point of view, Max's union with Nora, rather than being socially inappropriate, is socially appropriate, for it matches him with a partner from his inherited class. On this reading, the ending of *White Palace* demonstrates the futility of attempts to transcend one's inherited social class.

On both of these two interpretations, *White Palace*'s ending marks a retreat from the film's earlier affirmation of social difference. Through either an affirmation of working-class values or an assertion of the impossibility of social ascendancy, the film retreats from its earlier assertion that social difference in a couple can allow the partners to live more authentically. By adopting these more stereotypical portrayals of social class, *White Palace* retreats from its own attempt to make a statement about difference that transcends the standard views presented in Hollywood films.

This sense that the film's ending is a betrayal of its fundamental message is one that is not only an artifact of the viewers' responses and interpretations; it is present in the text of the film itself. The final shots of Max and Nora in the New York restaurant where she works show him symbolically screwing her on a table that he clears of its settings with a bold, sweeping, very masculine gesture. The cheers and applause of the other patrons of the restaurant who are now watching this scene, with much the same attitude as the actual film audience, disrupt the naturalistic assumptions of the rest of the film, creating a sense of disjuncture for the film's audience. The film thereby calls attention to the spectacle that the audience to the film has just witnessed by interposing a second audience—that of the restaurant patrons—between the real audience and the two main characters. The real audience becomes aware of itself as an audience to a spectacle through its perception of the restaurant audience's reaction to the scene.

But the film's invocation of the specular nature of itself and all film is not simply self-awareness on the part of the film. The parodic nature of the final shots arise out of the film's awareness that it has proceeded in bad faith with its audience in the final reconciliation. By calling attention to the process of viewing in this scene, *White Palace* also calls attention to the artifice of its own ending. The final parodic moment of the film is evidence of the film's own sense that it has itself acceded to the social demands of acceptability that it sought to criticize.

By adopting an ending of this type, *White Palace* allies itself with the reluctance of many Hollywood films to affirm the importance of social differences. It is particularly ironic that a film that shows how the demands of social conformity can impoverish the life of human beings winds up itself conforming to the social demand of the Hollywood system for narrative closure. Perhaps the ironic stance that the film takes towards its own ending is an attempt to tip off its audience to its own inability to achieve what it holds out as possible for its male lead, namely, the ability to live an authentic life beyond the confines of the demands of social conformity.

Notes

1 See, for example, my "'But Would You Want Your Daughter to Marry One?': The Representation of Race and Racism in *Guess Who's Coming to Dinner*," *The Journal of Social Philosophy* (forthcoming).

2 There are many other reasons for judging a couple to be unlikely, in the ordinary sense of that term. The category of unlikely couples focuses upon a specific type of unlikeliness in human relationships, one based on the assessment that the partners' membership in two social groups makes them inappropriate for one another.

3 There are a number of films that focus on age difference as causing a couple to be unlikely, including *Sunset Boulevard*, *All That Heaven Allows*, and *Harold and Maude*.

4 Although the parents of his friends are part of the group, Max's mother is not, a fact we learn when Rachel apologizes to Max for inviting her to Thanksgiving dinner. I discuss the relevance of this fact later in this chapter.

5 Sexual stereotypes thus function as the embodiment of class, religious, and age differences among women. This demonstrates the need to think of people's identities in non-additive terms. For an explicit argument concerning this point, see Elizabeth Spelman, *Inessential Other* (Boston: Beacon Press, 1991).

6 It is easy to see this film, as some feminist critics no doubt would, as reinforcing the stereotype that women are appropriate as nurturers of males. While such an interpretation is true to the film, I hope that it will not keep people from seeing that there is more at issue here than this level of gender stereotyping.

7 Virginia Wright Wegman argues, in *Creating the Couple: Love, Marriage, and Hollywood Performance* (Princeton: Princeton University Press, 1993), that the audience's awareness of the stars is central to understanding the appeal of these films.

8 For an interesting discussion of Monroe in light of this tradition, see Richard Dyer, "Monroe and Sexuality" in *Women and Film*, ed. Janet Todd (New York: Holmes and Meier, 1988), 69ff.

9 The "whore with a heart of gold" is another way to characterize the stereotype being invoked here.

10 Sex is therefore a symbol in these films, standing for an aspect of reality that is left out of lives determined by social stereotypes.

11 In this sense, we can see the entire narrative of the film as an allegory about the nature of film itself.

12 The film's portrayal of the working-class is not as positive as the ending suggests. Indeed, there are a number of respects in which it portrays working-class life and people in negative terms. There is the asocial nature of Nora's life, as if working-class people had no social life. This is especially stark in contrast to Max's highly social sense of his milieu. Second, there is the portrayal of working-class men. This occurs in the scene in which Nora and Max meet in the bar. The issue is why Nora is interested in Max. And at least part of the answer, aside from his physical beauty, is that he is not like working-class males, one of whom the film shows in the foreground as Nora circumnavigates the bar to talk with Max. The idea is that his androgyny is better than the macho style of working-class males. Thus, despite its valorization of the working-class in its ending, *White Palace* exhibits a highly ambivalent estimation of the value of working-class life.

13 The assertion of the superiority of working-class values also conflicts with the film's own manner of representing working-class males. In the initial bar scene in which Nora picks up Max, Max's appeal to Nora is presented by showing him to be different from the older, working-class males at the bar for whom Nora is simply a one-night stand. On this interpretation, the ending of the film completely undercuts the film's attempt to show class difference as affirming for partners in the couple.

part three ▊ **Specific Interpretations**

10 *2001*

Modern Art, and Modern Philosophy

Harvey Cormier

A ponderous amount has been written on the subject of modernism, but worthwhile things remain to be said about the relationship between philosophy and art in the modern era, especially where the art in question is film. In what follows I offer an account of the way modernist art in general is supposed to work, and then I attempt to apply this description to Stanley Kubrick's unique MGM science-fiction film *2001: A Space Odyssey* (1968). Doing so can help us to understand both this strange movie and the very idea of a modernist or avant-garde film.

The Shaggy Dog

Stanley Kubrick has asserted that he intends his films to work emotionally the way music does, that a film of his should be "a progression of moods and feelings."[1] This aspiration to music is typical of the kind of modern artist who thinks of music as the least imitative or "literary" of the arts, and who aims for similar nonrepresentational aesthetic effects in a different medium. Speaking specifically of *2001*, Kubrick has said:

> I tried to create a *visual* experience, one that bypasses verbalized pigeon-holing and directly penetrates the subconscious with an emotional and philosophical content.... I intended the film to be an intensely subjective experience that reaches the viewer at an inner level of consciousness, just as music does.[2]

But Kubrick has also deplored "modern art's almost total preoccupation with subjectivism," a preoccupation that has led, in his view, to "anarchy and sterility in the arts;"[3] and he is famous for obsessive and inventive uses of the latest technical cinematic artifices to create ever more objectively "real" scenes in his films. How can both of these attitudes go together? *2001* certainly reflects both, as impossibly realistic depictions of prehistoric earth and the future in outer space lead up to a climax that is an all-but-undecipherable light and sound show. As a somewhat roundabout way of approaching the question of what nonrepresentationality means in *2001*, I'd like to offer an analogy that seems to me an exceptionally good one for that film, and then defend in detail the idea that this metaphor reveals something about nonrepresentational modernist art in general. It is the metaphor of the shaggy dog story.

Here is a joke of a kind you might hear in any grade school:

> Two horses are stallmates in a barn. One looks up from his hay.
> First horse: Hey, aren't you Soandso? Didn't you win last week at Aqueduct Downs?
> Second horse: Yeah.
> First horse: What a great race you ran. I'll never be in your class.
> Second horse (modestly): Thanks, man.
> First horse: No, seriously, I'm no great racer. As a matter of fact, if I don't win the third race today, my owner's gonna send me to the glue factory!
> Second horse: Whoa!
> First horse: Wait. You're running in the third today, aren't you?
> Second horse: Yeah.
> First horse: Throw the race to me.
> Second horse (snorts): What? You can't be serious!
> First horse: Oh, please, I'm begging you! You're the only thing that can keep me and my meat by-products together!
> Second horse: I just don't know.
> A little terrier, kept in the stable to catch rats, trots up.
> Terrier (shouting): What do you mean, you don't know? He's begging you for his life! What are you, a horse or an ass?
> Second horse (looks wide-eyed at the dog, then back at the first horse): Look at that! A talking dog!

A shaggy dog story like this is supposed to be funny by virtue of being unfunny. It observes faithfully the decorum of joke fiction until the end, when an implicit compact between speaker and audience vanishes out the window, and, vanishing, becomes visible for the first time. Joke-tellers and joke-auditors discover themselves to be taking advantage of, and straining to have satisfied, conventional joke-type expectations, such as the convention that if a joke starts out taking a world full of talking animals for granted, that joke won't end by pointing out the absurdity of our idea that animals might be sitting around talking to one another. And it is the tiny shock of seeing ourselves now bare and blinking, stripped rudely of our silly, disposable protocols for laugh-giving and getting, that makes us laugh—or get mad—when we hear the punch line. We were expecting to take pleasure in the ridiculousness of someone or something else; now we find ourselves the buffoons on stage, with our way of life the target of even our own ridicule. "That's *it?*" we ask. "That's *stupid*," we say, either laughing or frowning.

Telling a joke is, of course, a small, homely performance, and jokes are, as it were, texts for little plays. Jokes like the one above can thus, with only a little straining, be seen as meager examples of what used to be called theater of the absurd: they at least display the preposterous dialogue and obscure meaning typical of absurdist theater. If this seems unlikely, consider the following two items. Samuel Beckett's dramaticule *Breath* goes like this: lights go up and the curtain rises to show rubble strewn around the stage, two loud cries are heard, then curtain and lights go down. And this is John Cage's *Theater Piece,* a work of musical theater, in its entirety: a soloist comes out on stage and throws a dead fish into a piano, then formally dressed helpers go out into the audience distributing cold pizza. These whimsical little works are not in themselves any more substantial than the little joke presented above, and they seem to be using similar humor to accomplish a similar end.

The goal that this play, this musical, and the above joke have in common is not simply the display of bizarreness or outrageousness or intentional simple-mindedness, but rather the *use* of those qualities both to stultify our expectations and, in the same gesture, to satisfy them. We are set up to expect a story with a beginning, a middle, and an end, and we don't get one; thereby we are told a story about ourselves and the way we tell and listen to stories, in theaters or on playgrounds. Usually, when we are told a story, we look through the artistic medium of storytelling to see what painful or funny things happened the other day to creatures like us, and that medium remains more or less transparent as we do so; but in the above specimens, instead of seeing the acts and misadventures of fictional others with whom we might identify ourselves, we see (nearly) nothing. The medium is as opaque as a switched-off TV tube. Nevertheless, as we look expectantly at the blank gray surface, straining to see an image, we shift focus a little, and there we are in the glass.

This strategem of self-disclosure (in a double sense) is, I would suggest, common in other, grander artworks in other media. Modern, modernist, or avant-gardist art in general toys with or discards narrative, verse structure and rhyme, pictorial representation, musical tonality, and all of the other typical, expectable features of Western art, thus producing low-plot or plot-free novels, plays, and films; paintings, photographs, and motion pictures of nothing and no one; music, verse, and drama that express no particular emotion; etc. How are these things supposed to work? What, if anything, are we supposed to see in them? They are all, in their different ways, shaggy dog stories. Through them we abandon our typical ways of looking at the world, hoping thereby to see ourselves as we really are.

Let me concede at once, even before I begin to argue for the usefulness of this little trope, that it may seem philistine and impertinent, and much too capricious a metaphor to use for the doughtily intellectualized artistic creations of high modernism. Is the claim that all these historic human works, in the making and defense of which women and men of genius strained and suffered, are just a lot of infantile amusements? Many people have felt that modernism is best understood as some kind of sardonic dig at the bourgeois who buy art, a way of pinching them and saying, "Look what I can get away with." This nearly does sum up the attitude of the early-twentieth-century Dadaists, whose furry teacups and inverted urinals were explicitly inimical to the whole idea of art;[4] and some who dislike modernist, avant-gardist art (as well as some who like it) have therefore assimilated all of it to Dada, construing it as anti-highbrow low comedy.[5] However, the analogy I draw here is not in respect of childish humor, or any other kind of humor, or any other kind of childishness. Instead, I mean to point out a symbolic function that is common to absurdist jokes, Dadaist sculpture, neo-Dadaist theater, abstract expressionist painting, atonal music, free verse, and—most importantly for our purposes here—films without represented subjects, dramatic organization, or emotional content. This symbolic function involves symbolizing by failing to symbolize.

The Opaque Object

Someone once asked Jackson Pollock why he didn't paint from nature, and he responded, "I *am* nature." Modern avant-gardists like Pollock didn't try to imitate or symbolize nature or anything else. Instead, like nature itself, they created *things*. The entities they produced weren't mere copies of the real world, but real objects in their own right, existing for their own sake. They were not to be studied simply as clues to a fuller and more interesting represented reality, but were to be studied as one studies natural phenomena. They were to be looked *at*, not *through*. Abstract painting had stopped mimicking three-dimensional space and started glorying in the intrinsic flatness of the paint-covered delimited support; atonal and aleatoric music stopped expressing happiness or sadness and started existing as structured, or purposely unstructured, patterns of sounds; absurdist theater stopped imitating life and providing catharsis, and began in various ways to examine the nature of theater and drama; and, since the 1920s, there had also been film that offered what Scott MacDonald calls "visual critique of convention as well as convention itself," that put its typical devices to work reflexively exhibiting the medium of film.[6] Appreciation of these creations was not a matter of grasping what the particular, historically locatable artist knew or felt and was trying to tell us, and therefore details of the particular artist's biography became irrelevant to the appreciation of the artist's work, along with all sorts of other historical details of the type academics typically ferret out and then use in cataloguing, institutionalizing, and taking possession of things.[7] Instead, what mattered was *the thing itself* that the artist had created, the thing there for anyone to perceive: the sound in the air, the paint on the canvas, or the human presence on the stage, and the *form* it had there. That form, if it turned out really to have aesthetic value, had it independently of its history, and was thus, to that extent, of supra-historical value.

What, then, was the nature of this formal transcendent aesthetic value? Pre-modern art was interesting and valuable at least partly because through it we could gain new insights into our world, ourselves, and others like ourselves. What was the putative interest of pure paint-covered canvas, pure sound, pure gallivanting around and talking on a stage, or the pure forms instantiated by these things? Ultimately, art works formalistically considered still retained a representational value, and moreover a value connected with representation of the beings who made and valued art. While formal arrangements of pigment, sound, and behavior did not represent us art-lovers or our world directly, one could learn about human beings from artworks in a special, shaggy-doggish way. Not just about human beings as they lived their ordinary lives in this or that socio-economic context: instead, one discovered the part of humanity that is separable from such particularities—the sensitive, reflective part of ourselves that is capable of feeling something like a moral imperative to create and appreciate these pure art works. Art was supposed to let us glimpse the part of humanity that sits above all of our petty and contingent desires.

Avant-Garde and Kitsch

The way in which avant-garde, formally innovative art reveals us to ourselves—and all the best art of history will be seen by the modernist evaluator as the formally innovative art of its time—can be observed by contrast with the way rear-guard art functions today.[8] One of the pillars of the modernist world view is the distinction between the high, serious, difficult art of the avant-garde and the low, popular, commercial art that is disparaged as kitsch. As Clement Greenberg describes the case in his classic 1939 *Partisan Review* article, "Avant-Garde and Kitsch," kitsch thrives by catering to just those desires that the avant-garde, in a way, rises above.[9] The common people who consume commercial art want to hear stories about people like themselves, with problems like theirs and in situations they can understand; they want to hear music that evokes emotions they recognize; they want to see pictures of things like things they've seen. Serious art neglects those contingent, exploitable wants, and thereby eventually provides its audience with exactly what it really values in art.

This really valuable aspect of art surfaces, in this picture, when even the vulgar herd eventually tires of consuming the identical product over and over, and minor variations on the same old themes have to be provided: new battles have to be depicted and described, new love songs have to be sung. This happens because the common folk do want familiarity, but only as long as the qualities of "the vividly recognizable, the miraculous, and the sympathetic" are present, too: the same old popular pictures, stories, and songs lose their vividness, miraculousness, and sympathetic kick after a while.[10] People generally, says Greenberg, have "instincts" that lead them in search of these qualities—and, in fact, these qualities represent the fundamental aesthetic values that we seek in even "high" avant-garde art. The popular culture industry is equipped to sate these desires by providing an endless rainbow display of novelties on a mass production basis; and, what's more, the popular artist "predigests art for the spectator and spares him effort" by keeping his repertoire of artistic devices within the range of what is familiar to his customer.[11] Thus, in that it provides a stream of vicarious experience that can penetrate even the blockheads of the insensitive, kitsch is even more artistic than fine art can ever be.[12]

But what, then, is the special value of fine art? It takes longer to get tired of violas than Moog synthesizers: so what, if they both do the same job? How, in any case, do the created things of modernism do this job at all? How do they provide us with the aesthetic values of vivid recognizability, miraculousness, or sympathy? With what are we to *sympathize* as we look *at* paint on a canvas? How can we have fellow-feeling with *things*? Greenberg will respond that since these aesthetic values are what lead persons to create these things, these objects do have to be imitations or copies of some kind after all: an aesthetic interest like an interest in feeling sympathy can't literally be an interest solely in paint, sound, etc. But formalist art objects aren't copies of any other individual entity: instead, they are "imitations of imitating."[13] They copy the processes of art production. And their amazingness, miraculousness, and sympathy come in by means of a reflected effect: as one looks at an abstract or formalist work and sees nothing immediately recognizable, one reflects on this and then recognizes that the aesthetic values are to be "projected" into the work.[14]

Projected how, though? What becomes *sympathetic* in, say, an easel painting considered as a formal arrangement of lines and colors on a canvas? And what mechanism, if any, puts us into a state of sympathy with this whatever-it-is? Greenberg doesn't sharpen and clarify his story any more than this—or, if you prefer, he doesn't make it any less allusive and any more literal and pedestrian—in any writings or discussion that I have seen. Still, we can make fairly straightforward sense of this story: something much like Kant's picture of aesthetic appreciation is at work.

Greenberg was, in 1939, a Trotskyite Marxist,[15] and the idea of a Marxist Kantian may seem self-contradictory.[16] Still, parts of Kant's aesthetic theory remain compatible with Marx's scientifically- and politically-centered outlook. Kant thinks that in creating and appreciating art objects, we leave behind our contingent, empirically conditioned emotional attractions to things we can use in this or that circumstance, and we create new values.[17] In doing so, we reveal ourselves to be amazing and miraculous creatures, capable of transcending, in a way, the scientifically knowable order. We are unlike animals, all of whose motivations and behavior are instances of regularities governed by natural law. We *give ourselves* laws concerning how to create and appreciate aesthetic forms, and thus we manifest our ability to be autonomous in another way, and give ourselves another law—the moral law, which also involves leaving behind empirical interests and the causal order. Thus, on Kant's view, our appreciation of a beautiful work of art, or a work that not only pleases us individually but *should* be appreciated by others as well, is a matter of sympathetic recognition of our transcendental ability to leave our natural, animal desires behind and be fully human.[18]

Not every part of this transcendentalist picture is compatible with the scientific materialist orientation of Marx and Greenberg, obviously, but there are plausible Marxist or Greenberg-esque analogues to what is miraculous and sympathetic in art according to Kant's view. Greenberg was at pains to deny that the preference for kitsch that existed among the lower classes in totalitarian countries was "conditioned" in the sense of having been consciously inculcated by state authorities: kitsch, he thought, employs instead a *natural* language of symbolization, *mimesis*. It is appreciating avant-garde art that requires artificial cultivation of various sensitivities. The Russian peasant, confronted with Picasso and Norman Rockwell, naturally takes pleasure in the recognizable picture and sympathy-producing situation in the Rockwell painting, and is naturally put off by the disinterested intellectual effort required to figure out what's going on in the Picasso. With effort and training, though, the peasant could learn to "reflect" and see not only a woman rendered in three dimensions on a fractured two-dimensional plane, but also the sympathy-producing *cause* of the painting, the process of leaving natural symbols behind and creating new artificial symbols. Thus, both creation and appreciation of avant-garde works involve leaving "nature" behind—nature outside of specifically human nature, perhaps—and becoming sympathetic to a miraculous, supernatural, autonomous creative process, one whose rules and right-nesses come not from natural feelings but from the process itself.

This picture remains a little murky, though. What is it to have "sym-pathy" with a creative *process?* And in what way is this process vividly rec-ognizable by the connoisseur of fine art? These ideas don't really make sense unless the process referred to here is some kind of *conscious* process, and Greenberg is indirectly referring to the *artist* who is responsible for it. It is the artist with whom we really sympathize, whose creative con-ceptions we recognize and appreciate, and who miraculously lays down the aesthetic law. Not the artist in the particular: not she or he whose his-tory and biography are, again, irrelevant. It is the artist in the abstract, the artist *qua* artist, whom we recognize and with whom we sympathize as we take pleasure in objects of fine art and their forms. When we lovers of avant-garde art "project" aesthetic value, we actively conceive of the art object with its given form as a sign that an abstract commonality exists between us and the artist who created that object in that form. And in the course of appreciating a given object-*cum*-form as constituting a work of art, we art-lovers conceive of ourselves in a novel way, as standing in a novel relationship to this strange, opaque new object and its creator. We and the artist are miraculous, supernatural co-participants in the process of leaving behind natural mimetic representations and using an opaque new object as a sign—a sign of our shared ability to do just this.

The Obscure Subject

We can think of a process like this as one of self-discovery, in which a lot of contingent social and psychological clutter is brushed away and some-thing like our transcendent, autonomous human nature is revealed. And, to the extent that we can generalize about this process of avant-garde inno-vation and appreciation, and regard it as characteristic of high art and cul-ture through history, we can see a special role for fine art generally that popular or folk art cannot play: fine art is the mirror of our true selves, opening up to our view our own infinite capacity for taking different objects and forms up in different circumstances for aesthetic uses.

A dehumanized attitude is to be expected in a modernist theory like this. The very idea of human self-knowledge has seemed terminally ill in the modern world since shortly after Descartes boldly announced the *cogito:* the great empiricist philosophers who followed and responded were far less sanguine about the prospects for true self-knowledge, and it's easy to think of someone like Hume as having already given up on that dream in the eighteenth century. In fact, some hold that the modern era in philosophy begins not with the *cogito,* but instead with the radical epistemological doubts that it is supposed to banish. This modern skeptical tendency culminates in the idea that man, like God, is dead: by the late nineteenth century we find Nietzsche and at least some Marxists arguing against the very idea that there *is* a persisting abstract humanity that could know its own nature.[19] Isn't it implausible, then, to read Greenberg, an heir to these writers, in the humanistic way I suggest?

I think it's interesting to notice that Greenberg's criticism of particular trends, shows, and artists tends to be highly personalized, even to the point of introducing biographical details about the particular artists he mentions—artistically relevant details, anyway. True enough, those artists sometimes get praise for leaving themselves behind for their art. But the artist, the human being who creates as well as signs art works, is central to this view because she or he is the source of the conceptions that the art works realize. The artist's conception is, in this view, what links an opaque art object like a Newman abstraction to the tradition of painting: it is what makes a Newman into a symbol of the process of painting, and thereby reveals the artist to us painters and connoisseurs of painting. It is the thing of fundamental value in the painting, and the main thing to be enjoyed: what is sometimes called "formal pleasure" appears when we reflect and discern the symbolic relation between this formal work and the tradition of painting that precedes it.

Greenberg's view can accommodate general modernist skepticism concerning the human by virtue of its Kantian features. Successful art, for Kant, is a *symbol* of the transcendent self, but does not provide *knowledge* of it: art doesn't provide the objective experience of the self that would be necessary for knowledge in Kant's theory.[20] Analogously, Greenberg's "projection" involves treating formal art works as signs of a shared autonomy, but it is never offered as a way to conjure up the mind or even the conceptions of the artist as objects of experience or knowledge. When we appreciate "reflected" effect, we see reflections of ourselves and our abilities, but the originals remain hidden.

There may not even *be* any originals: in this kind of theory, the dark possibility exists that, when we appreciate avant-garde painting, we are *merely* projecting our hopes and presuppositions onto paint-covered canvas, because there is nothing supernatural or transcendent to be grasped there.

It may be that the process revealed by "reflected" effect is one that, in the end, contains nothing for us to recognize or sympathize with, or at least nothing autonomous and enduring that only difficult, high art can show us. In that case, the avant-garde conception of aesthetic purity and self-governance reflects nothing more than a bias of taste, a rationalization of our local and contingent preferences. Nevertheless, thinkers like Greenberg and Kant can be both humanists and modernists because, if a theory like theirs is correct, our very lack of knowledge entails that it is also *possible* (as far as we're concerned, anyway) that man is not dead, or that we autonomous users of symbols share a universal but eternally fugitive human identity—one to which we can use works of fine art as strange clues. The very fact of our ignorance, the fact that we can't use art works or anything else as a transparent window on man, becomes, in this kind of modernism, grounds for hope and faith that a cosmopolitan human culture is alive and developing.

Avant-garde Film?

Once again, there have, since at least the 1920s, been modernist, avant-garde films about film that renounced conventional literary representation, presenting us with the medium of film itself, representing only the process of filmmaking. At least there have been attempts to create such things: those attempts are all made problematic by the issue of just what the medium of film *is*. Is a film made out of celluloid? Or is it light projected on a screen through celluloid? Maybe it is a succession of images made by that light. Maybe it is the "shape, motion, rhythm, chiaroscuro, and color" that characterize those images.[21] Or do photographs and movies contain, in Erwin Panofsky's famous phrase, "physical reality as such," in that they constitute a kind of visual "mold" of physical reality?[22] Stanley Cavell argues that films even manage to contain both physical reality and human "individualities" in a stronger sense, so that those entities are present to us when "the world is projected" on a film screen.[23]

A vant-gardism or modernism in movies, the effort to set not imitations or representations but *things* before the movie audience, becomes superfluous in Panofsky's and Cavell's views, because natural things rather than likenesses are already there in film. As Cavell says,

> Movies from their beginning avoided...modernism's perplexities of consciousness.... Media based upon successions of automatic world projections do not...have to establish presentness to and of the world: the world is there. [24]

Moreover, referring to modernist stylistic flourishes like quick cuts, moving cameras, surreal color, and radical camera angles which appear in many traditionally narrative films and which seem to constitute novel investigations of the possibilities of the cinematic medium, Cavell says that "mechanical intensification of the known quantities of filming" reflects the "desperation" resulting from an avoidable loss of touch with, and confidence in, the objective world in which film originates.[25]

2001, like all of Kubrick's films, is full of reflexivities, opacities, and stylistic devices of the kinds that characterize attempts at modernist film art. But it also offers plenty of traditional narrative devices, up until the last section anyway, and it succeeds in convincing us of its reality to an *amazing* degree.[26] The zero-gravity scenes, and especially the artificial gravity special effects, people jogging upside down and so forth, have never been equaled for realism in any other science fiction film I know of. (I can remember watching some call-in television show in 1968, and hearing a guest from NASA patiently explain to a caller that, no, *2001* had not really been shot in outer space, but in a studio.) And the "Dawn of Man" sequence, featuring the apes who are given intelligence by the monolith, was so realistic that some people think *2001* didn't win the Oscar for best makeup only because the members of the Academy who decided on the award thought the actors in ape suits were real apes.

The film constantly touches base with the reality of our frail human bodies and their constant need for care. The astronauts jog and sunbathe aboard *Discovery*, and when they perform their extra-vehicular activities, the hiss of canned air and the ominous-yet-plaintive sound of breathing fill the soundtrack. Throughout the film, everybody's always eating and drinking: leopards, apes, bureaucrats on the moon, the astronauts on their way to Jupiter, and the sole surviving astronaut in his Louis XVI suite of rooms somewhere beyond space and time. There is even the discreet appearance, at one point, of instructions for a "zero-gravity toilet"; and Dave's unseen hosts, at the end, have thoughtfully included in his suite a nicely appointed bathroom.

Moreover, speaking of touching base with reality, no extrapolation from our current condition can be convincing without signs of commercialism, and advertising logos therefore make various strategic appearances in *2001*—some of them amusingly out of date already, illustrating the danger of realism in depicting the future. A Pan Am space clipper takes Dr. Heywood Floyd, the space agency official who is to take charge of the strange magnetic monolith recently found on the moon, up to the Hilton Space Station in earth orbit. On board the clipper, we can spot "IBM" emblazoned on the main control panel. When Dr. Floyd gets to the station, a Bell Picturephone, the Pan Am desk, and the Howard Johnson's Earthlight Room are all waiting for him.

Nevertheless, despite the constantly multiplying realistic details, modernism keeps peeking through in *2001*, in the form of signs that we are watching a reflexive film about film. Max Kozloff describes here just one reflexive feature, as Kubrick uses virtuoso camera work to call attention to the curve of the Cinerama screen:

> Every moment of the lens [in *2001*] has a surprising yet slow lift and lilt to it. With their tangibly buoyant, decelerated grace, Kubrick's boom and pan shots wield the glance through circumferences mimed already by the curvature of the screen itself...equilibrium seems always to be winding itself through the panorama.[27]

And screens and screen shapes resonate through the film: we spend much of the movie looking through panoramic, or Cineramic, spaceship apertures; or watching people watch TV and computer screens; or, more curiously, watching letters and computer-animated shapes projected in reverse on the faces of people who are watching screens. This unrealistic effect is evidently meant not only to imitate the surface the audience faces, but also to identify the face and that surface, to construe them both as reflectors of projections, and to suggest that the screen itself "projects"—and all of these things together imply a reciprocal relation of projection and reflection, which seems to be pretty much the condition of the avant-gardist and her or his audience.

This watched-screen motif ties in with Kubrick's most famous obsession, the eye. An obvious metaphor for the camera, the eye figures prominently in many of Kubrick's films in various ways. The Kubrick stare, for example, is a trademark: locked out of the spaceship *Discovery*, Dave Bowman stares, trembling, into the camera as he reflects on HAL's madness and his own imminent death; in *A Clockwork Orange*, Alex the droog, stoned on drugged milk, stares lasciviously into the camera as he enjoys the goings-on at the Milkbar; and a rampaging "boot," driven mad by boot-camp, stares and smiles vacantly into the camera as he contemplates killing with his high-powered training rifle in *Full Metal Jacket*. The eye, receiver of information from the world, is also traditionally the symbol of reason: "theory," like "theater," has a root in the Greek *theaomai*, "to view." Yet Freud held that fear for the eyes was also a frequent substitute for fear of castration; and there are also familiar symbolic connections between the penis and the sword, the knife, and the gun. Thus reason, sex, and violence—dramatic obsessions in every Kubrick film, and arguably the elements that sum up human life—are all bound together in the image of the eye, which Kubrick turns on the audience again and again from the screen. Kubrick's screen and his audience are facing mirrors and projectors, reflecting into infinity the causes and effects of life and art.

This kind of allegorical reflexivity is not the specific kind of "mechanical intensification of known quantities" that Cavell criticizes in attempts to make movies modern; and this means that it is not the kind of use of formal qualities that Greenberg commends in painting and contemporary art generally. These reflexivities do not *block* associated ideas or objective interpretation: they don't make the film opaque. However, we can find that kind of opacity, too, in *2001*, if we turn to the final "Jupiter and Beyond the Infinite" section. When Dave Bowman leaves *Discovery* and approaches the monolith orbiting Jupiter, all the film's preceding representational conventions go out the window, just as the convention that animals can talk went out the window in the shaggy dog story above. In that joke, suddenly what is presented to us is not talking horses, but a remark that brings our understanding up short, thus showing us jokes themselves and how they work. In this part of *2001*, suddenly what is presented to us is not apes or astronauts, or even eyes and the like, as readable symbols of film and humanity. Instead we find unreadable sights and sounds, and apparently representational passages that rebuff our efforts to glean what is represented. What is then revealed, if anything, is the art of film itself.

Odyssey Out of Time

When Dave makes his plunge into the star-gate that is opened up by the monolith, Gyorgy Ligeti's chaotic "Atmospheres" swells on the soundtrack, and the screen fills with colors and sounds that imply fantastic acceleration. We can't tell what the little ship is accelerating past, but it looks as if it's going by *something* dangerously quickly. We see freeze-frames of Dave in the pod, terrified and in pain. Then, suddenly, as the music continues shrilling and thundering—which implies continuity with the images of the preceding few moments, and thus with those of the preceding two hours—patterns of color begin to appear that do not seem to record forward motion at all. In fact, they don't seem to record or reproduce anything. At moments they vaguely suggest such objects as a dolphin's face or a spermatozoon heading for an egg, but they are evidently not reproductions of those or any other things. An eye, apparently Dave's, its color solarized, is shown every so often: it's apparently watching what we're watching, but even that isn't perfectly clear. If we reflect for a moment, we realize that this is the way it's done in movies: an eye or a face is shown looking, and the next thing we see is the thing that the eye sees. But since what we're now seeing makes no clear narrative sense, and especially since it's not clear that we're seeing any *thing* at all, we may realize that this convention is being violated so that we can see it, and the art of which it is a part, perhaps for the first time.

The pod finally "stops" (it's no longer clear that it has really been moving) somewhere and some time, or nowhere and no time, in the neo-classical suite, whose very decor suggests timelessness by evoking the idea of timeless rationality. Now, in this setting, Kubrick plays around more with the movie convention of showing what the filmed eye sees. We see Dave, after his trip, aged perhaps twenty years, stunned and trembling in the pod, looking out the window. Then, through the pod window, we see Dave in the suite outside the pod. This image is ambiguous: are we seeing what Dave sees? How can that be, since what we're seeing is Dave himself?

Next thing we know, the pod seems to have vanished, and Dave, if the person we can see now is Dave, begins to explore his new home. We see him look in the bathroom mirror, and then we see a shot of him full on. Here we have another ambiguous image: is this the mirror image that Dave sees, or is it Dave himself? In any case, we and Dave then hear a sound, and he turns to look at something; the next thing we see is Dave himself, years older and at a different place in the suite. We watch the older Dave get up to investigate a noise apparently made by younger Dave, and we see that he finds no one in the spot we thought we occupied in the world of the film: it turns out we weren't seeing him through younger Dave's eyes after all. Once again, we have to contemplate a sequence of images that is unreadable because of ambiguity, and that therefore calls attention to the filmmaker's art, which typically eliminates this kind of opacity.

Then the elderly Dave goes back to his dinner, drops his wine glass, bends over to pick up the pieces, and catches sight of himself, ancient now, in bed across the room. This time, when we see the ancient Dave, we can see the merely elderly Dave from behind in the corner of the screen, so we know we're seeing what he sees—except that what he sees makes no sense in terms of typical movie time. And, finally, when ancient Dave reaches up toward the monolith and the luminous amniotic sac that have appeared at the end of his bed, we see that inside the floating, disembodied sac is Dave transformed once more, and we are stymied again in our attempts to look *through* the film at what or who it represents or reproduces. We don't know exactly what we're looking at, or whose eyes, if anyone's, we have been looking through. We are forced to project a meaning into what we see, and that meaning has to do with movies themselves and the way they conventionally use and represent time.

At the very end of the film, the Star-Child appears perhaps literally out of nowhere, to rival the earth in size. Apparently, the monolith has taken humanity up to the next rung on the evolutionary ladder, and, to the strains of the "World Riddle" theme from Wagner's "Also Sprach

Zarathustra," the *übermensch* has come home. But how did we and he get back to earth? How long did it take? Are we really here? How big is that fetus, anyway? What's going to happen if he touches the planet? Could he touch it? Is he a part of the same universe? The fact that two items occupy the screen at the same time typically means that the entities are close in space, but it's not at all clear that this convention is in operation here. We are now blocked from interpretation by violations of spatial conventions as well as temporal ones.

We have, at this point, no grounds for reading the events we see in any particular way. The film has slid into opacity, has become a jumble of colors, shapes, and disjointed images—and this includes the amazingly "real" parts before this final section, which were evidently continuous with what we now see. Kubrick has used the withdrawal of their meticulous realism to make these final scenes much more disconcerting and disturbing, and to make us viewers, when we try to make sense of the nonrepresentational images, much more aware of the power of conventional representation, and of what an achievement it is. These concluding images have an *intense* "reflected" effect on us: we are powerfully moved when we have to recognize what is up on the screen as "visual critique of convention as well as convention itself," or as a commentary on ourselves, the way we live, and the way we make and enjoy (film) art.

Another Inconclusive Ending

I spoke just now of how we have to understand this film: I meant only that this is how we must see it on this interpretation, not that the above is the only possible way to read—or rather, in this case, to avoid reading—*2001*. It is also possible to read the images that compose the ending of the film as a set of straightforwardly representational scenes, but scenes representing a world in which the usual physical laws don't apply. What would motion look like if you left space, or at least our space? Why shouldn't people run into themselves in a world without time, or one in which time worked differently?

And, what's more, we could even understand these representational scenes in a reflexive, sort of modernist way, as an allegory of artmaking. The creators of the monolith perhaps do for Dave what artists do for us art-lovers. They take Dave out of space and time, or out of nature, anyway, to the place they live, and they make this place his real home, in something like the way artists take us away from natural, conventional representation, and show us our ability to leave nature behind. However, this kind of allegorical interpretation does not regard the film as displaying Greenberg-type, avant-gardist modernism; and one might even argue that this interpretation would represent a postmodern reading of *2001*.

The postmodernist, if such a being really is any more than the up-to-date modernist, questions the ideal of art as pure, formal, and opaque, because she or he is also suspicious of, first, the idea that works or kinds of art have forms that can be appreciated in isolation from their representational content; second, the distinction between high art and low, or original art and imitative, that formalism trades on; and, third, the modernist picture of human beings as transcendent entities contingently trapped in various sociopolitical worlds. On this allegorical reading of *2001*'s final images, the film employs a complete rejection of conventional representation, not in order to display forms and represent by "reflected" effect, but instead to represent conventionally. The film, on this interpretation, defies narrative conventions while affirming them.

And, in affirming conventionality while throwing it away, perhaps *2001* both affirms and denies its own allegorical presentation of the infinite and eternal. Perhaps, that is, it displays a kind of *ironic* attitude toward human transcendence, a skeptical attitude that does not straightforwardly reject the modernist picture of humanity and art, but that instead emphasizes our human status as part of the natural, everyday world of familiar conventions and commonly seen things. Perhaps it suggests that, despite our aspirations to the eternal, attempts to leave behind local biases of taste are misguided, and that merely popular art—like movies—can reveal our true selves to us as well as high, formal art.

Perhaps, but that's another story.

Notes

1 *Great Movie Directors*, Ted Sennett (New York: Harry N. Abrams, Inc./AFI Press, 1986), 140.

2 From a *Playboy* magazine interview reprinted in Jerome Agel, ed., *The Making of Kubrick's 2001* (New York: New American Library, 1970); cited in Norman Kagan, *The Cinema of Stanley Kubrick* (New York: Holt, Rinehart and Winston, 1972), 145.

3 Cf. Michael Ciment, *Kubrick*, trans. Gilbert Adair (New York: Holt, Rinehart, and Winston, 1983), 148.

4 Matei Calinescu refers to the Dadaist motto "antiart for antiart's sake," in his *Five Faces of Modernity* (Durham: Duke University Press, 1987), 143.

5 Calinescu doesn't quite do this in *Five Faces*, but he does argue (124) that Dada's aesthetic nihilism "expresses an 'archetypal' trait of the avant-garde."

6 Scott MacDonald, ed., *Avant-Garde Film* (Cambridge: Cambridge University Press, 1993), 2.

7 See for example, Clive Bell, *Art* (London: Chatto and Windus, 1916), 25: "To appreciate a work of art we need bring with us nothing from life."

8 One can overemphasize this idea. Greenberg says at the end of "Towards a Newer Laocoon" (37) that "I am still able to enjoy a Rembrandt more for its expressive qualities than for its achievement of abstract values—as rich as it may be in them."

9 Originally published in *Partisan Review* VI, 5 (Fall 1939); reprinted in Greenberg, *Collected Essays and Criticism,* vol. 1, 5–22.

10 Greenberg, *Collected Essays,* 16.

11 Greenberg, *Collected Essays,* 16–17.

12 Greenberg, *Collected Essays,* 17. By the way, Greenberg voices latter-day regrets about the tone of his early writings in "Avant-Garde and Kitsch, Fifty Years Later," *Arts Magazine,* vol. 64, no.4 (December 1989), 56–57.

13 Greenberg, *Collected Essays,* 8.

14 Greenberg, *Collected Essays,* 15–16.

15 Greenberg also deplores his early doctrinaire Marxism in "Avant-Garde and Kitsch, Fifty Years Later."

16 In Greenberg's "Modernist Painting," originally published in *Art and Literature* (Spring 1963), reprinted in Gregory Battcock, ed., *The New Art* (New York: Dutton and Co., 1966), 100–10, Greenberg refers to Kant as "the first real Modernist" (100), and compares the goals of modernist art with those of Kantian critical philosophy.

This is a pretty late essay, and maybe Kantianism waxed as Marxism waned.

17 See Paul Crowther, "Greenberg's Kant and the Problem of Modernist Painting," *British Journal of Aesthetics,* vol. 25, no. 4 (Autumn 1985), and David Carrier, "Greenberg, Fried, and Philosophy: American-type Formalism," in George Dickie and Richard Sclafani, eds., *Aesthetics: A Critical Anthology* (New York: St. Martin's Press, 1978), 461–69 for (con-flicting) specific assessments of what Greenberg owes to Kant.

18 John H. Zammito, in *The Genesis of Kant's* Critique of Judgment (Chicago: University of Chicago Press, 1992), says that for Kant in the third *Critique,* "Art is the vehicle through which the supersensible gives token of its real presence. And it is just for this reason that the aesthetic experience is tran-scendentally grounded" (288).

19 Calinescu's *Five Faces of Modernity* features a section called "Avant-Garde, Dehumanization, and the End of Ideology" (125–32) that recounts the decline of the concepts of "man" and "the human" in the modern era.

20 Zammito's thesis is that Kant was led to the particular approach he took in the third *Critique* in part by a desire to use aesthetic judgments as a sign of the "unity of reason" and the "primacy of the practical."

21 Scott MacDonald says that the first "avant-garde" films directed our attention to these five things: cf. *Avant-Garde Film*, 3.

22 Panofsky suggests this in "Style and Medium in the Moving Pictures," in Daniel Talbot, ed., *Film* (New York: Simon and Schuster, 1959), 31; cited in Stanley Cavell, *The World Viewed: Reflections on the Ontology of Film, Enlarged Edition* (Cambridge, Massachusetts: Harvard University Press, 1979), 16.

23 Cf. Cavell, *The World Viewed* , esp. Chapters. 2–4 (16–29).

24 Cavell, *The World Viewed*, 118.

25 Cavell, *The World Viewed*, 62.

26 Of course, *2001* in its entirety is so chock-full of "special effects" and animation that one might well insist that its "projections" do not originate "automatically" in the objectively real world, any more than do, say, cartoons—which, Cavell holds, do not so originate and thus are not movies (cf. *The World Viewed*, 167–73). I don't know what to say about this except that it would seem an absurd result of Cavell's view if *2001* turned out not to be a movie.

27 Max Kozloff, "*2001*," *Film Culture*, no. 48–49 (Winter & Spring 1970); cited in Norman Kagan, *The Cinema of Stanley Kubrick*, 148.

11 ▌ Spike Lee's Morality Tales

Douglas Kellner

In this article I interrogate Spike Lee's aesthetics, vision of morality, and politics, arguing that his aesthetic strategies draw on Brechtian modernism and that his films can be read as morality tales that convey ethical images and messages to their audiences. I interrogate Lee's politics, focusing on the figure of Malcolm X in Lee's work and Lee's sometimes contradictory identity politics, which subordinate broader political aims to creating, affirming, and promoting one's identity. I argue that despite their limitations, Lee's films push key buttons of race, gender, sexuality, class, and black politics and provide a compelling cinematic exploration of the situation of blacks in contemporary American society and the limited political options they have within its current organization. I begin with an interrogation of *Do the Right Thing* (hereafter *DRT*), turn to a reading of *Malcolm X* (hereafter *X*), and conclude with more general critical comments on Lee's gender politics, his identity politics, and his aesthetic strategies.[1]

Do the Right Thing as a Brechtian Morality Play

DRT (1989) takes place in a Brooklyn ghetto on the hottest day of the year. Mookie, a young black man (Spike Lee), gets up and goes to work at Sal's Pizzeria on a Saturday morning. Various neighborhood characters appear as Lee paints a tableau of the interactions between blacks and Italians, and the Hispanic and Korean residents of Bedford Stuyvesant. Conflicts between the blacks and Italians erupt and when a black youth is killed by the police, the crowd destroys the pizzeria.

Lee set out to make a film about black urban experience from a black perspective and his film translates the discourses, style, and conventions of African-American culture, with an emphasis on black nationalism that affirms the specificity of black experience and its cultural differences from mainstream white culture. Lee presents black ways of speaking, walking, dressing, and acting, drawing on black slang, music, images, and style. His films are richly textured ethnographies of urban blacks negotiating the allures of the consumer and media society, and the dangers of racism and an oppressive urban environment. The result is a body of work that articulates uniquely black perspectives, voices, styles, and politics.

Yet Lee also draws on the techniques of modernism and produces original innovative films that articulate his own individual vision and aesthetic style. In particular, like the German artist Bertolt Brecht, Spike Lee produces a cinema that dramatizes the necessity of making moral and political choices.[2] Both Brecht and Lee produce a sort of epic drama which paints a wide tableau of typical social characters, shows examples of social and asocial behavior, and conveys didactic messages to the audience. Both Brecht and Lee utilize music, comedy, drama, vignettes of typical behavior, and figures who articulate the messages desired by the author. Both present didactic learning plays, which strive to teach people to discover and then "do the right thing," while criticizing improper and antisocial behavior. Brecht's theater (as well as his film *Kuhle Wampe* and his radio plays) present character types in situations that force one to observe the consequences of typical behavior. Lee does the same thing in *DRT* (and most of his other films), depicting typical work, familial, and street scenes and behavior. In particular, the three street corner philosophers, who offer comic commentary throughout, are very Brechtian, as is the radio DJ, Mister Señor Love Daddy, who tells the audience not only to do the right thing throughout the movie ("and that's the truth, Ruth"), but he repeatedly specifies "the right thing," insisting that the ghetto population: "Wake Up!," "Love one another," and "Chill!"

DRT posits the question of political and social morality for its audience in the contemporary era: what is "the right thing" politically and morally for oppressed groups like urban blacks? The film is arguably modernist in that the question of the political "right thing" is left open in the film. By "modernist," I refer, first, to aesthetic strategies of producing texts that are open and polyvocal; that disseminate a wealth of meanings without a central univocal meaning or message; and that require an active reader to produce the meanings.[3] Second, modernism is an aesthetic tendency dedicated to the production of unique works of art that bear the vision and stylistic imprint of their creator. Third, the type of modernism associated with what Peter Burger calls the "historical avant-garde" attempts to produce serious works that change individuals' perceptions and lives and strive to promote social transformation. Movements like futurism, expressionism, Dada, and surrealism meet these criteria, as do the works of Brecht and Lee, though I ultimately argue that Lee's films contain a unique mixture of American popular cultural forms and modernism, inflected through Lee's African-American experience.[4]

Because Lee's texts tend to be open, to elicit divergent readings, and to generate a wealth of often divergent responses, he is an auteur whose films project a distinctive style and vision, and together constitute a coherent body of work with distinctive features and effects. His work is highly serious and strives for specific transformative moral and political effects. Yet there are also ambiguities in Lee's work. While the disc jockey, Mister Señor Love Daddy, serves as a voice of social morality in *DRT*, it is an open question what, if any, political position Lee is affirming. Does he agree with the politics of Malcolm X or Martin Luther King? Is he advocating reform or revolution, integration or black nationalism?

Throughout the film, Public Enemy's powerful rap song "Fight the Power" resonates, but it is not clear from the film *how* one should fight the power, or what political strategies should be employed. Indeed, one could read *DRT* as a postmodern evacuation of viable political options for blacks and people of color in the present age.[5] That is, one can read the film as demonstrating that there is no "right thing" to do in the situation of hopeless ghetto poverty, virulent racism, and the lack of viable political options and movements. In this postmodern reading, the film projects a bleak, nihilistic view of the future, marked by hopelessness and the collapse of modern black politics. In this context, political reformism and Martin Luther King's non-violence appear questionable as viable instruments of change. In addition, one could read the film as questioning social violence, demonstrating that it ultimately hurts the people in the neighborhoods in which it explodes.

On this postmodern reading, it is not clear what power one is supposed to fight, what instruments one is supposed to use, and what one's goals are supposed to be. This nihilistic reading suggests that modern politics as a whole is bankrupt, that neither reform or revolution can work, that blacks in the United States are condemned to hopeless poverty and the subordinate position of an oppressed underclass without the faintest possibility of improving their situation by any means whatsoever.[6] Yet one could also read *DRT* as a modernist film that forces the viewer to compare the different politics of Malcolm X and Martin Luther King and to decide for him- or herself what the "right thing" is for blacks in the contemporary era.

Part of the politics in *DRT* is a cultural politics in which identity is defined by clothes, fashion accoutrements, and cultural style. The various characters wear distinctive clothes which define their cultural identity. The black DJ and Radio Raheem play exclusively black music, while the Puerto Rican street teens play Spanish-inflected music. A scene where Radio Raheem and the Puerto Ricans duel each other with loud playing radios signifies the cultural division and conflicts in the ghetto community. But it is the racial epithets that most pungently articulate the conflicts in the community. At a key juncture in the film, in modernist and Brechtian fashion, Lee interrupts his narrative and has the characters look into the camera and spit out vicious racial slurs, with Mookie attacking the Italians: "Dago, Wop, guinea, garlic breath, pizza slingin', spaghetti bender." Pino, the racist son, replies to the camera, assaulting blacks: "Gold chain wearin' fried chicken and biscuit eatin' monkey, ape, baboon, fast runnin', high jumpin', spear chuckin', basket ball dunkin' titso spade, take your fuckin' pizza and go back to Africa."

A Puerto Rican attacks Koreans in similar racial terms and the Korean grocer attacks Jews. This scene, thoroughly Brechtian, brilliantly shows the racial differences encoded in language, but equates all modes of racism as logically equivalent. One could argue, however, that the institutional racism against blacks is far more virulent than the variegated cultural racisms articulated and that Lee never really catches the reality of racism as part of a system of oppression.[7] On this view, society especially oppresses people of color: it is, then, not just that there is racism and hatred among all races and ethnicities, there is an unequal distribution of power and wealth in contemporary American society in which blacks and people of color tend to suffer disproportionately from racial and class oppression. Stated baldly, Lee does not understand that capitalism is a system of oppression that especially exploits and oppresses its underclass, particularly people of color.

In addition, Lee is constantly celebrating consumerism, the center of the film's focus and affective investments, rather than depicting how consumerism has come to centrally organize ghetto existence. Yet Lee does incisively show how clothes, music, language, and style separate the various ethnic groupings in his vision of a divided ghetto community. Such a situation is ripe to explode into violence and *DRT* presciently anticipated the L.A. uprisings that erupted in May 1992 after a white jury acquitted the policemen who were videotaped viciously beating Rodney King. Thus, the film has its insights, as well as its limitations.

After Radio Raheem is killed by white policemen when he and Sal start fighting, Mookie throws a garbage can through the window of Sal's

Pizzeria and violence breaks out that destroys the establishment. A close view of Mookie tossing the garbage can suggests that it was a conscious, deliberate act and that Lee *was* presenting it as "the right thing." The camera zooms in on Mookie deliberating about what to do after the police have accidentally choked Radio Raheem to death, in a fight that began when Sal smashed his beloved radio. Lee then pans a long and slow shot of Mookie studiedly walking away to pick up a garbage can and returning to throw it through the window of the pizzeria, starting the riot that ends in its destruction. It is clear that he is doing it because of rage over Radio Raheem's death and that Lee is depicting the act as a conscious, deliberate act on Mookie's part.[8]

In this reading, Lee is privileging human life over property and is suggesting that violence against property is a legitimate act of retaliation. One could also argue that Mookie is directing the mob's violence against the pizzeria and away from Sal and his sons, thus ultimately protecting them against the mob's wrath.[9] Although the act of violence is a clear rejection of King's philosophy of nonviolence, it is debatable whether it was "the right thing." One could even argue that this act only harms Mookie and the black community.[10] Smiley puts the picture of Malcolm X and Martin Luther King standing side by side on the wall, thus fulfilling Raheem's desire to have black images in the pizzeria. But they are shown burning on the wall, raising the question of whether this might be a sign of the futility of black politics in the present age, allegorically enacting the fading away of the relevance of Malcolm and Martin in the current moment.

In any case, the white conservative critique that *DRT* was "bad" because it was likely to produce violence and increase racial hatred is misplaced. Rather, Lee's film reveals the living conditions and the racial tensions and conflicts that are likely to produce urban violence. That is, *DRT* explores the social environment that produces violence and urban explosions. In interviews after the film, Lee protested that he was only depicting certain situations and not offering solutions, and this position seems wholly reasonable.

Although one could criticize Lee for deconstructing modern black politics typified by Malcolm or Martin as futile or irrelevant, thus giving voice to a postmodern nihilism, certain aspects of the film counter reading *DRT* as an expression of a bleak, postmodern pessimism.[11] The vision of *DRT* is in some ways consistent with Malcolm X's black nationalist teachings and thus affirms certain modern political positions. One of the streetcorner philosophers expresses wonder and chagrin that the Korean grocer can turn a boarded-up building into a successful business, while blacks cannot. This is a nod toward Malcolm X's views on black self-sufficiency and economic independence, and Spike Lee has enacted this philosophy as successfully as anyone in the black community. It is clear that Mookie is going to get nowhere working in Sal's Pizzeria and the other homeboys in the movie are also rapidly going nowhere. "Time to wake up, brothers, and get your shit together," following the examples of brothers Malcolm and Spike, is arguably a message in the film.

Likewise, Malcolm X put a heavy emphasis on black manhood, standing up to the white power structure, fighting back, and acting decisively to maintain one's self-respect. In that sense, Mookie's violent action instantiated certain of Malcolm's teachings, though one could raise the question whether this was in fact "the right thing." This confronts one with some questions concerning whether Malcolm X did or advocated the "right thing" politically at various phases of his life and what his legacy is for us today. I will interrogate *X* from these perspectives, arguing that the film, like *DRT*, is ultimately a morality tale and that Lee's politics slide into a black identity politics that can neither be pinned down to specific modern positions (i.e. Martin or Malcolm) nor to postmodern nihilism.

X as a Morality Tale

From the perspective of my reading of *DRT*, one could argue that *X* can be read as a morality tale interrogating what the "right thing" is for blacks in contemporary American society in both the individual and the political sense. In this reading, it is the figure of Malcolm X that is the center of the film and the key transitions involve his two self-transformations: from criminal to dedicated black nationalist working for the Nation of Islam; followed by becoming a more secular internationalist. The key is Malcolm X as moral ideal, as a model of a black transforming himself, becoming self-sovereign, and making something of himself, rather than any specific political position or message that Malcolm X taught.

Although Lee strongly affirms Malcolm X's politics, he is not an uncritical sycophant and hagiographer, and questions many of Malcolm X's views, while forcing the audience to decide whether the actions of Malcolm or other characters in the two films are indeed "the right thing." I thus see the two films as political morality plays and believe that Spike Lee was perfectly justified to tell black and other children to skip school to see the film *X*. Not only does one learn a great deal about one of the most important figures of our time, but one is forced to reflect upon what is the "right thing" for individual and political morality. Nonetheless, *X* focuses more on Malcolm as a role model for blacks and is more of a morality tale than a political drama. The figure of Malcolm X is certainly exemplary as a man able to undergo profound self-transformation and to forge his own individual identity under difficult circumstances (the delineation of such righteous models is also congruent with Brechtian strategy).

The first part of X shows what the wrong thing is for blacks today, that is, engaging in a life of crime, drugs, and shallow materialism.[12] Yet Lee invests so much time and energy to this phase of Malcolm's life that it makes the one-time criminal Malcolm Little almost attractive and certainly sympathetic. In his autobiography, Malcolm X presents Malcolm Little as a very bad dude and negative figure, though it does not seem that this image emerges from Lee's film.[13] Denzel Washington creates an engaging character and Lee's use of comedy and melodrama invests the Malcolm Little character with positive energies. Although he is caught in criminal activity and goes to jail, Lee fails to adequately criticize this criminal stage.[14]

In this sequence Lee uses the strategy of epic realist historical tableaux, heavily seasoned with comedy, satire, and music. As always, music is extremely important and X can be seen and heard as a history of black music over the decades and how it was an integral part of the texture of everyday life. Once again, parallels with Brecht are obvious, as Brecht used music to capture the ethos and style of an age and as a way of making or highlighting certain didactic points. Moreover, Lee presents certain forms of black behavior, such as "conking" hair, as bad and the early sequences contain the obvious moral that a life of crime leads to jail. The message concerning black men hanging with white women is less clear, though Lee tends to present interracial relationships negatively in X and his other films like *Jungle Fever*.[15]

The prison sequence shows Malcolm Little refusing to submit to the humiliations of prison life and then being broken by solitary punishment. But he is also shown coming to accept Black Muslim teaching and bettering himself through study. It is one of Lee's pervasive messages that education is the way to "uplift the race" (one of the mottos of *School Daze* and the title of the book on that film), and certainly Malcolm X embodies a positive model of this philosophy, as he is shown learning to study and to gain knowledge. Indeed, Malcolm X emerges from prison a totally changed man and an exemplar of an individual who undertakes a successful self-transformation.

So far, the aesthetic strategies of X have been read as a Brechtian morality tale that embodies specific lessons for blacks and others through showing tableaux of social and asocial behavior and thus contrasts of positive and negative values. Lee deploys a variety of genres and styles, mixing music, comedy, and dramatic flashbacks into key episodes of Malcolm X's early life (the mixing of genres is also Brechtian). The last third of the film continues this strategy, though it is too dense and compressed to present adequately Malcolm X's teaching and the complexity of his later positions. The key episode from the perspective of this paper is the shift from Malcolm X's adherence to the teachings of Elijah Muhammad and the Nation of Islam to his radical activist social philosophy. Yet there was too much of the religious and dubious racial teachings of the Nation of Islam and not enough of Malcolm X's later social philosophy, which many believe is his most valuable radical legacy.[16]

It is true that Lee does make clear the reasons for Malcolm X's break with the Nation of Islam and shows that Malcolm underwent a very significant transition to a radically new position, again making the point concerning the importance of radical self-transformation. He also dealt with the complexity of Malcolm X's assassination and the strong possibility that both the Nation of Islam and United States government agencies were involved in his murder—rather than just pinning it on the Nation of Islam. He also strongly emphasized that the mature Malcolm saw that all colors were equal in his experiences in Mecca. In fact, I am bracketing the question of historical accuracy in my discussion (upon which much of the critique of the film has focused, both from Lee's friends and enemies) and am focusing instead on the issue of aesthetic strategy and the politics of the film.[17]

Lee's Cultural Politics

I have focused on Lee's cultural politics and use of Brechtian aesthetic strategies. Yet there are some major differences between Brecht and Lee. Brecht was a convinced communist with very specific political values and a fairly specific Marxist political agenda (though there is some debate about this).[18] Lee, by contrast, does not seem to have as focused a political agenda. His politics appear more vague and indeterminate, thus perhaps coding Lee as somewhere between a high modernist position that refuses any determinate political stance; a more pragmatic contextualist politics that draws on disparate sources for specific political interventions in concrete political situations; and a postmodern politics, defined primarily through the production of cultural identity. Yet Lee privileges cultural politics over the politics of political movements and actions. Thus, a reading of Lee as a postmodern nihilist doesn't work because he affirms some very specific moral values with political overtones ("Chill!" "Wake up!") and at least tries to politicize film as a search for a viable politics.

Yet I wish to qualify my presentation of Lee as a Brechtian for I do not think that Malcolm X and the black radical tradition play the role that Marx and the Marxist tradition played in Brecht's work. Lee's politics are, for the most part, culturalist, focusing on black identity and moral decisions concerning race and gender. This was evident in *DRT* where Lee interrogated the visible badges of cultural politics and presented the conflicts of the community in primarily cultural terms. Lee excels in presenting small group dynamics and has not been successful in articulating larger structures—the structural context of black oppression—which impact on communities, social groups, and individual lives. He fails to articulate the dynamics of class and racial oppression in contemporary American society.

This leads to related questions about representations of gender, race, and class in Spike Lee's films. *DRT* focuses more on gender and race than class, seeing the antagonism between Italians and blacks more as a racial conflict than a class conflict. While the small businessman Sal can be seen as a representative of the class system that oppresses blacks, he is, like the Korean grocer, really part of the ethnic working-class himself, even though he owns a small business. Lee claims that he intended to deal with the black working-class in *DRT*, writing: "In this script I want to show the Black working-class. Contrary to popular belief, we work. No welfare rolls here, pal, just hardworking people trying to make a decent living."[19]

This passage, written before he made the film, is curious because the only blacks shown working are the DJ, Mookie, and a black cop. Mookie's sister is said to work, but it isn't clear if any of the other blacks are working or not. And although the neighborhood depicted is one inhabited by what could be called the black underclass, there is no exploration of their oppressive living and working conditions. All of the characters, as bell hooks notes, wear designer clothes and, as noted earlier, define their identity in terms of fashion and consumption.[20] Only the old drunk, da Mayor, dresses slovenly, and all of the other characters seem to be full-scale participants in the consumer society (much of the film, in fact, concerns consumption of pizza, ice cream, ice cones, beer, and other drinks, food, and various consumer goods, for which everyone always seems to have the money).

Thus, Lee fails to address the reality and dynamics of class oppression and does not explore black underclass exploitation and misery in his films. Reflecting his own middle-class perspective, most of Lee's characters are middle and even upwardly mobile blacks. The main characters in *She's Gotta Have It* are middle-class and, although some of the students in *School Daze* are of different classes and status groups, they are at least upwardly mobile. The one scene in a fastfood chicken restaurant, in which students confront working-class blacks, suggests hostility and difference between these sectors of contemporary African-Americans, but these differences are not adequately explored in Lee's films. *Mo' Better Blues* (1990) and *Jungle Fever* (1991) focus on black professionals and while the latter contains powerful images of a crack house and degradation through drug addiction, neither explores the reality of black underclass oppression.

Even though all of the characters of *DRT* are ghetto dwellers, the phenomenon of class oppression is not really explored, nor is it in his other films, including *X*. The ghetto blacks in the beginning of *X* are shown getting zoot suits, hair-conked, and dancing in dazzling ballrooms where they can pick up white women. In one scene, where Malcolm is working on a train and fantasizes pushing food into the face of an obnoxious customer, he is motivated more by race than class hatred. In the next scene where Malcolm encounters a Harlem crime lord who takes him on, Lee suggests that it is race hatred, rather than class oppression, that pushes blacks into crime. Nowhere does Lee adequately explore the world of class difference and exploitation.

The Malcolm who converts to Islam takes on resolutely middle–class values and the black underclass almost disappears from the film once Malcolm leaves prison and becomes a major political figure. Amiri Baraka claims that Lee "is the quintessential buppie, almost the spirit of the young, upwardly mobile, Black, petite bourgeois professional" and claims that these values permeate his films.[21]

Gender, like race, *is* a major focus of all of Lee's films, although he has been sharply criticized by black feminists for his treatment of the topic. bell hooks, for example, criticizes Lee's conventional construction of masculinity and stereotypical, usually negative, images of women.[22] His male characters often define themselves through acts of violence and typically engage in extreme macho/masculinist behavior. The women are generally more passive and powerless, though, occasionally, as with Mookie's sister Jade, and his Puerto Rican wife Tina, they verbally assault their men. Indeed, these examples show Lee's proclivity for utilizing images of stereotypical female bitchiness, although Jade, played by his sister Joie Lee, is a strongly sympathetic character.

As Michele Wallace notes, Lee privileges conventional heterosexual relationships and negatively stigmatizes oral sex, which Wallace argues demeans gays and "the rest of the vast range of illicit sexual practices and psychosocial developments beyond the pale of compulsory heterosexuality, in which such perverse passions as interracial sex and drug addiction are included."[23] Part of the underlying problem with Lee's gender politics is his tendency to use Brechtian typical characters to depict typical scenes. The typical, however, is a close breath away from the stereotypical, archetypical, conventional, representative, average, and so on, and lends itself to caricature and distortion. Lee is a realist in Brecht's sense of trying to depict real situations, but he does not engage the realities of underclass life or of gender oppression to any great extent. Indeed, like Brecht, he uses comedy, aesthetic interruption, satire, farce, and other devices to confront the problems of race, gender, and sexuality. These are hot issues at present, and much of the interest in Lee's work resides in pushing these buttons. Yet one could question whether Lee interrogates gender and sexuality any more seriously or successfully than he interrogates class.

Lee also heavily stresses skin color, dividing blacks in *School Daze* along these lines. In *Jungle Fever* too, there are constant contrasts between light- and dark-skinned blacks, and the wives of the two main black characters are extremely light-skinned. Both *Fever* and *X* fetishize white skin by showing white women to be an intense object of black male desire and a route to black male downfall. One of the jazz musician's girlfriends in *Mo' Better Blues* is light-skinned, while the other is dark black. Most of the sex scenes in Lee's films are shot at night and the lighting exaggerates skin color differences, highlighting his obsessive focus on skin color.

Yet as bell hooks, Michele Wallace, Ed Guerrero, Mark Reid, and others have argued,[24] Lee seems to rule out the possibility of healthy romantic relationships between people of different color—a quasi-segregationist position that a more progressive multiculturalist vision would reject. There are also stereotypical doublings of good and bad women in Lee's films, especially in *X*, where Malcolm's girlfriend Laura goes from good to bad. Laura is first depicted as Malcolm's good girlfriend in contrast to the white woman Sophia. Laura, however, becomes a junkie and a whore, and thus the good/bad opposition with Laura is reversed. Eventually, Malcolm's wife Betty appears as the ultimate good woman, against whom all other women appear as bad. Yet this replicates the stereotypical Madonna/whore opposition which has dominated classical Hollywood cinema. A possible exception to these stereotypes in *X* are the Muslim sisters who are seduced and made pregnant by Elijah Mohammed, but they too are ultimately presented as victims, as helpless objects of male desire and as breeding machines to perpetuate male patriarchy.

Moreover, in all of Lee's films women are relegated to the sphere of private life, while men are active in public life. This is most striking in *X*, where Malcolm's wife is primarily depicted as a dutiful spouse, raising his children and standing passively beside him. There are few positive images of women in Lee's films, or of egalitarian relationships between men and women.[25] Malcolm is shown as a harsh patriarch who seems to want a wife primarily for breeding. In *Jungle Fever* Flipper abandons his black wife for a white woman—later this relationship fails. In *She's Gotta Have It* Nola Darling plays off three black men against each other, resulting in tension that harms all her relationships. The jazz musician in *Mo' Better Blues* has two girlfriends and, once again, this situation is untenable; the main character marries the more conventional woman, has a family, and gives up his jazz career. Thus, in Lee's films one rarely sees strong, independent women, egalitarian relationships, or men who treat women with genuine respect and care.

In part, Lee's sexual politics fall prey to the stereotypes of classical Hollywood cinema and do not transcend this level. But they also reflect male chauvinism in black and other minority communities and the intensity of conflict between male and female—explosive tensions also articulated in rap music. But his cinema does not explore the causes of these tensions, or propose any solutions.

Conclusion

Lee privileges morality over politics in his films. They are best viewed as morality tales rather than political learning plays in the Brechtian sense.[26] Although his early musical *School Daze* thematizes class to some degree, on the whole Lee's films deal more with race and gender than with class (which is, of course, a major focus of Brecht's Marxist aesthetic). Before any final criticisms, however, I want to stress the progressiveness and excellence of Lee's films in relation to other products of the Hollywood cinema. His films are far superior to most other Hollywood films and it is good that a black person can use this system to articulate and disseminate black perspectives. It is difficult, therefore, to criticize him. Yet it is through critique and self-critique that cultural and political progress is made, so it is hoped that the criticisms presented here have positive effects.

Lee has been criticized from within the black community for not taking more specific political positions, for being politically vague and indeterminate, and for replacing nitty-gritty issues with cultural politics.[27] *School Daze* ends with the message "Wake Up!" proclaimed by the black activist hero, and *DRT* begins and ends with DJ Mister Señor Love Daddy proclaiming this. Fine, wake up. But to what, and what does one do when one is awake? Such concrete politics seem beyond the purview of Lee's vision and suggest the limitations of his politics.

Moreover, he seems to be primarily concerned with the situation and oppression of blacks and does not explore the oppression of other groups. This could be excused on grounds that it is useful for someone to undertake this effort, yet there are limitations to Lee's exploration of black oppression, which tends to ignore how a system of exploitation oppresses blacks and other people of color. Lee's color fetishism aids a divide-and-conquer perspective which, in essence, blinds the colonized and prevents solidarity among the oppressed. As Cornel West puts it:

> As long as we simply hide various particularisms...there cannot be a radical democratic project. So there must be strategies and tactics that cut across identity politics, cut across region, and gender, race, and class.... We're in the bind we're in partly because we've been unable to generate the transgendered, transracial, transsexual orientation of social motion, social momentum, social movement. And if we can't do that, then there will be many, many more David Dukes by the end of the twentieth century, even while we engage in our chatter about identity.[28]

Identity politics keep oppressed peoples apart and tend to reduce politics to the search for a cultural identity and style. Lee never portrays political movements in any serious fashion. He fetishizes leaders, which, as Adolph Reed puts it: "also reflects an idea of politics that is antidemocratic and quietistic. Great Leaders don't make movements."[29]

Although there is confusion between his affirmation of Malcolm X's modern politics and his evocation of a postmodern identity politics, the central problem is that Lee ultimately comes down on the side of a culturalist identity politics, which subordinates politics in general to the creation of personal identity. Identity for Lee is primarily black identity and he constantly operates with a binary opposition between black and white, us and them. Lee's identity politics, moreover, are primarily culturalist. This was clearly the case in *DRT*, where every character's politics were defined in terms of cultural style. None of the various characters were involved in any political organization, movement, or struggle, and Buggin' Out's boycott of Sal's Pizzeria is a pathetic caricature of the real struggles by people of color for rights and survival.

Concrete issues of black politics in *DRT* were reduced to slogans on walls—graffiti such as "Tawana Told the Truth," "Dump Koch," or "Jesse," referring to Jesse Jackson's 1988 run for the Presidency. Here black politics are reduced to slogans and images, and Lee's culturalist identity politics never really rise beyond this level. As bell hooks notes, Lee never explores alliance politics and fails to realize that:

> Combatting racism and other forms of domination will require that black people develop solidarity with folks unlike ourselves who share similar political commitments. Racism...is not erased when we control the production of goods and services in various black communities, or infuse our art with an Afrocentric perspective.[30]

hooks also argues that even Malcolm X becomes reduced to an image in Lee's presentation, both, I would add, in *DRT* and *X*.[31] Lee thus ultimately falls victim to a consumerist image culture in which value, worth, and identity are defined in terms of images and cultural style, in which one's image determines who one is and how one will be received. Film is, at its best, a feast of images, but critical film interrogates these images, deconstructs those that serve the interests of domination, and develops alternative images, narratives, and aesthetic strategies. Lee does not rise above the repertoire of dominant images already established and reproduces many questionable images of men, women, blacks, and other races. Although his films show that cinema can address issues of key political importance and generate interesting discussions that may have progressive political effects, so far his films are limited, specifically in their identity politics.

Yet his films do attack some of the many forms of sex, race, gender, and class oppression. While they might not ultimately provide models of a "counterhegemonic cinema" as hooks desires, they provide some engaging and provocative cinematic interventions that are far superior to the crass genre spectacles of Hollywood cinema.

Notes

1 I am aware that there are problems with a white male professional in a privileged race, class, and gender position, writing about black culture and politics, but it is important for people of different subject positions to cross over and explore the terrain of difference. I also consulted with a number of black and feminist critics on this project and am grateful to many people for critical comments on various versions of this article, which was first presented in a symposium on *Malcolm X* organized by Mark Reid at the 1993 Society for Cinema Studies, and was then presented in a workshop on contemporary film at the 1993 American Sociological Association conference.

2 I do not know whether Brecht specifically influenced Lee, or if Lee (re)invented something like a Brechtian cinema out of his own experiences and resources. I have not yet found any specific references to Brecht in the book publications that Lee regularly produces on his films, and have found only one mention of a Brecht/Lee connection in the growing literature on the black director. See Paul Gilroy, in *The Washington Post*, 17 November, 1991, 63. For a fuller presentation of Brecht's aesthetics and politics, see Douglas Kellner, "Brecht's Marxist Aesthetic: The Korsch Connection," in Betty Weber and Herbert Heinin, editors, *Bertolt Brecht: Political Theory and Literary Practice* (Athens, Ga.: University of George Press, 1981), 29–42.

3 On "the writerly" modernist text that requires an active reader, see Roland Barthes, *Pleasures of the Text* (New York: Hill and Wang, 1975).

4 Jameson stresses the role of individual vision and style in modernism, while Burger analyzes the "historical avant-garde" that attempts to change art and life, as opposed to more formalistically oriented modernist art. See Fredric Jameson, *Signatures of the Visible* (New York and London: Routledge, 1990) and *Postmodernism, or The Cultural Logic of Late Capitalism* (Durham, NC: Duke University Press, 1991); and Peter Burger, *Theory of the Avant-Garde* (Minneapolis: University of Minnesota Press, 1984).

5 This reading was suggested in conversation by Zygmunt Bauman after a series on postmodern film at the summer 1992 10th anniversary conference of *Theory, Culture, & Society*. In addition, Lee's *Do the Right Thing* is read as a "postmodern" film in a somewhat indeterminate sense in Norman Denzin, *Images of Postmodern Society* (Newbury Park and London: Sage Press, 1991), 125ff.; likewise, Baker describes Lee as a "true postmodern" with an "astute, witty, brilliant critique of postmodern, urban hybridity" in *Do the Right Thing*, but without giving the term "postmodern" any substance; see Houston A. Baker, "Spike Lee and the Commerce of Culture," in Manthia Diawara, ed. *Black Cinema: History, Authorship, Spectatorship*, (New York: Routledge, 1993), 174–5.

6 Of course, there are many postmodern politics, ranging from the nihilism of the post-1980s Baudrillard to the pragmatic reformism of Lyotard and Rorty, to the multiculturalist identity politics of many women and minority group postmoderns; see the survey in Steven Best and Douglas Kellner, *Postmodern Theory: Critical Interrogations* (London and New York: Macmillan and Guilford Press, 1991).

7 Put differently, Lee's portrayal of racism does not take into account logical types, that there is a hierarchy of racial virulence, usually dictated by color (blacks being subject to the most extreme racism, followed by Hispanics, Asians, and ethnics like Italians), gender (with women below men), sexual preference (with gays subject to prejudice from straights), and so on (in which black, lesbian women would suffer significantly more oppression than, say, Hispanic men). The scene under question portrays all forms of racism in terms of linguistic equivalence of cultural difference and racial hatred (I am grateful to Rhonda Hammer for this insight).

8 In interviews after the release of the film, Lee said that he was constantly amazed at people indignant over the destruction of property, but ignoring the black youth's death. Lee was initially concerned to interrogate the conditions that could lead to wanton killings of black youth, spurred on by the Howard Beach killings in which white youth gratuitously assaulted black youth, leading to one of their deaths. Thus, Lee seems to believe that violent protest is a legitimate response to the senseless killing of blacks, as would, presumably Malcolm X himself. In a book on the making of *Do the*

Right Thing, Lee remarks: "The character I play in *Do the Right Thing* is from the Malcolm X school of thought: 'An eye for an eye.' Fuck the turn-the-other-cheek shit. If we keep up that madness we'll be dead. YO, IT'S AN EYE FOR AN EYE." (Spike Lee (with Lisa Jones), *Do the Right Thing* (New York: Simon and Schuster, 1989), 34, stress in original.)

9 This reading was suggested by Kelly Oliver in a comment on an earlier draft of my paper. Indeed, as indicated in note 8, Lee was angry that many viewers and reviewers seemed to be very upset by the destruction of property, but were overlooking that a black youth was killed by the police.

10 In a throw-away line, Mookie's sister Jade mentions that she'd like to see something positive happen for the community, but it isn't clear what she has in mind and in the absence of a more complete development of her political views, one can only guess.

11 It is precisely this nihilism that Cornel West warns blacks against; see "Nihilism in Black America," in *Black Popular Culture*, ed. Gina Dent (Seattle: Bay Press, 1992), 37–47.

12 It was generally overlooked in the reviews of the film that a good part of *Jungle Fever* was spent attacking the crack scene, portraying it as a dead end and in extremely negative terms as a major force of destruction in the black community. Lee avoided the issue of drugs, however, in his earlier films, for which he was criticized.

13 Alex Haley and Malcolm X, *The Autobiography of Malcolm X* (Baltimore and London: Penguin, 1965).

14 Brecht too was sympathetic to criminals and often presented them positively, as in the *Three-Penny Opera*.

15 Although the narrative suggests that Malcolm was attracted to the white woman, Sophia, as a means of exerting sexual power and gaining racial revenge, there are both positive and negative images of the relationship, which is more favorably presented ultimately than the image of interracial relationships in *Jungle Fever*, despite the fact that Malcolm X himself came to sharply condemn black men pursuing white women. I interrogate Lee's controversial sexual politics below.

16 The Nation of Islam, for instance, preached black superiority, presented the white man as a "devil," and in general engaged in racist teachings, advocating black separatism rather than structural social transformation. For some years, Malcolm X shared this perspective, but eventually distanced himself from such teachings and developed more revolutionary and internationalist perspectives. See such collections of Malcolm X's later writings as Malcolm X, *The Final Speeches* (New York: Pathfinder, 1992).

17 Obviously, the question of historical accuracy is important in evaluating a film that has the pretense of telling the truth about Malcolm X's life. Lee's

Spike Lee's Morality Tales ▌ *217*

book on the film indicates that he was attempting to uncover the truth of Malcolm X's life through research and interviews (Lee and Wiley, *By Any Means Necessary*), so one could validly examine the film for its historical accuracy; such a project, however, goes beyond the scope of this study. For some reflections on historical accuracy and distortions of *X*, see the symposium in *Cineaste*, vol. XIX, No. 4 (1993): 5–18 and the review by bell hooks, "Malcolm X: Consumed by Images," *Z Magazine* (March 1993): 36–39.

18 Douglas Kellner, "Brecht's Marxist Aesthetic."

19 Spike Lee (with Lisa Jones), *Do the Right Thing*, 30.

20 bell hooks, *Yearning. Race, Gender, and Cultural Politics* (Boston: South End Press, 1989).

21 Amiri Baraka, "Spike Lee at the Movies," in Manthia Diawara, ed. *Black Cinema*, 146.

22 hooks, *Yearning*, 173ff.

23 Michele Wallace, "*Boyz N the Hood* and *Jungle Fever*", in *Black Popular Culture*, ed. Gina Dent (Seattle: Bay Press, 1992), 129.

24 hooks, *Yearning*; Wallace, "*Boyz N the Hood* and *Jungle Fever*"; Ed Guerrero, "Spike Lee and the Fever in the Racial Jungle," in Jim Collins, Hilary Radner, and Ava Preacher Collins, eds., *Film Theory Goes to the Movies* (New York and London: Routledge, 1992), 170–81; and Mark Reid, "African-American Cultural Studies: Towards a Politics of the PostNegritude" (forthcoming).

25 A curious set of images for interpreting Lee's sexual politics are found in the opening dance by Rosie Perez in *Do the Right Thing*. hooks (*Yearning*) notes how this dance replicates male behavior (male dance forms, boxing, fighting, etc). But Lee possibly intends this as a powerful image of a woman of color; the dance is accompanied by the rap song "Fight the Power" which puts positive energy into the scene. It is a striking, but ambiguous sequence, perhaps signalling the film's modernism which requires viewers to construct their own readings.

26 For Brecht, a political learning play would impart exemplary political insights and behavior to its audience, helping to politicize them and to incite the audience to participate in social change. It is not clear that Lee's films function in this way, but rather, as I am arguing, serve instead primarily as black morality tales.

27 See, for example, Adolph Reed, "The Trouble with *X*," *Progressive* (February 1993): 18–19 and Baraka "Spike Lee at the Movies," 145ff.

28 Cornel West, "A Matter of Life and Death," *October* 61 (Summer 1992), 23.

29 Adolph Reed, "The Trouble with *X*," 19.

30 hooks, *Yearning*, 183–84.

31 bell hooks, "Malcolm X: Consumed by Images," 36–39.

12 ▮ Passing in *Europa, Europa*

Escape into Estrangement

Julie Inness

> My main aim was to save myself and in this process to retain a Jewish soul.[1]
> —Oswald Rufeisen discussing passing as German during World War II

Oppression produces superb actors. Jews take on gentile roles. Homosexuals learn to play the part of heterosexuals. African-Americans mask themselves as whites. All learn to live life as a masquerade, donning costume after costume in order to survive in a hostile world. It seems like the ideal escape. No wonder many members of dispossessed groups decide to "pass," that is, masquerade as their own oppressors. By doing nothing more than concealing a socially despised identity and taking on a new one, people who pass transform their lives, escaping moral biases such as anti-Semitism, homophobia and racism while seeming to harm none.[2] Despite the apparent desirability of passing, movies, novels and everyday life abound with people who risk their relationships, jobs, and even lives because they can no longer bear to pass: Jews revealing their concealed identity in Nazi Germany; homosexuals in the military declaring their homosexuality to officers; African-Americans divulging their race to potentially racist whites.[3] What drives these people to take such quixotic risks? This is a difficult question to answer if passing is thought about in the abstract; for people who have not passed, to imagine living in a divided world is challenging. Film, however, aids a faltering imagination. By exploring the complexity of the passing person's world, film provides an entry into the puzzling dynamics of passing.

Numerous films explore passing, including *Pinky*, *A Gay Deception*, *Imitation of Life* and *My Fair Lady*. This abundance of films about passing is not surprising: the nature of film makes this problem difficult to avoid. Watching a film, the viewer is accustomed to the split between the actor and the role she plays on the screen. Both viewer and actor must monitor this division: the actor needs to recognize that her own life is not that of the character she plays; the viewer must distinguish with proficiency between the actor and her plethora of roles. It takes only a slight stretch of imagination to transform this double vision into triple vision; whereas there was once an actor and a role, now there is an actor playing the role of someone playing a role. The viewer's previous training in distinguishing between the actor and her role is pushed one step further; now the viewer must attempt to distinguish between the actor, her primary role and her passing role. As for the actor, she is faced with the issue of how to distinguish between her false role, her true role, and her life. In this process, a question that is always in the background of all films gets pushed into the foreground, becoming the content of the film itself: Can we separate the person who acts from the role(s) she plays?[4] Films on passing provide insight into what happens when the role a person plays dominates her life, throwing into confusion the division between self and role. Just as the person who passes is led to confront the question of who she is becoming, the viewer and actor must both engage the question of how we distinguish between actors and characters, individuals and the masks they wear. And both viewer and actor are forced to confront the danger that lies in failing to make these distinctions.

The issue of passing is central to *Europa, Europa* (Agnieszka Holland, 1992), a film about Solly, a Jewish boy who survives the Holocaust by passing as a gentile member of the German Army and Hitler Youth.[5] Throughout the film, the viewer is always aware that Solly is acting to save his life; the threat of discovery is never far off. For Solly, passing seems the only rational choice. Yet he is always on the verge of revealing his true identity, and sometimes even does; from publicly tracing a Star of David in a mist-befogged window to blurting out his Jewishness to the mother of his German girlfriend, Solly's behavior seems suicidal. Watching, the viewer may empathize with Solly's struggle against passing without fully understanding the source of this empathy. Why accept Solly's resistance to passing, rather than dismiss it as irrational?

There are several extrinsic reasons why Solly might yearn to abandon passing. Political commitments, for example, might motivate him to claim his true identity in an effort to transform society. Or he might be spurred on by some notion of heroism, a desire to stand by other Jews who were facing death. The crucial interest of *Europa, Europa*, however, lies in how it *fails* to appeal to such extrinsic factors to explain Solly's behavior. Solly is never portrayed in the grip of political commitments or heroism. His surroundings provide him with no reason to believe he could help other Jews by announcing his identity; he would only be sent to a concentration camp. The film develops, instead, a phenomenological unraveling of the internal structure of passing, suggesting that passing distances the person who passes from other people. We watch as Solly's friendships disintegrate. When his friends never truly see him as he is, he suffers.[6] The initial euphoria of passing fades away, leaving him increasingly lonely due to his inability to claim his own identity in the eyes of his friends. But this explanation only leads to another question: how could passing alienate Solly from his friends when it appears to be a way to avoid the certain estrangement of hatred? By entering Solly's world through the film, we discover how passing conceals a logic of escalating estrangement.

Passing: Opaque Friendships

The camera pans to the left and we hear a burst of gunfire. Solly jerks in response to the noise, realizing the fate of the Jews that were just led away, then hastily conceals his incriminating papers. Solly first decides to pass as German when his life is threatened. Yet the film does not treat self-protection as the central reason for his passing; more fundamentally, Solly is on a quest for human connection in a world that has been turned upside down.

Before Solly passes, his deep loneliness is apparent. He is continually getting separated from others he cares about. His parents decide to send him out of the country with his brother, but the two are separated as they try to escape. Drifting, Solly is picked up by the Russians and makes friends at a Russian school, only to lose track of his classmates as they flee from the Germans. Each time Solly is separated from others, the camera draws back to provide us a long shot of crowds of people desperately trying to escape the war, reminding us that getting lost is a real possibility in a world where all reference points are uprooted.

When Solly finally gets picked up by some German soldiers, he blurts out that he is German because he is scared. Yet, although Solly does not freely choose to pass, he comes to accept what was initially only a survival strategy when he discovers that he has apparently escaped from loneliness. For while passing as German, Solly discovers affection in abundance; not only do the soldiers make a pet of him, but the officer in charge even announces that he wishes to adopt him. Yet Solly is constantly reminded that this affection does not extend to acknowledged Jews. The soldiers who have befriended him display their anti-Semitism, one forcing him to look at Jewish corpses to develop "appropriate" hatred, while the officer who seeks to adopt him tells him about the need to cleanse Europe of Jews. Faced with a choice between life and friendship based on denial and estrangement or death based on honesty, Solly reaches for friendship.

Solly's strategy is simple. Faced with his own dangerous difference, he realizes that he can regain control of his life. Although it is impossible to change the views of his prejudiced German friends, the same is not true of remaking himself: he can shape himself to fit the expectations of his friends and to conform to their values. Once he conceals his difference, nothing will stand between him and friendship. He will be free to reveal things about his life; his revelations will be understood by his friends, not overshadowed by his being a Jew. As Solly reflects, it seems ridiculous to allow himself to be hated because of a circumcised penis.

Initially Solly's denial of his Jewish identity seems a small price to pay; in exchange, he leaps over the hurdle to his acceptance by Germans. Numerous friends appear in his life: Leni, his girlfriend; Gerd, his Nordic roommate; Leni's mother; the officer who wishes to adopt him; his Hitler Youth companions. Solly's surge of popularity is not surprising. Blind to who he is, his friends still find him useful and pleasant. And use and pleasure are sufficient for friendship of a sort, as Aristotle knew:

> These friendships then are a matter of result: since the object is not beloved in that he is the man he is but in that he furnishes advantage or pleasure as the case may be.[7]

Solly's friends gain both advantage and pleasure from his company, for they feel secure around him when he passes. He is the perfect mirror, reflecting back to his friends not the truth, but their own idealized image of themselves, thereby reassuring them that their way of being in the world is the standard for which others strive. Solly offers no disconcerting criticism of the values he reflects, including anti-Semitism. Feeling at ease, others experience no hesitation in disclosing themselves to him. Liking follows fast in the footsteps of disclosure, for it is difficult not to like someone who reflects yourself back to you at more than life size. Solly also seems to thrive in this relationship. Remaining silent about his religion, he seemingly frees himself to talk about his life, hopes and desires.

Passing into Estrangement

> I was exhausted by being "on stage" all day long. Even just talking was trying.... Never a mistake, never a minute to relax the vigil.[8]
> —Yehuda Nir discussing passing in Nazi-occupied Poland.

Things seem simple at the start. When Solly is questioned by the Germans, all he does is claim to be a purebred German rather than a Jew. But Solly soon learns that passing requires isolation. His initial concealment rapidly ripples outward, forcing him to conceal increasingly large portions of his life from his friends. His family is the first to go. When friends ask about his family, Solly must lie, claiming that he is an orphan.

Even when a German officer offers to adopt him, Solly must remain silent. Next Solly conceals his past. Friends ask him about people he has known, places he has lived, and even his seemingly heroic service in the German Army. In response, he offers them a false persona, a facade. He recreates his past, relocating his home and renaming the people he has known. Although he remains silent about his career in the German Army, he allows others to fall in love with their own vision of him as a hero. Finally, he hides his body and emotions. While his friends frolic nude in the showers, Solly goes to extreme lengths to conceal his circumcised penis. Surrounded by his Hitler Youth comrades taking pleasure in singing about killing Jews, Solly conceals his hatred and fear, even joining in the singing himself to conceal the truth.

As Solly discloses progressively less, he becomes more of a puzzle to his friends. Failing to understand him, they either respond incorrectly or not at all. Sometimes they unintentionally aggravate Solly's fear and pain. When, for example, Solly's intense loneliness causes him to become close friends with a German soldier, the soldier finds homosexual implications in Solly's actions. The friend makes a sexual overture as Solly soaks in a bathtub, only to have Solly leap from the tub and flee, terrified about revealing his circumcised penis. Thinking that Solly is upset by the show of homosexuality, his friend pursues him, hoping to calm him down. Other friends offer no comfort when Solly needs it, failing to see his carefully concealed agony; for example, his girlfriend ridicules him when he refuses her invitation to make love—only we as viewers see the close shot of Solly's face, torn between adolescent desire and the need to safeguard his life by concealing his penis.

As Solly continues to pass, this failure of understanding thoroughly taints his friendships with Germans. His angers and depressions become increasingly inexplicable to his friends, for Solly discovers that passing demands an especially tight rein on these emotions. As far as anger is concerned, Solly often encounters situations that call for anger on his part: the surrounding anti-Semitism makes anger a morally commendable response. But passing allows no outlet for justifiable anger. Since Solly cannot react to the real cause of his anger, he must choke it down, leading to sudden and, to his friends, inexplicable outbursts. Along with anger, he encounters reasons for depression, including his inability to make contact with his family and his continual fear for his life. Once again, he must struggle to transform his depression, trying to make it seem reasonable; yet this only aggravates the problem. His friends believe that his depression stems from the death of his fictitious German parents "because of the Jews," so as a way of lifting his spirits they encourage him to hate

Jews. Solly finds himself in an almost unbearable trap with his friends: because he seeks to pass to gain acceptance as well as to preserve his life, he must struggle to conceal all aspects of his life that might cast doubt on his allegiances; yet the more successfully he conceals his life, the more challenging he becomes to understand.

When others find Solly difficult to understand, their friendship some- times suffers, such as when his girlfriend rejects him. She does so because he shows sympathy for Jews, slapping her when she makes an anti-Semitic remark. Shocked, she is poised to report him to the authorities for his crime of slapping a German woman in defense of Jews, a plan she aban- dons in favor of breaking off their relationship. More often, however, Solly's reticence sets up a barrier in his relationships, a barrier that main- tains distance without uprooting all affection. Yet the remaining affection is never based on acceptance of who Solly is. The film emphasizes how many of his friends would reject him if they knew he was Jewish. One of Solly's friends talks about cutting Jews to death with knives, while the officer who seeks to adopt him explains that Jews must all be sent to "some place like Madagascar."

Solly becomes a blank slate for friends to write upon, composing narra- tives that enhance their own sense of value at the expense of understand- ing Solly himself. And write they do, inscribing narratives that reveal more about themselves than Solly. From the woman who seduces him because he reminds her of Hitler to the German officer who seeks to adopt Solly because he sees him as the son he never had, few people hesitate before casting Solly in fantasies of their own. His soldier friends take him for a war hero, interpreting his failed attempt to escape to the Russian side as a daring and successful move to capture the enemy position. At the school for Hitler Youth that he attends after being sent to Germany from the front, his friends admire him as the ideal Hitler Youth. His girlfriend warms to him once she discovers that he can play the role of the German hero in her own drama.

Herein lies the source of the rift Solly senses growing between himself and his German friends—he realizes that he is invisible to them, and that they love him in his invisibility. His friends feel free to project on him what they will, accepting him because he makes them feel certain about their own ideals and prejudices: the brave Hitler Youth; the horrible Jewish horde that contributed to the death of Solly's fictitious German parents; the German son fighting for the Fatherland. Ralph Ellison's words about another invisible man express Solly's discovery:

> I've never been more loved and appreciated than when I tried to "jus-
> tify" and affirm someone's mistaken beliefs; or when I've tried to give

my friends the incorrect, absurd answers they wished to hear. In my presence they could talk and agree with themselves, the world was nailed down, and they loved it. They received a feeling of security.[9]

Denied mutual recognition, Solly must continually confirm the identities of his friends, strengthening them in themselves as he denies himself. The more lopsided confirmation he offers, the more he is loved; the more he is loved, the more inconceivable it becomes that his friends should recognize him for himself. They have too much to gain from his invisibility.

Passing opens up a rift that separates Solly not only from German friends, but also divides him from other Jews, leaving him trapped in a no-man's-land. He learns that passing is a one-way street; once he goes down it, he must break off contact with Jews, including his family. To do otherwise would compromise his passing. Solly makes a wrenching discovery of this rift when he goes to visit his family, but finds that they now live in a ghetto closed to Germans. Boarding a streetcar, he travels through the ghetto, but there is no going home again. The world he has passed into is sealed against his escape as long as he passes. The literal dimensions of this seal become evident when Solly sees a woman in the ghetto who resembles his mother; desperate for contact, he tugs wildly at the streetcar window, trying to open it, only to be reprimanded for a forbidden act—the seal between the Nazi and ghetto worlds must not be broken. Not only must Solly keep away from other Jews, they also understandably keep away from him. Most mistake his passing persona for himself, never imagining his Jewishness. But there is an exception: at the film's conclusion, an officer of the liberating army gives a gun to a former concentration camp inmate and hands Solly over, telling the former prisoner, "He's one of yours." The prisoner prepares to fire. There is no room for friendship here. To those he has left behind, Solly appears a traitor, just as those among whom he passes would see him as a traitor if he revealed his identity.

Boomerangs seem like harmless toys. But they can prove treacherous, arcing back and harming the unsuspecting thrower. Passing, in this respect, is like a boomerang—just when it seems certain to lessen estrangement between friends, passing ricochets and contributes to estrangement. Solly passed in order to lessen his loneliness, seeking community in a hostile world. But he discovered the boomerang: passing created a gulf between him and the possibility of either German or Jewish community. There are several problematic twists in the process of passing.

Mutual disclosure is essential to true friendship. Without it, we feel distant from others, not part of their world. With it, we feel trusted, invited into another's life. Such communication of trust is essential, since trust is a fundamental marker of friendship. Along with expressing trust, mutual disclosure has the potential to draw us closer: we often feel a surge of affection for the person who responds to our words with open and sincere conversation. Perhaps most importantly, mutual disclosure allows us to see into each other with greater perspicuity, distinguishing between the shallow and deep, the trivial and essential, the contingent and foundational in each other's characters. Such insight allows us the chance to like each other for the people we are, not merely the people we seem to be. In a world where it often seems rational to live in estrangement from one another, mutual disclosure is the first show of faith necessary for friendship.

> One had to talk, one could not always talk about books, one had to be ready to talk about oneself. Which self? The issue was the limit of one's inventiveness and memory, because the lies had to be consistent—more consistent...than the truth.[10]

—Louis Begley describing Jewish passing in Poland.

Limiting disclosure would be tantamount to enhancing disclosure—this was the promise that passing held out to Solly. By closing one door on his life, he sought to free himself to open others, talking almost at will for the price of momentary periods of silence. But paradoxes have a way of reasserting their power. Solly discovers that passing does not involve simple exclusions from what you reveal to others. It involves progressively hacking away at your life; the markers of the difference Solly must conceal include more than his circumcised penis and place of religious worship. He must also worry about such markers as his first name, his choice of friends, and his place of birth—difference can emerge anywhere.

Because of the pervasiveness of difference, Solly is faced with the problem of constantly maintaining the fiction he has created. Starting by not admitting to being Jewish, Solly finds that he has to take meticulous care to conceal himself around his German friends, hiding facts about his life as well as his own emotions. Family information is locked away. His body is concealed. His fears and terrors cannot be given voice. Longing for other Jews must never be spoken. Caught in this escalation, the only path to safety is ever-increasing silence on Solly's part, especially around his friends since they are close enough to notice with ease if his facade begins to crumble; upon hearing him mention to her mother that he is unaware of his parents' current location, Solly's girlfriend protests, "You said the Bolsheviks killed them!" To avoid such moments, Solly sometimes seeks a cessation of speech by pushing away from certain friendships. With his remaining friends, Solly learns to curtail his disclosures. As disclosures cease to flow, his friendships wither. Not being trusted with any disclosure of significance, his friends sense they have become serviceable adjuncts rather than true friends. They cut back their own disclosures, unwilling to suffer the pain of lopsided trust. For his part, he must censor himself almost out of existence.

Friendship demands a depth of understanding not shared by strangers passing each other on the street. This is illustrated by how often we as strangers turn to someone's friends when we wish to understand her actions, asking, "Knowing her as you do, what do you think she meant by that?" We would be puzzled if the friend responded, "I'm certainly her friend, but why do you think I know her any better than you do?" This depth of understanding places more stringent demands on friends than simply collecting data from one another, knowing each other's birth date, favorite vacation spots, and family history. It also requires insight into each other's point of view, including her motivations and values—insight into, for example, why she hates birthdays, seeks out vacation spots by the ocean, and never mentions other family members. The understanding of friendship consists of insight into how another imbues her world with meaning. Such understanding is not only intrinsically part of friendship, it also provides an atmosphere in which the trust and affection characteristic of friendship can thrive. Without a certain depth of understanding, our trust suffers, there being little reason to assume that another will do well by us if we seriously doubt that she understands what we seek in the first place. Sensing a lack of such understanding, we begin to cool toward one another, wondering whether the other values us so little that she is interested only in our surface.

Passing promised to promote understanding in Solly's friendships. But this promise has proven hollow: not only does passing generate a sustained deficit of understanding, it *must* produce one. The markers Solly conceals under a cloak of silence—from his family surname to his hometown—are not inert material as far as understanding is concerned: They are its necessary matrix. His friends cannot understand his actions as though they were isolated beads on a string, contingently linked to one another. They need to embed his actions in what they know of his life, turning, for example, to what he has told them about his own family in order to understand why he bursts into tears when a blessing for orphans is given. Understanding another's action always requires situating it within a narrative of his past, present and projected future. Yet the concealment demanded by passing makes it impossible for others to formulate such a narrative of Solly's life. Lacking a context in which to place him, his friends' understanding suffers. When, for example, his girlfriend's mother learns that he has rejected her daughter's sexual advances, she wonders whether he is homosexual. Lacking access to Solly's own narrative, the girlfriend's mother has no recourse but to spin her own narrative to explain his actions.

Solly becomes not merely a puzzle with missing pieces, but a puzzle that has had some of its missing pieces replaced with misleading ones. Passing demands not only the concealment of difference, but also the projection of a new set of allegiances. Keeping silent about his own culture, Solly must strive to convey his approval of German culture. Yet he must never forget that his task is to blend in with his surroundings; in an ironic twist, overly-enthusiastic support of Nazi values might render him an object of dangerous scrutiny. So he mimics those around him, hoping to remain unnoticed. Encountering Solly's mimicry, the Germans who seek his friendship interpret his motivations as similar to their own. Seeing him salute Hitler, they imagine he acts for the same reasons they do. His friends always get Solly wrong—reading him as though he were themselves rather than himself. The understanding characteristic of friendship, seeing into another's motivational core, is precluded by passing.

Solly's friendships are undeniably distorted by passing. Gaps and stutters in disclosure and understanding make it impossible for him to be the closest of friends with those among whom he passes. He is always faced with the rift of trust and understanding that passing demands. But this lack of depth in his friendships may not be critical. Although some people, such as his girlfriend, reject his passing self, others accept him without depth of trust or understanding. Solly is well-liked by his soldier buddies and his school comrades. Passing does not enable Solly to speak freely, but apparently it still allows him to satisfy his craving for affection.

Consider the tale of Cinderella. When the Prince meets Cinderella at the ball, we are not surprised that he is infatuated. The enchanted facade provided by Cinderella's fairy godmother, including fine clothing, jewels and an expensive coach, is designed to produce such a result. Yet we remain uncertain whether he truly loves her until he meets her at home, surrounded by squalor, and carries her off. At this conclusion, we are content, satisfied that the Prince loves Cinderella for who she is, not for her elegant appearance at the ball. As our response reveals, we have a deeply-embedded intuition about true acceptance in a relationship: it has to stem from seeing another as she is, not as she merely appears. As Aristotle pointed out, true friends love each other for who they *are*.[11] Although it is easy for our friends to be impressed with our outward show, we yearn to be accepted because of the characters we have formed throughout our lives, not due to the glittering or merely safe personae we put on when we go to our own version of the ball.

If we are to be accepted for who we are, we must both present ourselves honestly and be seen accurately by others. Deceit and error are antithetical to such acceptance. Systematically deceiving another, we never allow him to accept us for who we are—it is as though Cinderella never set aside her enchanted costume, yet still married the Prince. We would also reject a friendship upon discovering that our friend liked us out of error, liking us, for example, because he mistakenly believed us to be heroic. In both of these situations, the affection rings hollow, but not because we doubt its psychological existence. We want more from our friendships than being liked due to deceit or error; such liking is dismissed because it seems to have nothing to do with who we truly are. Instead of our friends liking a myth, we wish them to accept us in the harsh light of truth, warts and all.

This desire to be accepted and liked for ourselves is central to the structure of true friendship. When we encounter people with whom we are not friends, we often experience a mutual desire to change one another, going so far as to make our acceptance contingent upon such transformation. True friendship, however, is different. Friends do not seek to change one another's essential traits; their mutual acceptance depends upon an explicit rejection of such transformation. This acceptance reveals that friends must acknowledge each other as possessing distinct wills, respecting one another's essential freedom to create their own selves by not insisting that they change. It is this drive to be accepted as self-creating beings that makes our desire to be accepted for who we are explicable. We wish our friends to accept us in our freedom; to do this, they must accept the self we have created, the self that embodies the cumulative weight of the choices we have made over our lives. Yet they cannot do this if they are blind to who we really are, seeing a hero rather than a coward due to deceit on our part or fantasy on theirs.

With respect to his friends, Solly ends up in a situation far worse than Cinderella's since she only had to change her clothing to blend in at the ball.[12] Solly disguises himself with more than an enchanted costume; his friends know him as someone who not only dresses as they do, but also shares the same values. And they never discover his masquerade. So their affection is unavoidably flawed, directed as it is at the role Solly plays yet does not accept as being truly himself. Worse, Solly cannot discover whether he would be accepted as a Jew by any of his friends since he cannot set aside his passing and then take it up again. By passing, Solly thinks to gain acceptance. His friends end up accepting someone, but it is the mask he wears that they love; accepting his semblance, they accept only themselves, in an act of unnoticed narcissism. Such narcissism makes a mockery of the idea that friendship involves the mutual recognition and acceptance of two independent wills.

The Invisible Man

> The man with the sad eyes believes he has been changed inside forever, like a beaten dog...[13]
>
> —Louis Begley describing the effects of passing on a Jewish character.

Solly's one real friend has just died, shot next to him as they were fighting together in the German Army. Before his death, he and Solly were best friends. They had bonded together despite the fact that the other man had made a homosexual pass at Solly while he was bathing, pursuing him as he fled. In fact, perhaps this is why they bonded—without the pass, the pursuing soldier would never have known the truth. Only the chase around the bathhouse transforms the situation, revealing Solly's circumcision. Halting his pursuit, the pursuer declares that he will be like a brother to Solly, accepting him for who he is. And so they become friends, the homosexual who passes as heterosexual and the Jew who passes as German. Yet, when his friend dies, Solly does not stay by his body to grieve. Framed by a crane shot, we watch as Solly makes his one serious, although unsuccessful, attempt to dispense with passing by trying to join the Russians. Is there a connection between losing his friend and his sudden decision to set aside passing?

Always reflecting back an idealized image of those close to him, never seen for himself, Solly slowly disappears. It is easy to imagine that identities can be created without recourse to others. But the individual does not exist without others, as Hegel recognized:

> Self-consciousness exists in and for itself when, and by the fact that, it so exists for another; that is, it exists only by being acknowledged.[14]

Friends are central sources of recognition. Friends anchor each other's identity, enabling both to know who they are; we tell our friends who we imagine ourselves to be and they, in turn, teach us who we are, convincing us of our own solidity. No wonder Solly cries out with such pain when his real friend dies; he understands that he has lost the last person who truly saw him, helping him retain his concealed identity, fixing him in himself. Feeling the sudden weightlessness of being without the fixing gaze of his friend, Solly's immediate response is to flee to people who may still see him for himself. But his flight fails as he is once again caught in an image: his German Army buddies interpret his attempted flight as a heroic attempt to take the enemy position and follow him to victory against the Russian position. His friends need Solly to be the hero so that they can confirm themselves as brave soldiers following him; by denying Solly access to the recognition he craves, his buddies ensure that he remains an actor in their narrative, a narrative that calls for him to be almost anyone other than himself.[15]

No longer seen as himself, Solly grows increasingly uncertain about who he is; looking into the eyes of those who claim to be his friends, he never finds himself mirrored back as Jewish. Lacking friends to fix him in his identity, Solly faces the ultimate terror for a person who passes: Is he disappearing behind the disguise he assumed? Nietzsche warned,

> Such an instinct [for acting] will have developed most easily in families of the lower classes who had to survive under changing pressures and coercions, in deep dependency, who had to cut their coat according to the cloth, always adapting themselves again to new circumstances, who always had to change their mien and posture, until they learned gradually to turn their coat with every wind and thus virtually to become a coat...[16]

Solly becomes skilled at changing his "mien and posture." Starting by changing his name, he goes on to wear German uniforms, sing Hitler Youth songs, and stare without speaking at Jewish corpses. Whereas he is initially confident about the Jewish identity hidden beneath the coat he wears, this confidence fades. As Solly's behavior increasingly becomes that of a Nazi, his fear grows that he is becoming nothing more than an actor without a core; from screaming out that he is Jewish to attempting to flee to the Russians so that he will be seen as Jewish again, Solly desperately tries to convince himself he still exists. This terror is what drives him to reveal his identity to his girlfriend's mother, despite his ignorance of her political sympathies. After asking him about his sexual restraint with her daughter, the mother questions, "Tell me. Are you really a German?" Faced with another lie, Solly blurts out the truth: "No, I'm a Jew...I had to tell someone. I couldn't stand it anymore." This burst of dangerous revelation underscores Solly's realization that his identity is slipping; he needs to have friends who can reflect him back to himself, friends to anchor his Jewish identity. Passing, he finds only the semblance of friends—others who have a stake in *not* reflecting him back at himself.

Passing is quite different from friendship, for friendship requires open disclosure, mutual understanding and affection based on acceptance of who we are. Solly discovers that passing involves necessary estrangement from the Germans who surround him: disclosures silenced, understanding compromised, and affection directed at a facade. Reeling back from this estrangement, Solly finds that he is also separated from other Jews; if he were to allow himself to get close enough for friendship, his passing cover would be put in jeopardy. And probably to no avail: when another Jew points a gun at him, Solly discovers that he is no longer trusted—in the process of masquerading as the enemy, he has crossed a line and is now seen as the enemy. As for being accepted for who he is, passing cannot permit this; those who do not know Solly's secret obviously cannot know him as he is, but neither can those who are in on the secret, for who he is becomes increasingly unclear as his passing progresses. Passing produces the bitter loneliness of being within touching distance of friendship yet never close enough.

This paper began with a puzzle: why should people yearn to escape from passing? After our close look at *Europa, Europa*, this puzzle is less perplexing. Passing has revealed its hidden logic of escalating estrangement. People who pass neither make a complete transition into the world in which they pass nor do they effortlessly step back into the world they left behind. Attempting to develop friendships with people who occupy the passing world, they find themselves trapped. Wishing to talk freely, they discover that they must censor themselves. Seeking understanding, they find misunderstanding. And those who pass know that even the limited understanding that remains is flawed since it is no more than understanding of the role they play. Turning to those who refuse to pass, attempts at friendship also fail. Fraternizing would render them suspect in the world in which they pass. Should they disregard this danger, they know they may find that those they wish to have as friends are not equally eager. No wonder people cast aside the masks they once donned, refusing to belong to neither person nor place.

> No doubt real friendship ties would have reduced Solly's burdens. But in his case the need to confide and lean on someone competed with the need for safety. Safety prevented him from establishing closer ties to the Jews. Because of safety, he could not be fully open with anyone else....
> [He] felt like an outsider, like someone who does not belong to anyone and to anyplace.[17]
> —Nechama Tec describing the life of a Jew who passed.

Notes

1 Nechama Tec, *In The Lion's Den: The Life of Oswald Rufeisen* (New York: Oxford University Press, 1990), 120.

2 The transformative possibilities of passing are discussed in James Weldon Johnson's novel, *Auto-Biography of an Ex-Coloured Man* (New York: Garden City Publishing Company, 1972).

3 For examples, see Paul Monette, *Becoming a Man: Half a Life Story* (New York: Harcourt Brace Jovanovich, 1992); Jessie Fauset, *Plum Bun* (London: Pandora Press, 1985); and Walter White, *Flight* (New York: Negro Universities Press, 1969).

4 This question is particularly explicit in Douglas Sirk's *Imitation of Life*, where the problems of the fictional character Lora Meredith in deciding between her "real life" and her acting career echo the confusion experienced

by Sarah Jane Johnson, a black character who decides to pass as white.

5 For other accounts of Jews who passed to escape Nazi persecution, see Louis Begley, *Wartime Lies* (New York: Alfred Knopf, 1991); Yehuda Nir, *The Lost Childhood* (New York: Harcourt Brace Jovanovich, 1989); Nechama Tec, *In the Lion's Den: The Life of Oswald Rufeisen*; Nechama Tec, *When Light Pierced the Darkness* (New York: Oxford University Press, 1986).

6 In this paper, I question whether Solly is capable of true friendship because of the requirements of passing. Due to this, it would be most accurate to speak of Solly's "friends" throughout, thus calling into question the nature of his relationships. However, this is stylistically awkward. Also, common usage allows for several uses of the word "friend"; as Aristotle remarks, "…men commonly give the name of friends to those who are connected from motives of profit…and to those who are attached to one another by the motive of pleasure" [*Nichomachean Ethics*, trans. D.P. Chase (New York: E.P. Dutton, 1920), 1157a]. So I have set aside the quotation marks. Yet the reader should remember that Solly's friends may not end up truly being friends.

7 Aristotle, *Nicomachean Ethics*, 1156a.

8 Nir, *The Lost Childhood*, 102.

9 Ralph Ellison, *Invisible Man* (New York: Random House, 1990), 573.

10 Begley, *Wartime Lies*, 105.

11 Aristotle, *Nichomachean Ethics*, 1156a.

12 The story suggests that Cinderella's fairy godmother is not faced with the more demanding task of changing Cinderella's speech, manners and values. This is due to her concealed class background. Despite appearances, Cinderella's class background is seen as suitable for a match with the Prince. Cinderella does not need to learn how to speak "like a lady" because, in a sense, she is seen as already being one. When the Prince finally places the glass slipper on her foot, he sees her as she is while also acknowledging her true status in the world. My thanks to Thomas Wartenberg for helping me develop this point.

13 Begley, *Wartime Lies*, 5.

14 G.W.F. Hegel, *Phenomenology of Spirit*, trans. A.V. Miller (Oxford: Clerendon Press, 1977), 178.

15 As Alasdair MacIntyre points out, we are all actors in multiple narratives; we act our own story as well as play roles in the stories of others. It is only when we set aside our own story that the narratives of others threaten to overwhelm us. See Alasdair MacIntyre, *After Virtue: A Study in Moral Theory* (Notre Dame, Indiana: University of Notre Dame Press, 1981), 213.

16 Friedrich Nietzsche, *The Gay Science*, trans. Walter Kaufman (New York: Random House, 1974), 316.

17 Tec, *In the Lion's Den*, 96–98.

13 ▏ The Politics of Interpretation

The Case of Bergman's *Persona*

Kelly Oliver

What is the Relationship Between Film and Theory?

Marxist and feminist film critics alike often engage in the exposure and identification of subterranean—or not so subterranean—ideologies within films. Marxists look for inherent capitalist structures and images while feminists look for inherent patriarchal structures and images. This raises the question of the relationship between film and ideology.[1] For the purposes of my analysis here I will define ideology as the naturalization of structures and modes of domination. Ideology, then, is the process and effect of various structures and institutions that causes certain beliefs and values to appear natural or true for all time, when by examining their histories and engaging in crosscultural analysis we see ways in which they are socially and culturally created and evolving. It seems, however, that all discourses are engaged in this process of naturalization and therefore all discourses are engaged in naturalizing structures of domination—even while they may resist it. All propositions in our language to some extent operate by assuming that there is a natural set of facts. Even as I try to argue that language creates a naturalization effect I am engaged in the process of using language to create such an effect: I am trying to persuade you that my hypothesis about ideology is true and that it accurately describes the way language works. If language operates by assuming that there is a set state of affairs, matters of fact, or nature, then ideology is everywhere. If ideology is everywhere then the critique cannot merely be engaged in a process of exposing ideology and the truth. The critic is also creating ideology, replacing one mask with another. In the case of film, the question then becomes, what is the relationship between film and criticism or theory? Or, in this context, what is the relationship between film and philosophy? Does the critic or philosopher discover the ideology in the film or does she actually create it? Does she do both of these at once?

Another way of asking these questions is to ask what is the relationship between the primary text—the film—and the secondary text—the commentary, criticism, or film theory. But this relationship between primary and secondary text deconstructs, especially when we are talking about ideology or philosophical models; for the critic engaged in the project of uncovering a film's ideological or philosophical pretext, structure, or content, presents a text—the subterranean text—that is prior to the so-called primary text. Suffice it to say that philosophical models also represent, manifest and perpetuate ideologies. In this project I am using Ingmar Bergman's *Persona* (1966) in order to subvert the Hegelian-Lacanian philosophical model that proposes that subjectivity is the result of an antagonistic struggle to the death with the other. In this case the film can be used to show the place at which the philosophical model breaks down.

The relationship, then, between film and criticism or theory is a productive relationship. The film engenders criticism but various readings recreate, resignify, and recirculate the film. Reading the film does more than merely uncover its ideological or philosophical presuppositions. Criticism and film theory can change the ideological or discursive context of film, in some cases in order to make the film subvert the very ideology or philosophical model that it might appear to exemplify. To say that the relationship between film and theory is productive is to say that there is a dynamic interchange between the film and the theoretical analysis of it.

The film never exists in itself. Film is always interpreted. Even if the viewer does not analyze it, she still engages in some interpretation of what is happening in the film and some interpretation of what she is watching. Her interpretation creates the film that she watches. She may watch it a second time and have a different experience of the film; it may become a different film for her. Film critics and theorists actively engage in interpretations that create different readings of films. The critic can bring elements in a film together to create a different film for her readers. A very powerful analysis may change the way that we view a particular film.

The ideology is not inside the film. The film exemplifies a philosophical model or an ideology only after it has been interpreted as such. The visual images in film, however, can provide striking examples of ideologies once they are read. This is not to say that the critic or theorist has control over the film or that any reading is just as good as another. Rather, the film can resist the critic's or theorist's interpretation of it. The critic must accept her responsibility not only to actively interpret the film—not merely pretend to describe the film as something whose meaning is transparent—but also she must accept her responsibility to the film and its integrity as a complete work.

In addition, interpretation has a larger goal: to effect social change. The film critic or theorist hopes that her interpretive work can make a difference in the way people think about each other and thereby make a difference in the way people treat each other. For example, Marxist critics hope that by exposing capitalist structures and modes of domination within films they can make people aware of exploitative relationships and thereby take one small step toward changing the social order. And feminists hope that by exposing patriarchal structures and modes of domination within film they can demonstrate that what we take to be natural ways of relating to each other are actually modes of socially constructed domination that should be called into question.

There are at least three possible strategies with which film criticism and theory can attempt to subvert the naturalization of structures of domination as they are represented, manifested or perpetuated within film.[2] First, the critic/theorist can diagnose and identify the ideological structure of the film. The question here is, what is the ideology behind this film? Second, the critic/theorist can dismantle the ideological structure of domination by showing how the naturalization effect is produced within the film. The question here is, how does the film naturalize power structures? What techniques does it use? Third, the critic/theorist can present an alternative to the apparent ideological structure of the film by showing places where the apparent ideology of the film breaks down or cannot sustain itself. Or the critic/theorist can read the traces of something other with the film itself in order to suggest an alternate power structure. The question here is, how does this film break down or subvert dominant ideology?

In this essay I will attempt to use all three strategies in order to diagnose and subvert the structure of relationships between women in Ingmar Bergman's 1966 film *Persona*. First, I diagnose and identify the structure of relationships as a Hegelian-Lacanian struggle to the death. Within this film women relate to each other by identifying with the mother. And all relationships between women become struggles to separate from the mother. The mother represents antisocial silent nature and must be abjected (to use Julia Kristeva's term) so that the daughter can become a subject. Second, I denaturalize those structures by showing how they have been constructed within the film using various dialogic and cinematic techniques and camera angles. In addition, I use the theories of Hegel, Lacan, Kristeva, and Irigaray to show how this antagonistic model of relationships has been constructed in both philosophy and psychoanalytic theory. And finally, I suggest an alternative conception of intersubjectivity by both showing how the model represented in the film cannot sustain itself and by providing an alternative model to the one represented in the film. In *Persona* the Hegelian struggle for recognition breaks down when the maternal body is involved.

The Struggle for Self-Recognition

In Hegel's master/slave model, self-recognition is the result of a life and death struggle with another self-consciousness. The self can only recognize itself after it is recognized by another self-consciousness. The recognition of the other, however, turns the self into an object of its own consciousness. Unable to take the position of an object and a subject for itself at the same time, the self must recuperate its subjectivity by first recognizing itself *in the other*, thereby identifying with the other's recognition, and then *supersede the other*. This last moment is crucial. In order to return to itself from the place of the other, the self must supersede the otherness of its self-recognition. It must overcome its self-alienation in its relation to the other. This dialectical struggle between self and other is a violent battle in which the self must either kill the other or commit suicide to avoid the inevitable murder of the other.

The French Freudian psychoanalyst Jacques Lacan amends the Hegelian scenario. He claims that the self-alienation inherent to self-recognition continues throughout self-conscious life. Lacan describes what he calls the "mirror stage" as a developmental process that takes place at about six months of age. The subject can only see itself as the image reflected in the mirror or in the body of another; the self is reflected in the other. This recognition becomes the model for subsequent relations and self-definition. For Lacan, like Hegel, self-consciousness comes only through an encounter with an other. Or as Lacan puts it, the subject must split into its reflection and itself in order to become one subject. In the mirror model this splitting is the splitting between the child's body and the mirror image through which the child recognizes itself. Without this splitting the child would not have recognized itself as unified. This is the paradox of self-consciousness: to become one you must become two. The tension that Lacan describes is the tension between Hegel's master and slave. Ultimately, it is a dialectical struggle for recognition. This specular relation, where the subject can only see itself through the other, leads to an absolute rivalry with the other. The subject wants to annihilate the other so that it might exist.[3]

Once the subject sees its image in the mirror or in the body of another, it realizes that it is separated from the rest of the world and from its mother to whom it had an intimate and satisfying attachment. Following the mirror stage, the mother takes the place of the mirror image as other—the child is beginning to see her as another being. Now it becomes dependent on her to fulfill its needs in a new way. If she is another being, then it is alienated from her in a way in which it wasn't before, in its imaginary unity with her. The child realizes that the mother can go away and that it has no control over her. At this point, since the child cannot communicate its needs and does not yet have access to symbolic substitutes, its only options for satisfaction are either to extinguish its desire or annihilate the object who controls the satisfaction of its desire.

Before the subject enters language and a symbol can stand in for its desire, "desire is seen solely in the other."[4] After the subject can express itself in language the imaginary struggle with the other is no longer life-threatening. Language mediates between the two subjects, and their interdependent existence, which appeared on the imaginary level as mutually exclusive, is reconciled. Through language one subject can recognize and acknowledge another subject *qua* subject. Desire is given a voice, however inadequate.

French psychoanalyst and cultural theorist Julia Kristeva reconceives the Hegelian-Lacanian model so that self-recognition becomes not a question of killing the other but a question of embracing the other. We can imagine that if self-recognition necessitates the alienation of this mediate other, rather than killing off the intermediate, we could embrace it. Rather than denying our alienation we could accept it. For Kristeva this is the project of psychoanalysis. This was Freud's project; showing us how to live with, even embrace, the return of the repressed. Kristeva maintains it is the other that is repressed both in the individual psyche and in the society. Both the individual and the society need to learn to embrace the return of the repressed rather than trying to kill the other. That which we try to exclude from our identity as individuals and societies is that within ourselves that we project onto the other in order to repress it. As Kristeva describes it, this repressed other can safely make its way back into our psyches and society through language (in the broadest possible sense). Something of this repressed other, what Kristeva calls the "semiotic," is discharged into language. The semiotic is the affective tonal rhythmic element of language, the element that means without referring. It is the linguistic trace of a repressed material drive force.

If we return to the Lacanian model, it is only through representation, through the image in the mirror, that the subject has any recognition of self.[5] It is only through representation that self-recognition takes place. By the very nature of representation, however, that self-recognition is always other, always split, always alienated. Because we can never adequately or completely represent ourselves, we keep trying, we keep talking.

Ingmar Bergman's *Persona* is a study in the psychic dynamic of self-recognition through an encounter with an other. It is a study in the inability to represent semiotic drive force. It is a study in the breakdown of identity inherent in the very process of becoming self-identical. It is also a study in the patriarchal construction of relationships between women and maternity.

Persona begins with a visual poem full of images of sacrifice, crucifixion, vampires, and death. Next we meet Sister Alma (Bibi Anderson), a nurse who has been assigned to care for an actress, Elisabet Vogler (Liv Ullman). Elisabet Vogler, we are told by her doctor, stopped during the second act of a performance of *Electra*, fell silent for a minute, then continued as usual, went home as usual, but refused to get out of bed the next morning and has refused to speak for three months. After the performance, Elisabet Vogler claims to have had a fit of laughter during that second act. The doctor sends Elisabet and Sister Alma to her beach house for a therapeutic summer rest. At first the women seem to enjoy each other's company and the restful life at the beach house. They pick mushrooms, read, and walk on the beach. Alma begins to open up to Elisabet and tell her things she has told no one else. Although Elisabet still refuses to talk she occasionally writes a letter. One day she sends a letter addressed to her doctor with Alma to town. In the car on the way to town Alma notices that the envelope is not sealed. She yields to her temptation and reads Elisabet's letter. This is a turning point in the film when Alma discovers that Elisabet claims to be studying her, using her, and Alma feels betrayed.

The Sacrifice

Elisabet gives up speaking because her words seem empty and false. She realizes that all representation is just acting and all self-representations are just so many personae, so many masks. In a long monologue in the first part of the movie, her doctor suggests that she no longer talks so that she will no longer lie:

> I do understand, you know. The hopeless dream of *being*. Every tone of voice a lie, an act of treason. Every gesture false. Every smile a grimace. The role of wife, the role of friend, the roles of mother and mistress, which is worse? Which has tortured you most? Playing the actress with the interesting face? Keeping all the pieces together with an iron hand and getting them to fit? Where did it break? Where did you fail? Was it the role of mother that finally did it?[6]

While Elisabet futilely resorts to silence to try to shed her masks (her personae), Alma encourages her to accept the lies. Alma suggests that all we have are lies; in fact lies might be the truth of human communication:

> Is it so important not to lie, always to tell the truth, always to have the
> right tone of voice? Can you even live without talking as it comes?
> Talking nonsense, excusing yourself, lying, evading things? I know you
> have stopped talking because you're tired of all your parts, all the parts
> you could play perfectly. But isn't it better to let yourself be silly and
> sloppy and lying and just babble on? Don't you think you'd be a bit bet-
> ter really, if you let yourself be what you are?[7]

Alma seems to accept that communication necessarily breaks down, that
every representation is a false image. She encourages Elisabet to accept
the fact that all forms of communication are surface attempts to represent
the unrepresentable semiotic. In *Persona*, however, this failure of language
to represent semiotic drive force and affect leads to violence. Like the
monk who early in the film appeared on Elisabet's television burning himself in Vietnam as a protest, Alma resorts to violence in order to be heard.
Late in the film, after Alma has read the fateful letter which makes her
feel betrayed, she breaks a glass on the porch. She sweeps up the glass
except for one piece. She decides to leave this one piece when she hears
Elisabet coming out from inside the house. She leaves the glass for Elisabet
to step on. Eventually Elisabet steps on the glass while Alma is watching
through the window from inside the house. They exchange hostile glances
and at that moment the film appears to dissolve Alma's image and burn
up. No form of representation, including the film, can adequately represent human affect. Throughout *Persona* Bergman makes allusions to the
shortcomings of various forms of representation and communication
including radio, television, photographs, music, letters, and speech. In all
of these cases there is something that exceeds the medium, something that
cannot be communicated. That which motivates representation itself cannot be represented.

This excess of language bursts out in moments of violence; it is spoken
by the movements of the body, but it is sacrificed to the symbolic order,
the social order. The force of affect is cut off from language because the
material bodily drives that give rise to affect are repressed in symbolic representation. For Kristeva, the original seat of these drives is the maternal
body. It is in relation to the maternal body that human beings first experience the excitation of drives. In its first years of life, typically, a maternal figure regulates the child's bodily processes so that these processes and
the drives connected to them become associated with the maternal body.
The repression of drives, then, is the repression of the maternal body,
especially the autonomous subject's relation to and dependence on that
body. What Kristeva calls the semiotic element in representation, which is

repressed within and yet motivates signifying systems, is associated with the maternal body. Both Elisabet and Alma feel the inadequacy of language and all forms of representation. Both of them feel frustrated because they cannot represent that which seems closest to them, most important to them. And for both of them this frustration is deeply associated with maternity, as I will explain later. While Elisabet protests her frustration through silence, Alma expresses her frustration through talking continually; silence and empty speech are both reactions to the inability of language to express affects connected to bodily drive force.

During the course of their stay at the doctor's beach house, because Elisabet won't talk and Alma does all of the talking, they begin to exchange roles. Alma takes the place of the patient while Elisabet takes on the role of the listening therapist. Alma begins to hear herself through Elisabet's ears. She begins to see herself in Elisabet. In the first half of the film when the two women had separate identities, Bergman usually showed them together in the same frame. In the second half of the film as the boundaries of their individual identities blur and it becomes impossible to separate them—as if depicting the Lacanian mirror stage in which identity is always set up on a splitting—Bergman shows the two women almost exclusively in separate frames.

In their exchange, Alma is figured as the sacrificial lamb of the opening visual poem, while Elisabet, the therapist/actress, is figured as the vampire. Here women are portrayed as either sacrificial lambs or vampires, virgins or dangerous, powerful women. Women's power must be sacrificed or it remains dangerous. Women must be sacrificed or they are dangerous. There are two scenes in which Elisabet's association with a vampire is striking. In one scene Elisabet sucks the blood from a cut on Alma's wrist. In another Elisabet appears in the night like a shadow, creeps into Alma's room and bends over to kiss her neck. Like a vampire, Elisabet, artist/therapist, sucks the life out of Alma. Elisabet is using Alma, studying Alma for her own purposes, and gives her nothing in return except alienated images of herself. Elisabet is a mirror that reflects Alma's words and her silence eventually makes Alma's words seem empty and false.

Just as the monk shown on television protesting the Vietnam war sacrifices himself in order to warn us that we have reached the limit of the social, so does Alma. She is willing to sacrifice herself and be sacrificed so that Elisabet will talk and reenter society. Free-floating violence, violence that cannot be represented, threatens the social order. Kristeva argues in *Revolution in Poetic Language* that ritual sacrifice is foundational to the onset of society because it channels violence and makes it representable.[8]

Sacrifice makes violence representable—society cannot exist without representation, even though something always exceeds it. It is also interesting that for Kristeva, Biblical sacrifice and prohibitions, especially dietary prohibitions, are associated with and analogous to the maternal.⁹ As Kristeva describes it, even sacrifice is an attempt to come to terms with the mother. Certainly it makes sense within the framework of psychoanalytic theory to emphasize the importance of separation from the mother. If both sacrifice and representation in general are forms of separation, then they are at least associated with a separation from the maternal body. This separation, the primary separation, within the Hegelian and Lacanian scenarios anyway, is a violent struggle with the mother for recognition of the self as an autonomous subject.

Matricide

In *Persona* the struggle for recognition between self and other becomes focused on maternity and the relationship between mother and child. For example, near the end of the film, there is a scene that is replayed from two angles. We see Elisabet and Alma sitting across the table from each other and it is unclear whether this is Alma's fantasy or whether it is real. The first part of the scene is shot from Alma's point of view and we see Elisabet's reactions while Alma is talking. Then the scene is replayed from Elisabet's point of view and we see Alma's face as she is talking. Alma is describing Elisabet's experience of motherhood as if it were her own, by switching between pronouns "you" and "I." She describes a pregnancy that is the result of pressure from others, a pregnancy that operates as a threat to her bodily integrity. She describes her/Elisabet's desire to terminate the pregnancy. Even after the child is born it is threatening and Alma/Elisabet wishes that it would die:

> So Elisabet Vogler, the actress, got pregnant. When I realized I couldn't change my mind, I got frightened. In the meantime you tried several times by yourself to abort. And you failed. In the end you went to a doctor. He realized it was no longer possible. When I saw there was no way out, I became ill and began to hate the baby and wished for it to be stillborn. In the end, the baby was pulled out with forceps. Elisabet Vogler looked with disgust and terror at her crippled, piping baby. Left alone with her first-born, she kept hoping and muttering: Can't you die now, can't you die. And I thought what it would be like to kill the baby, smother it under the pillow as if by accident, or crack its head against the radiator. But he survived.

Alma could be describing her own experience of pregnancy that ends in abortion. Elisabet's doctor suggests that it was her role as mother that led Elisabet to silence: "Where did it break? Where did you fail? Was it the role of mother that finally did it?" Even the radio play that Alma turns on to soothe Elisabet in the hospital reminds her of the pain of motherhood. A woman's voice from the radio says: "Forgive me so that I can breathe again—and live again. What do you know of mercy, what do you know of a mother's suffering, the bleeding pain of a woman?"[10]

Persona presents us with a mother who wants to kill her child, a mother whose identity is threatened by her child. Maternity becomes the emblem of the subject's struggle with otherness. In the case of the maternal body, the other is within the self. The maternal body presents the quintessential undecidability of the subject—is it one or two subjects? Within the dialectical dance of subjectivity described by Hegel we do not see a moment of such questionable identity. Because with maternity alterity is within, in this case, Hegel's struggle to the death with the other becomes a struggle within the self. In Hegel's scenario we are involved here with infanticide and possibily matricide. *Persona* shows us that the case of maternity breaks down the Hegelian model of self-recognition as the struggle to the death. For in the case of maternity the death of the other amounts to the death of the self: there can be no clear separation between self and other.

Is it an accident that Elisabet Vogler stops, falls silent, laughs to herself, not to speak again during the second act of *Electra*? We don't know which character Elisabet plays in the drama. Does she play the vengeful childless daughter Electra or the murdered and murdering mother Clytemnestra? One of the subtexts of Sophocles' *Electra* is that words are worthless compared to actions; actions speak louder than words. What would be the second act of his drama is an argument between Electra and her mother Clytemnestra in which Electra derides her mother for the murder of her father, Agamemnon, and Clytemnestra defends her action. This exchange becomes an argument over speech and the right to speech. Their argument is interrupted by a messenger who delivers the news that Orestes, Clytemnestra's son and Electra's brother, is dead. This news should be good news to the mother and bad news to the daughter because Orestes was Electra's ally in her vengeful plots against the mother. What is at stake in Orestes' death is also silence:

> Clytemnestra: Will you and Orestes silence me?
>
> Electra: It is we who are silenced, and have no power to silence you.[11]

Through the son the mother is silenced. In the end she is silenced for good when Orestes kills her. Perhaps this is what makes Elisabet laugh in the middle of act two when, upon discovering that Orestes, her son and enemy, is dead, Clytemnestra says, "There is a strange power in motherhood; a mother may be wronged but she never learns to hate her child."

Elisabet laughs because she never learns to love her child. She laughs at how, in *Electra*, infanticide begets matricide.

Using Kristeva's theory of feminine sexuality, Alma and Elisabet's infanticidal desires can be read as matricidal desires. In *Black Sun* Kristeva describes something akin to what she calls the abjection of the maternal body in *Powers of Horror*. Abjection

> is an extremely strong feeling which is at once somatic and symbolic, and which is above all a revolt of the person against an external menace from which one wants to keep oneself at a distance, but of which one has the impression that it is not only an external menace but that it may menace us from inside. So it is a desire for separation, for becoming autonomous and also the feeling of an impossibility of doing so.[12]

At the weaning stage the child needs to experience its mother as abject, as something both repellent and fascinating. Alma and Elisabet seem to have a kind of abject relationship to each other: both are fascinated and yet repulsed by the other. In the end, Alma especially wants separation from Elisabet; she insists, "I'm not you, I'm only trying to help you, I'm Sister Alma. I'm not Elisabet Vogler. It's you who are Elisabet Vogler. I would very much like to have—I love—I haven't…."[13] And yet she cannot separate; she desires separation and feels separation impossible. This is the experience of abjection.

In *Black Sun* Kristeva's notion of abjection becomes more extreme. It is not merely the case that the maternal body must be abjected so that the child will not abject itself. Now, on the imaginary level, the maternal body must be killed so that the child will not kill itself. "Matricide," says Kristeva, "is our vital necessity."[14] It is necessary that the child leave the maternal body. The child must agree to lose the mother in order to be able to imagine her or name her.[15]

Kristeva argues that female sexuality is more likely to be a depressive sexuality because it is more difficult for females to commit the necessary matricide.[16] Because of the female's bodily identification with the maternal body it is difficult for her to kill the maternal body without also killing herself. In the case of the female, matricide does not ward off suicide; rather, matricide is a form of suicide. Kristeva suggests that part of the reason why female sexuality is melancholy is because within our heterosexist culture a woman cannot have a mother-substitute as an object of desire in the way that a man can. In other words, female sexuality is melancholy because it is fundamentally homosexual, which must be kept a secret within a heterosexist culture. It is possible, however, that if the dependence on the maternal body can be separated from the dependence on the mother then the necessary matricide can take place and a woman can lose the maternal body and still love her mother. This means that she can lose the maternal body as maternal container and love her mother's body, her own body, as the body of a woman. Unlike Freud who maintains that in order to develop normally females must change their love objects and erogenous zones by *denying* their original love objects and erogenous zones, Kristeva suggests that females must admit, even (re)*embrace*, those original loves and pleasures.

For Kristeva, one way that a woman identifies with her mother on this semiotic level of bodily drives is through childbirth. This reunion is bittersweet because it reminds the new mother what she has lost. Kristeva argues that through the experience of maternity and birth a woman identifies with her own mother. It is this identification with the mother that both Elisabet and Alma find difficult to bear. It is their recognition of themselves in the mother that is both terrifying and fascinating. Perhaps their infanticidal desires are really matricidal desires, desires to separate from the mother whose identity has become overbearing and claustrophobic. In *Persona*, feminine sexuality winds around these matricidal desires.

One of the strangest scenes in *Persona* is near the end of the film when Elisabet's husband Mr. Vogler visits the beach house. In an hallucinatory scene, Alma greets Mr. Vogler who speaks to her as if she is Elisabet. At first Alma insists that she is not Mrs. Vogler. When Elisabet comes out of the house to watch, Alma begins to respond as Elisabet. Mr. Vogler says that "the most difficult thing is to explain to—your little boy. But I'm doing what I can. There's something deeper there, that it's difficult to see."[17] Alma responds with tender words for "our little boy." After her expression of love for "our little boy," Mr. Vogler is overcome with passion and begins to kiss Alma. Alma passively admits Mr. Vogler's caresses while Elisabet watches from the side. Alma looks at Elisabet the whole time that she is speaking to Mr. Vogler. Her identification with Elisabet and specifically Elisabet's motherhood is consummated in this scene with Mr. Vogler. Hers is a sacrificial sexuality. She displaces her desire for Elisabet by identifying with Elisabet so that she is able to have sex with Mr. Vogler. It is only because Elisabet is there and for the sake of her son that Alma can go through with it.

Midway through the film Alma describes another voyeuristic sex scene involving two women. Slightly drunk one evening, she tells Elisabet about one summer afternoon on a beach sunbathing with a woman from next door whom she did not know. They were sunbathing nude and noticed two young boys watching them from the rocks above. The neighbor woman invited them down and the two women took turns having sex with one of the boys. Alma describes how excited she was by this voyeuristic scene. She watches her neighbor Katarina both while Katarina is having sex with the boy and while she, Alma, is having sex with the boy. She affectionately describes Katarina's naked body. All the while Elisabet listens intently nodding her head.

Within the film this scene is overdetermined. In the visual poem that begins the film, a young boy of the same age that Alma describes on the beach is watching and caressing the face of a woman, Alma/Elisabet, on a big screen.[18] Also, in one of their first encounters, Alma reads a letter to Elisabet and enclosed with the letter is a picture of Elisabet's son. Elisabet tears the picture in half and hands it back to Alma in disgust. The recurrence of these young boys—the young boy in the beginning of the film, Elisabet's son, and the young boy on the beach—is charged with both sexual and maternal desire. The recurrence of these scenes also marks Alma's identification with Elisabet. Like Elisabet, Alma had been pregnant, as the result of the afternoon on the beach with the boy. And it is through the experience of pregnancy that Alma takes over Elisabet's discourse in the scene shot twice from both of their perspectives in which Alma refers to herself as "I" when telling the story of Elisabet's unwanted pregnancy. She knows about unwanted pregnancy from her own experience. Only unlike Elisabet, she has an abortion. Now, in this twice-shot scene, Alma wants to have a child. She wants to be Elisabet, the mother, even while she tortures Elisabet with her account of Elisabet's unwanted pregnancy.

Even Alma's name is an allusion to the mother. "Alma," Latin for bounteous, is an allusion to the Alma Mater, the bountiful mother, the Virgin Mary. Kristeva suggests that, like sacrifice, the myth of the Virgin contains the violence of semiotic drives by turning violence against them. And like sacrifice, the violence of the semiotic returns within the very ritual that attempts to repress it. Through the myth of the Virgin Mary the mother's power is brought under paternal control. It is domesticated:

> It is as if paternity were necessary in order to relive the archaic impact of the maternal body on man; in order to complete the investigation of a ravishing maternal *jouissance* [ecstasy, total joy] but also of its terrorizing aggressivity; in order somehow to admit the threat that the male feels as much from the possessive maternal body as from his separation from it—a threat that he immediately returns to that body.[19]

Man returns the threat to the maternal body through the myth of the Virgin. The maternal body is allowed only joy in pain. Her body has only ear, milk, and tears.[20] The sexed body is replaced by the "ear of understanding," the Virgin Mary of the Catholic Church.[21] Kristeva suggests, however, that the silent ear, milk, and tears "are metaphors of nonspeech, of a 'semiotics' that linguistic communication does not account for."[22] The

Virgin mother becomes the representative of a "return of the repressed" semiotic. Although the myth of the Virgin can *control* the maternal semiotic, it cannot *contain* the semiotic.

Like the Virgin Mary, Sister Alma, bountiful mother, a mother without boundaries, gives herself over for the sake of the social. The boundaries of her self dissolve. She is lost so that the social relationship might be restored and Elisabet will talk again. French philosopher and psychoanalyst Luce Irigaray suggests that it is only because we associate the mother with nature over and against culture that we believe she must be sacrificed for the sake of the social and language.[23] We imagine the mother as a silent, natural body which must be left behind in order to enter culture. This matricide, argues Irigaray, is necessary only within patriarchal culture.

The bountiful mother does not have to give herself over to culture. Irigaray imagines a Virgin Mary who is not sacrificed for the sake of her son. She imagines a divinity made flesh that engenders a loving relationship with the other that is not violent and destructive. She suggests that perhaps with the figure of Mary we have the word made flesh and the advent of a nonviolent erotic divinity.[24] In the body of Mary we have the fertile marriage of logos and cosmos, spirit and body.[25] Mary's maternal body is the incarnation of otherness. She is neither merely the body-object, since she is the incarnation of the divine spirit, nor merely the spirit, since the god-child must be born from a body. For Irigaray, Mary represents the in-between, the "sensible transcendental," through whom we might imagine another economy of exchange that does not require sacrifice. Only when the mother is seen as a speaking, loving, desiring human being will ethics be possible. Irigaray's ethics of sexual difference requires a rearticulation of maternity which rescues the mother from the patriarchal association with nature/death.

Against Lacan, Irigaray maintains that we don't have to substitute the law of the father for the body/desire of the mother. It is not the case that language necessarily replaces the corporeal relationship to the mother. Rather, we need to find a language with which to speak the corporeal. This speech is possible because the mother is not what Lacan and traditional psychoanalytic theory take her for.

Within Freudian and Lacanian psychoanalytic theory the mother is seen as the infant's first object. She is merely the container that meets the infant's needs. She is nature against which the infant must struggle to enter culture. Within traditional psychoanalytic theory, the primary identification with the mother is a threat to the autonomy and normal psychic development of the child. It is necessary that the child break off its identification with the mother through the father in order to become social, in order to become a human being. The identification with the mother is a threat, however, only because this identification is seen as an identification with nature. Only if the mother operates merely as the container of needs and not at the level of desire (in the Lacanian sense) is she anti- or presocial. In *The Ethics of Sexual Difference* Irigaray says that the mother is a threat because she is denied a desiring body; hers is an anti-social body without the relationship to something outside the mother-child dyad which is necessary for sociality.[26]

Irigaray emphasizes the need to reconceive of the mother-daughter relationship, a relationship completely annihilated within patriarchy. She says that "in this perspective, the relation between the genders is determined by the necessity of man and without consideration for the identity of woman, who rather admits the desire for and with another. Woman, born from the same as herself, knows much less and more artificially the nostalgia for regression in the mother."[27] Rather than experience her relationship with the mother as a nostalgia for reunion with the maternal body, a body that she carries with her in her own, she experiences this relationship as a longing for reciprocal exchange, intersubjective language.[28] Unlike the man's, hers is not a desire to reunite with nature in the place of the maternal body motivated by Thanatos; rather hers is a desire to communicate with the mother-woman motivated by Eros. In place of the Hegelian-Lacanian model, Irigaray imagines a mother-daughter relationship, a relationship between two women, that founds intersubjective relations and the social rather than threatens them.

Bergman's *Persona* is a visual display of the limit of the Hegelian-Lacanian model when its actors are mothers, women who relate to each other as mothers and daughters. By the end of the film, although there is no final resolution, both women seem to realize that in some ways they need each other in order to be whole. This realization, which was in the beginning the source of self-alienation and violence, may in the end be a kind of consolation as they each go back to their respective lives to take up their duties, their personae, as they did before.

In sum, I have argued that Bergman's *Persona* represents a violent Hegelian model for intersubjectivity. More specifically, it represents two women's struggle for recognition within a patriarchal structure of intersubjectivity and relationships between women. I have identified this patriarchal Hegelian structure as the ideology manifest in the film. In addition, I have attempted to show how the film constructs this violent sacrificial relationship between two women in order to begin to dismantle the patriarchal structures that figure relationships between women as violent struggles. Moreover, using the theories of Julia Kristeva and Luce Irigaray, I have proposed an alternative conception of the relationship between women by reconcieving maternity. I have shown that maternity is the limit case for the Hegelian model of intersubjectivity, since in the case of the maternal body the two subjects do not engage in a struggle to the death. In addition, following Irigaray, I propose a model of maternity that does not reduce the mother to some natural thing that is opposed to culture or the social. This new conception of the mother makes it possible to imagine an identity with the mother that does not threaten society or subjectivity. Within this alternative conception of maternity, women can identify with each other through an identification with their mothers as women.

In *Persona*, Alma and Elisbet fight against any identification with the maternal. Theirs is a struggle to the death that insures that they cannot identify with each other and maintain their own individuality at the same time. Within the Hegelian model displayed by Bergman, one is sacrificed for the other; there cannot be two. In my analysis of this film I have given answers to the three questions with which I began: "What is the ideology behind this film?" "How does the film naturalize power structures?" "How does this film break down or subvert dominant ideology?" As a critic or theorist I have attempted, first, to use Bergman's film *Persona* to analyze some patriarchal institutions and representations that go beyond this particular film and that contribute to women's oppression; and, second, to suggest less oppressive alternatives.

Notes

1 I am using "ideology" in a very broad sense here. I am not using it in a strict Marxist sense.

2 This is a complex question in itself—does film merely represent, manifest or perpetuate structures of domination? I address this question only indirectly throughout my analysis.

3 Jacques Lacan, *The Seminar of Jacques Lacan, Freud's Papers on Technique, 1953–54*, Book I, trans. John Forrester (Cambridge, England: Cambridge University Press, 1988), 170–73.

4 Lacan, *Seminar*, 170.

5 For a discussion of the relation between film images and the Lacanian mirror stage, see Janet Bergstrom and Mary Ann Doane, eds., *Camera Obscura: A Journal of Feminism and Film Theory* (1989), 20–21; Mary Ann Doane, *The Desire to Desire: The Woman's Film of the 1940's* (Bloomington: Indiana University Press, 1989); Christian Metz, *The Imaginary Signifier: Psychoanalysis and the Cinema*, trans. A. Williams, B. Brewster and A. Guzetti, (Bloomington: Indiana University Press, 1977); Laura Mulvey,

"Visual Pleasure and Narrative Cinema," *Visual and Other Pleasures* (Bloomington: Indiana University Press, 1989).

6 Ingmar Bergman, *Persona and Shame: The Screenplays of Ingmar Bergman.* trans. Keith Bradfield (New York: Marion Boyars Press, 1972), 41.

7 Bergman, *Persona*, 80.

8 Julia Kristeva, *Revolution in Poetic Language*, trans. Margaret Waller (New York: Columbia University Press, 1974), 75–78.

9 Julia Kristeva, *Powers of Horror*, trans. Leon Roudiez (New York: Columbia University Press, 1980), 100.

10 Bergman, *Persona*, 29.

11 Sophocles. *Electra and Other Plays*, trans. E.F. Watling (Baltimore: Penguin, 1953/67), 92; translation slightly altered.

12 Kristeva, *Powers of Horror*, 135–6.

13 Bergman, *Persona*, 97.

14 Julia Kristeva, *Black Sun*, trans. Leon Roudiez (New York: Columbia University Press, 1987), 27.

15 Kristeva, *Black Sun*, 43.

16 Kristeva *Black Sun*, 28–29.

17 Bergman, *Persona*, 84.

18 There is a strong resemblance between the two actresses, Liv Ullman and Bibi Anderson, who play Elisabet and Alma.

19 Julia Kristeva, "Motherhood According to Giovanni Bellini," trans. Thomas Gora, Alice Jardine, and Leon Roudiez, in Leon Roudiez, ed., *Desire in Language* (New York: Columbia University Press, 1975), 263.

20 Kristeva, "Stabat Mater" in *Tales of Love*, trans. Leon Roudiez (New York: Columbia University Press, 1976), 248–49.

21 Kristeva, "Stabat Mater," 257

22 Kristeva, "Stabat Mater," 249.

23 In several places Irigaray suggests that the mother must be seen as a desiring subject. I interpret this to mean that she should not be seen as merely a part of nature. See Luce Irigaray, *The Irigaray Reader*, ed. Margaret Whitford (London: Blackwell Press, 1991), 43, 52, 170–17. For an elaboration of this thesis, see my *Womanizing Nietzsche: Philosophy's Relation to the "Feminine"* (New York: Routledge, 1994).

24 Luce Irigaray, *Marine Lover of Friedrich Nietzsche*, trans. Gillian Gill (New York: Columbia University Press, 1991), 181.

25 Irigaray, *Marine Lover*, 190.

26 Irigaray, *Irigaray Reader*, 170–71.

27 Luce Irigaray, *J'aime à toi* (Paris: Grasset, 1992), 212, my translation; all subsequent references to this text are my translations.

28 Irigaray, *J'aime à toi*, 213.

Index

Contributors

Noël Carroll is Professor of Philosophy at the University of Wisconsin at Madison. He is author of *Mystifying Movies* and *The Philosophy of Horror*, among other books.

Stanley Cavell is the Walter M. Cabot Professor of Aesthetics and the General Theory of Value at Harvard University. His books on film include *The Pursuits of Happiness: The Hollywood Comedy of Remarriage* and *The World Viewed*.

Harvey Cormier is Assistant Professor of Philosophy at the University of Texas at Austin. He is currently writing on William James' concept of truth.

Cynthia A. Freeland, Associate Professor of Philosophy and Director of Women's Studies at the University of Houston, has published widely in ancient philosophy, feminist theory, and aesthetics. In 1992 she curated a horror film series for the Museum of Fine Arts, Houston.

Robert Gooding-Williams is Associate Professor of Philosophy and Black Studies at Amherst College. He is editor of *Reading Rodney King/ Reading Urban Uprising* and author of *Nietzsche's Pursuit of Modernism*.

Karen Hanson, Professor of Philosophy at Indiana University, teaches and writes on topics in ethics, philosophy of mind, and aesthetics. She is author of *The Self Imagined* and co-editor of *Romantic Revolutions*.

Julie Inness teaches philosophy at Mount Holyoke College. Her publications include *Privacy, Intimacy, and Isolation*. She is currently working on a manuscript tentatively titled *Passing Thoughts*.

Douglas Kellner is Professor of Philosophy at the University of Texas at Austin and is author of many books and articles on social theory, politics, history, and culture, including *Camera Politica: The Politics and Ideology of Contemporary Hollywood Film*, co-authored with Michael Ryan. His most recent book is *Media Culture*.

Kelly Oliver teaches philosophy at the University of Texas at Austin. She is the author of *Reading Kristeva: Unraveling the Double-bind*, and *Womanizing Nietzsche: Philosophy's Relation to "the Feminine."* She edited a special issue of *Hypatia* on Feminism and Language, and *Ethics, Politics and Difference in the Writings of Julia Kristeva*.

Nickolas Pappas is the author of *Plato: The Republic* and other articles on Plato and poetry. He is currently writing on Plato's affiliations with Aristophanes and on *Bram Stoker's Dracula*. He teaches at the City College of CUNY, New York.

Naomi Scheman teaches philosophy and women's studies at the University of Minnesota. Her papers in feminist epistemology are collected in *Engenderings: Constructions of Knowledge, Authority, and Privilege*. She is working on a book on Wittgenstein and feminism, exploring issues of marginality, privilege, home, and diaspora.

Thomas E. Wartenberg is Professor of Philosophy at Mount Holyoke College. He is the author of *The Forms of Power: From Domination to Transformation* and editor of *Rethinking Power*. He has published widely in the history of philosophy and social theory as well as on film. He is currently working on a manuscript entitled, *Unlikely Couples: Film and the Representation of Difference*.

George M. Wilson works in philosophy of language, philosophy of action, and aesthetics. He is author of *Narration in Light*, *The Intentionality of Human Action*, and articles in various leading journals. He is Professor of Philosophy at The Johns Hopkins University.